"Philip is a phenomenal teacher of human language, behavior, and psychology who deepened my understanding of our shared experience in many remarkable ways." ~ *Michael Guenza, USA*

"Philip far exceeded any expectation I had of what a good teacher should be. He asked deep questions which planted the seeds of continued self-development in his students. Philip encouraged us to go beyond just teaching English, to considering our role as one in which we could make the world a better place. He has a true teaching spirit." ~ *Oliver Dilly, England*

"I have come across many outstanding teachers, but Philip is an extraordinary teacher who is able to connect with his students of all ages. He always respects every student's ideas and opinions with a positive attitude and wonderful rapport." ~ *Nang Ji, Myanmar*

"In Philip's classroom, we didn't just learn principles and ideas, we experienced them through his presence and actions. His wisdom, professionalism, calming spirit, gentle sense of humor, wealth of experience, and respect for human dignity have shaped me as a learner and as a university faculty member. I consider him one of the all-time best teachers I've ever had." ~ *Dr Oliver S. Crocco, Assistant Professor of Leadership and Human Resource Development, Louisiana State University, USA*

"I always looked forward to his classes as they were so interactive and were infused with a strong sense of learner autonomy." ~ *Sudharani Subramanian, India*

"Philip is an exceptional teacher. He challenged students to express, reason and make the process of learning enjoyable." ~ *Grace Dee, Myanmar*

"Philip is undoubtedly one of the best teachers I have ever had. He has unique ways to involve his students and get authentic opinions out of them, promoting a peer learning experience... we evolved and became a better teacher. He taught with passion... and his classes were a source of joy to us." ~ *Bonny Toufic, USA*

"I remember Philip especially as being a superb role model for us to follow." ~ *Samantha Burman, Thailand*

"Philip's non-conventional approach to language learning has truly been an eye-opener for all who have attended his classes, and has personally contributed greatly to my success as an English educator." ~ *Joshua Wax, USA*

"I have grown as the professional I am today because of great teachers like Philip, who allowed me to be myself and encouraged me to follow my dreams." ~ *Tatiana Aline Mohler, Brazil*

"I knew that my class taught by Philip would be well organized, engaging, reflective, and most importantly, meaningful." ~ *Eric D, USA*

"He knows how to teach. He showed me, not taught me, how I should behave in a second language classroom." ~ *Liz Ning, China*

"From the first lesson with Philip I always felt highly engaged in the learning process he created. As the course went on, my classmates and I always knew that Philip's forthcoming lessons would be absorbing, energising, and fulfilling experiences." ~ *Rick Mann, England*

"He did his research and was deeply knowledgeable on whatever subject he introduced. Philip's classes often challenged me to think for myself and question my own ideas and strongly-held beliefs… one of the few teachers in my life that really inspired me to look at learning as a lifelong pursuit." ~ Chris, USA

MENU for a SPIRITUAL REVOLUTION

Health Harmony & Happiness

PHILIP KEAY

Menu For A Spiritual Revolution: Health Harmony & Happiness

www.aspiritualrevolution.com

Published by Philip Keay

National Library of Thailand Cataloging in Publication Data

Keay, Philip.

Menu For A Spiritual Revolution: Health Harmony & Happiness.-- Chiang Mai : Blueprint Graphic and Web Design, 2021.

370 p.

1. Spirit. 2. Spiritual life. I. Title.

128.1

ISBN 978-616-586-143-4

Disclaimer: This book is intended as a reference volume only. It contains the author's perspectives and understandings, not any existential truths or facts. The ideas and information within are not intended as a substitute for any professional advice from the medical profession.

Cover Design by Danijela Mijailovic, Cutting Edge Studios

Edited by Michael Pilgrim, Helping Authors Succeed

Created with Vellum

Dear Reader

This book is specifically dedicated to ***you****! The universe invited* ***you*** *to be here, and would love* ***you*** *to flower and flourish.*

Spiritual living *means entering into a conscious agreement with Mother Earth, to protect, promote and enhance your life and hers, to the best of your ability. This agreement asks you to forevermore push the boundaries of your best, and to love and cherish yourself along the way.*

It is a commitment to lifelong learning: learning to learn, and learning the art of living. ***A spiritual revolution*** *sets you up for life. The menu within invites you to decondition, self-educate and empower yourself into health, harmony and happiness.*

Have a fantastic adventure.

CONTENTS

PREFACE

You can't change anything about your life tomorrow. Nothing whatsoever. Because you'll never get to tomorrow, it's always one step ahead of you. However, if you do want to make beneficial changes, you can do it today. You can change anything you want to change today. In fact, this is the only time you can make a change. So, don't aim to reach a better tomorrow, simply make today a better today…

At 4.30 pm on Saturday 7th September 1991 the Aeroflot flight from Moscow touched down on the tarmac at the old Bangkok airport in Thailand. My travels to the mystical Oriental Far East were officially underway.

Unbeknownst to me on that tremendously exciting evening I had just accidentally emigrated from England. I was 27.

Before Christmas the money was all but gone and I was faced with an early trip home. Not only that, I had arrived on a one-way ticket, had no money to get back to England, and no credit card. I had fallen in love with the Thai people and their country, and, in equal measure, dreaded being pitched back into a cold dark depressing winter. I simply had to do something.

And I did. I landed myself an English teaching job. The last time I'd been in a classroom was nine years previously, desperate to get my schooling behind me and myself out into the big wide world.

A brand new line of work and a brand new life had just begun. I still haven't bought that return ticket.

Throughout the 90s I lived in almost permanent bliss. I loved my job, loved my students and the Thai people, loved Bangkok, loved the food, and I especially loved a trip to the southern islands of Samui, Phangan or Tao every three months. I loved it all. Thailand is called The Land of Smiles and it suited me down to the ground.

There was, though, one problem that intermittently punctured my heavenly life. Rage.

In my new multicultural and international life I was reading books about 20th century politics and history, in particular since the end of the second world war. It was brutal. It was beyond my comprehension what powerful humans were doing to ordinary humans while constantly getting away with it, and it tore at me like nothing ever had before. Empire invasions of sovereign nations, wars, genocide, testing nuclear bombs in other people's backyards, not to mention the ransacking of our planet's resources. And then reading about the Cultural Revolution in China, the killing fields of the Pol Pot years in Cambodia, the extreme army repression in Burma just next door to where I was living... no words to describe the brutalities, impossible to conceive human beings could act like this.

I had never come across any of this in the British media. Emigrating was when I started to learn about the real history of our world, and my country of birth and upbringing had serious blood on its hands.

Whenever I read the books, and I had to read them for I am a reader and researcher of life as well as a player of it, my body and mind would fill with a horrible rage at the injustice, unfairness and barbarity of it all. It would feel like my whole body was made of metal, and my mind was volcanic.

After a couple of years or so, I realised I had to do something about my enraged feelings that would consume my being when thinking about these crimes. I had to stop feeling like this.

And so my spiritual odyssey was consciously born, somewhere about 97 I think. Living in Thailand there was no shortage of books on Buddhism, Taoism, gnosis, the Dalai Lama and various other spiritual offerings. I dived into them and found a beautiful new inner world arising in me. I began to understand both the bliss and rages that characterised my new life. The bliss remained and the feelings of rage began to dissipate. Nowadays, feelings of hatred or anger in me simply don't exist.

Meanwhile in my educational work, I completed my diploma in teaching English to adults in 1998, and my already decent ability at offering a learning experience that my students loved just shot through the roof. Being in the classroom almost became a spiritual experience to me, so much did I love being there! Still with a youngish body, my mental and spiritual health were now flourishing.

In 2000 I left my well-paid job and blissful life to return to London to study for my Master's in Applied Linguistics and English Language Teaching. The rules, regulations and laws of Blair's Britain were a shock to my system and felt really stifling to me; 'no' and 'not allowed' were the common refrains everywhere. It felt like a semi-police state. I had to put my head down, postpone my new spiritual journey and focus on my studies.

However, the bright light was that I thoroughly enjoyed the course and learned tremendous stuff relating to language, meaning, communication, and the psychological and sociological driving forces behind them. It illustrated to me precisely how marketing, propaganda and indoctrination could be effected, and I finally understood the absolute power contained within language; I could now analyse and see through the media's messaging and manipulating of public opinion with crystal clear vision.

In a one week period in September 2001 the plane attacks of 911 in America shook the world, I handed in my thesis to officially complete my degree, and three days later, with a copy of my thesis in her hands, my mum died after a nine month battle against cancer (if only I knew then what I know now). Life deals its cards to us in strange ways sometimes. I used my spiritual learnings from Thailand to help me, focusing my mind on my profound luck at having such a beautiful mum and life teacher for 37 years, rather than what I would no longer have. She would forever live on in my mind and soul, of that I was sure. And yes, she still does.

A month or two later, after her memorial service, I returned to Thailand, effortlessly pulled back there by my heart. I joyfully got back onto my spiritual path. Presently I got a teaching job teaching other teachers doing their own master's. I was back in my favourite country, back in the magnificent challenge of the classroom, back in my spiritual way of life, and then I met a beautiful and lovely human being who I later married, and life was rewarding me again. Yet…

In 2008, beset by frequent lower back pain which no medical professionals could help me overcome, I finally paid attention to my deteriorating physical health. I had spent nearly 20 years focused on the psychological and spiritual domains of human life while barely giving my body a moment's thought.

With help from a natural healing practitioner, I healed myself through diet within a week, and what a revelation to me that was! I quickly discovered that a fitter, leaner and more flexible body allowed my psychological and spiritual wellbeing to flourish like never before. I had found the missing piece to my life's work: realising our body is a temple to be cherished, not something to be taken for granted.

Being a researcher in my work, I immediately and voraciously set about researching all matters relating to nutrition, disease, healthcare modalities and so on. Having set out on my spiritual journey to counter the rage I felt towards our geopolitical world, I now discovered the perfect challenge to my newfound spiritual credentials: I learned of even greater crimes against humanity in the spheres of food and medicine! But generally I passed the test, and felt no hatred or disgust, merely a determination to try and do my best to add to the solutions.

This book was born.

Dear Reader and fellow Earth Dweller, I am a traveller, a soul adventurer, a transformational educator, a communicator, a learner, and a lover of life. In this book you will find a smorgasbord of my experiences, understandings, insights, research findings and awareness-raising tasks, all knitted together and informed by my own spiritual revolution. My intention is to enthuse you into launching your own spiritual revolution, because…

… so far as we know, we only get the one life, there are no dummy runs, no dress rehearsals, no second goes, this is it, this is your lot. I say give yourself the very best shot at it, today, and every other today you get. It will be my pleasure to guide you along the way.

Spirituality to me is when we discover our own essence and purpose for living, and then set about expressing ourselves fearlessly, lovingly and joyfully. The revolution part is discovering who we really are and how life works. We become properly intelligent, we heal ourselves, and we help heal Mother Earth.

What more could a human being want out of life??

I should like to mention a couple of crucial things relating to a successful reading of this book, and how you may get the most out of it. I do this with my rebel teacher's hat on!

Firstly, I have not written this book to tell you what is right or wrong, what is good or bad, nor how you should live your life. I am sharing with you my understandings and ideas, and my truths gleaned from my experiences and observations, not some fixed facts and knowledge which I declare to be true for everybody, no, not at all.

The truth of being a human being is not *out there*, it cannot be taught or handed on to us by others, only we ourselves can find it, and that's because it's inside of us. Any teacher, life coach, guru or leader who makes you dependent on them is doing you a disservice. The only guru who should lead you is yourself. The contents of my book are designed to help you become that guru, by acting as a trigger and springboard for your own evolving understandings of yourself, and of life.

Secondly, and to that end, I should like to emphasise that this is a book of learning, and I mean *real* learning, the genuine article, the real McCoy. Such learning should be fun, challenging and liberating. I therefore bring many of my classroom teaching techniques to the book, to enhance the learning process, and to make your journey as enjoyable and successful as possible.

I invite you to conduct frequent tasks along the way to help you raise your awareness of key issues, and to personalise your learning experience. I further invite you to buy yourself a beautiful notebook in which to do the tasks (beauty and good quality are motivating).

You may also come to feel that I repeat myself sometimes. This is no accident, a judicious use of repetition is but one useful strategy to deepen the learning process. In addition, I use a fair smattering of acronyms and initialisms for important concepts integral to your spiritual revolution, and therefore which I feel are worth learning by heart. These abbreviations may slow you down a bit, but that's usually necessary when the brain has to learn key stuff. However, once learned, you will nicely benefit from your extra work done.

Don't be shy either to reread sections or chapters. And use your notebook to record insights and understandings as you progress along your journey.

The *Starters* are to whet your appetite, open your heart and mind, and put the foundations for your revolution in place. The *Main Courses* are for developing your cognitive explorations and understandings, and for learning about yourself and how life works. The *Desserts* have strategies, tips, techniques and tools for helping you put all you learn into practice.

May the spiritual force be with you, and I trust I can be a friendly helpful navigator during your journey!

STARTERS

This section is to put the foundations for your spiritual revolution in place. It serves to whet your appetite, get your digestive juices flowing, get you thinking and reflecting, and to inspire you for the learning journey ahead. Without strong foundations, any old storm can blow the building down.

In any journey we undertake to improve our health and our life, we first establish and become aware of our situation as it is; then we discover and identify what is optimal, what constitutes best practice, where we would like to get to; then we look at how others have succeeded in getting to the better place, and how we can get there. And then we do it!

Uncover, discover, recover. Question and challenge, learn and understand, do and reflect. Repeat forevermore.

In this section the emphasis is getting one's journey firmly underway. Some unpalatable facts may present themselves to you, but if so, then be sure not to flinch, for then your journey will be a cinch!

By the end of the *Starters* I think you should be nicely grounded and set up for the main task at hand: learning key knowledge, acquiring core life skills, putting it all into practice, and then enjoying the rewards for your endeavours.

Let's start strong, build strong, and become strong!

1

WELCOME TO YOUR SPIRITUAL REVOLUTION

'Be the change you want to see in the world.' ~ attributed to Mahatma Gandhi

'I never let my schooling interfere with my education.' ~ Mark Twain

Brothers, sisters, friends, citizens, this book is a call to arms. Humanity has committed a dreadful crime against itself and against Mother Earth. It is surely time for us - all individual human beings - to wrest the initiative and solve our existential crisis. Not by overthrowing or fighting anybody, but by empowering ourselves and transforming our lives one by one into the beautiful, miraculous, individual, interconnected human beings that we were born to be.

And never let anyone tell you we are not worthy to be such beings.

We live in turbulent tempestuous times, times characterised by massive change, yet marked by political weakness, corporate corruption, and unfit for purpose education and healthcare systems. Oh, and a downright disrespect for our environments.

We are well and truly up shit creek without a paddle in sight.

As human beings, on a global scale and collectively speaking, we treat our planet as if it's our personal and limitless resource to be exploited as we see fit. Yet it is the source and provider of all life, without which we would be high and dry and without even a rancid old creek for our sins. What on Mother's Earth do we think we are doing?

This book says 'enough!' Enough of all our wars, poverty and injustice, enough of the corporate mindset that seeks to control and dominate us all. Its mantra is that 'enough is never enough', always more it seeks, inexorably marching like a gigantic swarm of locusts devouring all in its path; and it will take us all to oblivion if we don't stop it. We are already halfway there, perhaps closer.

And focusing on our own individual lives, I wonder if you have observed the sad and ailing state of the physical, psychological and spiritual health that marks the lot of so many of us human beings all over the world, and which is ever more keenly seen in the developed nations? Does technological and material progress carry a horrible sting in the tail?

It's hardly surprising we're sick, lost and unhappy, and psychologically floating around in that creek, because if we, as indeed we do, pollute and poison the very air, waterways and land of Mother Earth that gives us all life... from which we breathe, drink, eat and derive our sustenance... then it stands to perfect reason that we are polluting and poisoning our own lungs, our own bloodstreams, and our own flesh and bones. Trash our planet, trash our bodies. And sick bodies lead to unhappy minds. But hey, we directly pollute our minds too, and as for our souls and spiritual essence... virtually out of mainstream society sight, nowhere to be seen nor heard from.

Our own inner ecosystems mirror the external ones. Both are in a mess.

Now, you may be wondering, nothing is new, we all know this, we know our world and our human family are struggling due to the crimes we have committed against it and ourselves, but what can you and I do about it? We are mere individuals, we can't change the world, we can't fix its ills, there's nearly eight billion other people out there. And in any case, it's the job of the governments and corporations to manage things, and they are to blame, right?

Maybe, and they both certainly have to step up to the plate, but you and me can't control or stop them. You can, however, control your own life. You have the temple of your body, the miraculous magic of your mind, and the spiritual protection of your soul you can nurture. It's time for you to heal the only person you can heal in life: yourself. It's time to come home, to reveal your immense beauty to yourself. Yet, as my experience vividly tells me, the more one heals oneself, the more one can bring inspiration to other people's lives. If you carry energy and enthusiasm around with you then you naturally emanate it, and this is hardly going to cause other people a problem!

And by healing your own inner ecosystem you cannot help but improve the health of our planet at the same time. When we focus first on ourselves, we empower ourselves and in this way we can and will easily help take care of our beautiful Gaia.

That's what this book is about, and that is what spiritual revolution is about. Life is about what we *can* do, not what we *can't* do; and it's about conscious gratitude for what we have got rather than subconsciously taking it for granted or bemoaning what we don't have. So many people arrive at their deathbed and then think what they could have done, how they could have lived, and wonder why they didn't. But by then of course it's just too late.

I can't doesn't mean that, it means *I won't*. You *can*, but *will* you?

Will *you*?!

Spiritual revolution is my proposed answer to all the aforementioned problems - for individual human beings, for humanity, and for the natural world. Its premise is that we heal ourselves first and this will automatically add to the collective pot of positive energy for use by all others. Our focus must be on changing what we can, not what we can't. The idea is we that can't change the world directly, but we can change our own outlook, mindset and actions in positive ways, and in this way, we can contribute to a better world.

It is a revolution **of** the individual, **by** the individual, **for** the individual. It's purely a one-man or one-woman personal affair, with the onus on the revolutionary to do all their own work, but with some super useful guidance from me, simply because I'm in a good position to be that guide and am writing it down here.

And **you**, my friend, are that individual! You've found the book, you've found a navigator, and wherever you already are on your journey is your personal starting point for this revolutionary journey that is now up and running.

I've done mine and I happily and loudly declare that I am a spiritual warrior, a soul adventurer, and a sovereign human being who celebrates and reveres the sanctity of life. I am tuned in, switched on and plugged into the life grid of Mother Earth, and I'm connected to the cosmic consciousness and the very life force of the universe. I journey along in my life on my personal *wellness wagon*, traversing and navigating all the physical and psychological landscapes and challenges that come my way. I fall off it sometimes, for life does not always go according to plan or desire, but I'm usually able to get back on it in pretty short order. And I stay on it for longer periods of time these days. I have found that exchanging negative thought patterns and harmful habits for good habits and a spiritual outlook on life, and practise practise practise, is the key.

Now, I'm an educator, an accidental but proper educator, and I have always loved writing, so I wanted to write for all fellow citizens the full and complete guide for conducting one's own spiritual revolution. I want to share with you my own journey and understandings, and provide you with the means and framework for you to become your own spiritual warrior.

And the emphasis is on 'guide' for it's *your* revolution and you will be doing all the work, I am merely here as a navigator for you. I am nobody special, just an ordinary human being, and anything I can do, so can anybody else; a successful spiritual revolution awaits anybody who desires positive changes in their life.

What I *have* done, though, is thousands of hours of research and reflection upon all the important matters of what it means to be a human being, and in this way, I feel I can help speed up your own progress.

We are talking only about activating and utilising what is our birthright as a human being, but which I say society has repressed in us: the force of intuitive intelligence. All you have to do is reveal your inner intelligence to yourself and bam, you're up and running and won't look back. This is our central work here, helping you to fully activate, embrace and act upon your innate intelligence.

What I feel I can do that many others might struggle with, thanks to my line of work, is collate the whole caboodle into one resource and help others to empower and transform themselves. Education is my work, and my life. My teaching style is to facilitate learning to take place - your learning, by yourself. When we commit to being learners in life, things begin to magically happen and fall into place.

From all my observations and reflections, I conceive that millions of spiritual revolutions conducted by individual human beings all over the world is our only way of finding a paddle to row ourselves out of that smelly old rancid creek we're collectively mired in, and into a beautiful clean fresh river where all around us heavenly sights delight and melodic sounds abound.

Many have begun the journey, for even in the midst of all these troubles, human consciousness, spirituality and intelligence is on the rise. Wherever you are at in your own station of life, I invite you to step aboard and journey into the real and true you.

But what exactly is this revolution, what does it do, what do we get, how do we do it?

I suggest, when all is said and done, the deepest yearning and highest objective of all human beings is to be healthy and happy. 'I just want be happy' is always the crux of it, and that's not so easy if we aren't healthy. They go hand in hand. How it is done we may not care, but to feel happy and to experience good health is to give us the real sense of freedom that a human desires and deserves.

With good health and a content mind, we can achieve anything we are motivated to.

Yet, happiness, and certainly good health, is rather elusive for so many people in our modern frenetic world, and for me the reason is simple. We live in a material world where possessions are the objective, but you can't go out and buy happiness or fill up your tank with it. No, first we must ensure certain conditions in our life prevail, and only then will good health and happiness reveal themselves to us. This is your spiritual revolution: learning what those conditions are, how to put them into place, how to maintain them, and how to get them back when things have gone awry. My book navigates you through all of this.

In life we can be discouraged and disempowered, or we can be encouraged and empowered. My reflections tell me we got too much of the former and not enough of the latter in our formative years. Unless we proactively set about empowering ourselves, we may never really recover. In these pages I shall emphatically show you the way to empowering and motivating yourself to sail into a pristine lagoon of magic!

Spiritual revolution turns things around in our life, we find out who we are, how life works, and we become skilled livers of life. My book seeks to help you do this in just the time it takes you to read it. Then you can continue spiritually evolving at a somewhat more sedate pace.

My contention is that **stress** is the single cause of just about all ill-health, unhappiness, procrastination and spiritual emptiness. I have read this in a few places in my research and it makes full sense to me based on my experiences in life. It's just that there are so many ways to stress ourselves, not just mentally but physically too - for example through poor posture, poor food choices, too much sedentary living, lack of movement and exercise and so on. Our body and mind are designed to deal with stress, it's part of the whole mechanism of living, but in our modern world humanity has created an uber-stressful experience for ourselves in multiple ways. It comes at us like bees to a honeypot, but without any sweetness.

And this is why so much sickness, disease and unhappiness are to be found in so many communities and nations. We live with inner conflict in ourselves, which leads to conflict between us.

There are many kinds of stress - for example nutritional, psychological and environmental - and they weaken us in mind, body and spirit. Sometimes we know we're stressed, but often we don't realise it, and it gradually builds up inside of us, one day erupting like a long, apparently but it turns out not, dormant volcano.

When we feel and become overly stressed, we look any which way we can to alleviate it, and this is where your alcohol, drugs, and comfort foods come in. They give us temporary pleasure and help us forget our stressful world for a while, only for it to come back the next day because we never sought out, nor addressed, the root causes of our stress.

This is our grand human mistake: we ignore the laws of nature because we were educated that way, eschewing the life lessons that an understanding of karma and karmic law offer us, which in plain English is that every effect has a cause, and every sowing leads to a reaping. Every action leads to a reaction, this is simple energy mechanics in action. We try to numb our negative feelings and emotions, and we take pills for aches, constipation and myriad other bodily ailments. Instead of using our stressful state of being to investigate the causes and then make changes to reduce and get rid of the stressors, we simply carry on. If external conditions don't change, then we are building up future problems inside our being like a ticking time bomb.

And, before you know it, we have developed harmful habits and addictions which further exacerbate the stress to our body and mind, depleting our spirit, robbing us of our essence, and we are caught up in a vicious cycle from which there can seem no escape. Often, as time goes by, we need more and more of our 'drug' because its pleasurable effects become weaker and wear off faster.

Our body has got used to our source of pleasure, and so demands more of it. The cycle gets ever more vicious.

Small hits of pleasure sandwiched by much physical and emotional unhappiness become our lot, and happiness and sound health have now long since become a distant dream. Our relationships suffer, life gets ever harder, we see doctors more often than friends, and then one day the biggie comes along, a diabetes, a cancer, you know the score.

All because we ignored the cast iron law of nature: out of your action comes a related reaction. Spiritual revolutionaries very much learn to live according to karmic law for you will have to be super lucky indeed in this spiritually warped world to accidentally live happily and with wellbeing.

You may have reflected that both the original stress and our subsequent addictions arise from our relationship and interaction with the world outside of us. Either our interactions with the external environment are harmonious to our being or they bring us stress. Our starting point in our journey out of this physiological, psychological and spiritual mess, is to address stress and its root causes, and that means becoming aware of all our interactions and relationships with the world out there beyond our skin. We need to understand not just the stressors out there, but also our own reactions which will be based on acceptance or resistance.

Verily so, stress is the big enemy!

I should note that on occasion we get stressed for our protection. If you suddenly come across a big dangerous animal - in the jungle, in the Australian seas, in a bar on a Friday night - your body is immediately flooded with adrenaline and is most certainly stressed. But your body has reacted this way to send extra strength into your limbs so you can fight the beast or get the hell out of the scene at a rapid pace of knots.

However, if this bodily reaction happens frequently, and however small the trigger, then this is the cause of our troubles, health-wise. All those hormones are running riot, our body overheats and becomes tense, and our mind is overtaken by negative energy. And if we are in a virtual constant state of stress, well, that's when our health can spiral downhill. Pain, emotional distress, negative feelings… they are our body's message to make changes to our life. But are we listening? Often we are not, nobody taught us, and we pop that pill, drink that bottle, snort that line, and so on.

The last word on stress for now is that physical stress leads to mental stress, and mental or emotional stress leads to physical stress, and in this state of being our spiritual essence is chased right out of town. Mind and body are intimately linked, contrary to the orthodox views of western medical science and thinking. Just reflect upon your own life and you can verify this law of nature.

One of the quickest ways out of mental stress is to clean up one's diet. Eat whole foods, avoid corporation-made foods and drinks, and just see how your body and mind feel after a week or two. Start right now why don't you?? No sense in hanging around, this is your revolution, act quick! This is the simplest yet best diet to support your wellbeing in body and in mind. Once you've successfully changed over to this diet then you can refine things further. You can read about all of this in the final section of the book.

THE OPPOSITE STATE of being stressed is being in balance, in **harmony**. You feel balanced within your being; your mind and body are stress-free and both are in fine working order, your soul is alive and dancing, and you are living harmoniously with the people and world around you. It is by spending most of your time in harmony that you create the conditions which allow happiness and good health to flourish. Harmony is your key, my friend. But harmony just does not come to us on a plate. We literally have to work to get it. There's no escaping this, one simply must do the hard yards to get the rewards. We are going to learn that wellness and wellbeing is a way of life, a consciously chosen lifestyle, which requires our ongoing commitment forevermore until the janitor from heaven arrives for our collection.

The only way is through intelligent living, and in fact my definition of intelligence is 'the ability to live harmoniously with the world around us'. And if the world around us is going to pot then we need to get seriously intelligent, but we can do it, we are human and we have huge reservoirs of resources inside our minds and hearts. But it must be a conscious thing.

Intelligent people seek harmony because they know that good health and contentment and joy come out of it. Academic intelligence, or intellect, is quite another thing, and no indicator of good health at all. Trouble is, in our schooling they focused on academia and ignored the crucial stuff. Know the stuff in books they said, but be ignorant of how to live happily, healthily, harmoniously. Bad deal! I say let's have both.

Harmony, then, arises within us from our intelligent interactions with the world out there, and that means in all our relationships - from food to ideas, from people to the environment, and everything in between. Nothing exists in isolation, all is interlinked and interdependent, and it's all energy flow. Energy flows into you, and it flows out of you back into the world. Harmonious energy flow between you and life out there means health and happiness, inner peace and contentment, joy and fun for you. And all life on Mother Earth will love you for it.

The key to ensuring we live intelligently is becoming consciously aware of all our relationships, whereupon we are now able to make informed changes to any that are not serving us well. It may be we need to temporarily choose stress, to resist something or somebody out there (an injustice, bullying behaviour), but at least we do it with conscious choice and because we feel such resistance will return us to harmony. *'No pain no gain'* comes to mind.

So there you have it, less stress, more harmony, and Bob's your uncle (hey Steve!), all will be tickety-boo in your life. I call our active pursuit of it the **'Triple-H lifestyle'**: living with **health, harmony** and **happiness**. Each of the three Hs lead to the other two, it is a holistic triple-H. I ask you what objective for our daily life could possibly be more important??

Our journey together in this book all relates to learning how to pursue, achieve and maintain the 3Hs. And when lost, to retrieve.

Challenging times and problems will still come knocking on your door for sure, such are the vagaries and vicissitudes of life, but you will have the wherewithal and skills to navigate yourself through the challenges, and to solve problems in short order. You will have created your own *personal wellness wagon* to journey upon for the rest of your life. Just one book will do it. You get the full compendium, the total guide, the full course dinner!

Your work then, my friend, is all about learning how to bring harmony into your relationships and your life, keeping it, and being able to recover it when it's temporarily lost. My work, in these here pages, is to take you on a guided and fun discovery to do just that, to be your navigator and to facilitate you in your journey. The key word is *learning* - and only you can do it. I can guide, but you have to learn for yourself, hence the personal nature of the spiritual revolution; we each of us must conduct our own. But there is a problem…

… and that is, until we do our own inner work, we are not very good learners.

IF WE'D HAD an education worth its name this book would be redundant, so would all the tens of thousands of diet books and self-improvement books. You will discover that my views, as an educator of educators, are not very complimentary about the state of mainstream education systems in our human world. And I don't mean to knock teachers at all, they have a hard job; I knock the system. A feature of spiritual living in my view is that we do our level best to not blame anybody, rather to just seek out what is broken or crumbling, and then fix it.

There are only really two ways to effect change in, or modify, people's and society's behaviour: education and law. That we have tens or hundreds of thousands of laws to govern our behaviour strongly suggests our education has gone wildly wrong.

The fundamental flaw in education systems nearly everywhere - I know Finland to be a noble exception, as are some individual schools dotted around the world - is that the teachers were taught to *teach*, they do not facilitate and develop in us the skill of *learning*; that is, they teach stuff to the kids, they don't teach the kids how to learn the stuff. This handicaps us all right from the off. We sit at our desks for 12 years being taught, being told, being spoken at, being tested, being silent, complying, behaving, memorising… this is our lot. And 12 years is a *very long time* for a young human being. I argue later in the book that it near about breaks us.

This absolutely is not learning, nothing to do with it! Being human can be tough, and to successfully navigate our way through life we need, as well as useful knowledge, skills, and we need plenty of them, especially *cognitive skills* such as learning, communicating and problem-solving.

But we get none of that during our schooling.

We can embark upon our own spiritual revolution to rectify this terrible mistake.

To skilfully acquire all those skills we must first learn the mother of all skills: how to learn. And they never trained us how to do this, insanity!! As a teacher, I know the most important attribute I need is the ability to learn for myself, and never to stop doing so. If I, the teacher, can't learn properly how can I teach properly? If we citizens can't learn, how can we learn to live properly?

Look at these key words, which by the end of the book will be a friendly feature of your mental landscape: *learning, discerning, intelligence, integrity, authenticity, understanding, happiness, inner calm, attention, awareness, observation, reflection, conscious living.* We shall find that the last one is the engine room of your revolution and brings all the others into action.

Their common denominator? None of them can be taught to you, none of them can be handed over to you, you cannot get them from anybody else, you have to make them happen yourself, they come from within you. Others can help point us in the right direction, but only if we are willing, able and ready to learn ourselves; I read it once, 'when you are ready to learn a teacher will appear'.

Facts, knowledge, and information are of course super useful in their own right, yes, but the real stuff of life - intelligence and harmonious living - comes from within us, and since the schools didn't empower us to be skilled learners, we shall have to do it ourselves. Spiritual revolution is in many ways a revolution of learning through self-education to make up for what we didn't get, to liberate ourselves from what I call our 'conditioned ignorance'.

My mission as an educator has always been to empower all my students, many of them teachers, by helping them develop themselves into highly skilled learners. Once we can learn properly, we can do anything we want in life. If you ever had a really good teacher, I can tell you it will have been because she or he was a skilled learner themselves.

Learning is an art, a science, a dimension even. If there was one thing I was brought into life for by the universe, it seems to me, it was to help people learn and develop themselves into autonomous citizens. Autonomy is your absolute passport to experiencing as much freedom as an individual human being can get for themselves, and by freedom I mean having good health to pursue and realise your dreams.

My effort here is to transfer my classroom work into this book, and help you become a super skilled learner. My objective for the chapters in the *Starters* section is to pique your curiosity and activate your digestive juices, to get you thinking about some of the core issues we shall discuss in the *Main Courses section*, and in general help you get your mind to be fully open and attentive for the learning journey ahead of you.

Real learning comes from hearing about the story *and* the storyteller because no story, no life, exists without the experiencer. I will share with you many anecdotes from my experiences in my own spiritual revolution to better illustrate to you my truths and understandings. The intention is smooth your path to your own truths and understandings.

Only by us individual citizens doing inner work on ourselves can we begin to turn things around at the global level for our whole human family and Mother Earth alike. It makes the impossible possible. Nobody can change the world, but they can change *their* world, and ultimately speaking that *will* change the world.

. . .

THERE ARE many ideas of what it means to be spiritual, to live spiritually, and I shall close this chapter with one of my own.

Spirituality combines living for today with an intention to cause no harm to oneself or to others. It is a recognition that we are an interconnected part of the whole (world and universe), and that we represent the whole, and therefore to harm others is to harm oneself. The act of this recognition is to unleash a revolution in the noticer's life - it is 'flicking the switch of awareness' and is a single act of revolution within an evolution already begun. Once you have flicked this switch, everything becomes clearer.

Awareness comes from conscious living, and this book is all about developing one's conscious living. I bid you a warm welcome to our journey together, drive well and enjoy the scenery!

2

SOME BAD NEWS, AND THE GOOD NEWS

The only guru you need is you. Don't be a Buddhist, be your own Buddha. Others can medicate you, others can mediate for you, but only you can meditate for you. Meditation is your own medication and mediation in life.

Ignorance in a land of milk and honey may well be bliss. Ignorance on Planet Earth, at the outset of the third millennium, is far too dangerous to entertain.

We have established that humanity faces many challenges, not least their own wellbeing and the wellbeing of Mother Earth, both of which we ourselves have attacked. If we are to emerge from this twin threat with effective solutions which individual citizens can implement for themselves, we must discover the root causes behind all of our stress and strife which causes us to mistreat the sanctity of life. Life should be more of a joy, and less of a struggle.

We often look at the huge world out there and think we can't change it, for we are just one person, what power do we have, the governments hold all the power, etc etc. But take a look at a football team, a sales team within a company, or two families going out together to the countryside for a picnic. All are groups of people and we can say that the group's work is the sum total of the work by all the individuals. Each group will have an anointed or implicit leader or main organiser and it will have other members who have their own roles to play. The success, or not, of each group's activities rests upon whatever work each person brings to the table within their own role. The group is the auspices under which each person works, but the group itself does no work, only its members do the work at the individual level, which combines to form the group's output.

The point being that everything in the human world comes down to the actions of individual human beings. We have the ultimate, largest group membership of the lot in *humanity as a whole*. But humanity doesn't do anything, it does not exist as a physical person, it is an idea, a thought construct, an understanding. Whatever goes on globally and collectively in our world is still the consequence of the deeds and words of each individual member of humanity, but aggregated together to form 'humanity' and its output.

Now, if you disagree with me here, and want to argue that what you or I do has no impact on the world, because we're only one person, then fair enough, but what about yourself? Don't you want to enjoy health, happiness and vitality?! Don't you want to have a positive impact on yourself and on others? Of course, we all do. Can we? Yes we can! So what is stopping so many people? Why so much misery and mayhem in us, blocking us?

We said stress was the cause of most if not all ill-health, and we said harmony was our way out of stress. But we need to dig further, we need to get behind the causes of stress and ill-health if we are to find our solutions, and we need to look into how we can achieve harmony. We have to look at the bad stuff as well as the good stuff. If you want the good news, you can't avoid the bad news.

For a long time I've observed the ways of us humans, and for me the issue is a psychological one.

We make excuses against changing our ways, sticking to what we are used to, seeking the easy life. We fear the unknown and prefer our routines. We're too busy and don't have time to change. Maybe tomorrow...

Negative self-talk, and reasons for non-action, are rife. Self-limiting beliefs block change and often cripple us. We suffer, we are unhappy. It's in our mind, the blockage is in our mind.

Lots of more important, powerful, educated people are out there to make the changes, it's their job to fix our world we say, they are trained, and they are the experts, we are not. We lack useful information to even know what changes we can make. It's another excuse for non-action on our part. And, don't we just love our comfort zones?!

We can say that unrealistic expectations of others, our own fears, and not taking personal responsibility hinder us from making beneficial changes. In a word, ignorance. Nobody wants to think of themselves as ignorant, but what if we all are? What if we were *taught* into ignorance? We shall certainly be exploring this idea later. What if ignorance will continue to haunt us until we take personal responsibility for our own life, our own thoughts, actions and reactions?

Ignorance, we should note, includes two types: not knowing about something, and thinking/assuming we know about something but unknowingly being wrong. The latter is the dangerous type, for here we are deluded that we know, yet we are acting upon wrong assumptions. We have been unknowingly misinformed or misled.

Humanity has always grappled with two core negative psychological manifestations: *greed* and *ignorance*, and each feeds into the other. Both *arise* from desire and fear, and both *cause* desire and fear. If you were to press me to go even further back and link all our problems down to one thing only, for me it's ignorance. This is our Achilles heel. Out of ignorance comes fear and delusion, out of ignorance comes cravings and greed, and out of ignorance we become dependent and impotent.

If we can get to grips with our ignorance, chase the pesky chap out of town, shine a light onto its darkness, then we will assuredly transform our life into such a better experience. It's my view that we were literally conditioned into varying degrees of ignorance during our childhood which, when we enter adulthood, seriously handicaps us in our efforts to live harmoniously with robust health and a sound mind.

A WRONG UNDERSTANDING of **time** is a serious impediment...

Life is now, life only happens and takes place in the current moment, always and forevermore it is *now*. This is the truth of everything. Life is not to be found in the yesterday, for that has passed, now just a memory in our thoughts or pages in the history books. Life is not in the tomorrow, that is just an idea - an ambition, an imagining, a worry.

Past and future time are constructs of our mind, useful in some ways, but frequently we dwell in our minds, going over past memories and future projections, and consequently, sadly, today passes us by in a blur. In the super busy mode we hardly notice today. In this way we miss whole chunks of life, we miss the journey of life. We pass a lot of our time in the not-now.

You cannot change anything about the past or the future, you can only change your attitude towards the not-now. Changes are related only to now, change is a flow of energy which only takes place in the current moment. We can only change things now, today, this minute. Giving up something tomorrow is not giving it up, starting afresh tomorrow is merely an idea.

We can make intelligent changes now by reflecting upon the past, or considering the future consequences of our actions today, and letting such considerations influence our choices and decision-making in the here and now.

Considering that today is where life is to be found, the only place and time that you can experience life, it makes perfect and intelligent sense to reorient our life such that we aim to experience health, harmony and happiness *today*. And when you wake up the next morning to the new today, more of the same please vicar. If it goes wrong today, consider why, make changes, then work on the next today being a better one. Just one day lost, not whole chunks of time.

But no, this was not on the education curriculums when we went to school! Society, in its uber-materialistic guise, doesn't care too much for today at all. All it wants to do is aim for a better tomorrow and get success in the future, whereupon, it has been conditioned to believe, it can then be happy and do all it desires to do. Put your head down, work hard, don't make waves, make acquisitions and gains along the way, and happiness will be yours.

And if it doesn't happen in this lifetime, no worries, be a good person and then you can enjoy heavenly rewards in the next life.

NO! I exclaim 'NO', that's no good at all! Who knows if heaven is up there, or if it's true? I want to celebrate and enjoy *this* life, and would you not agree that our world is a true heaven itself? Her beauty and offerings could hardly be bettered in my imagination. We are already in a heaven, but if we're caught up in too many thoughts we can't see it. The soul and heart connects us; the mind, when in the wrong mode, disconnects us and we can't see the beauty.

What we emphatically do know - because here we are now - is that we only get one life, there are no dress rehearsals, no dummy runs, no second goes, this is it my friend, this is your lot. So what are we doing about it? What are we going to do about it?! Yes, it may be we are reincarnated and get another life, but we don't know for sure and so I'm not taking the risk. We know we have this life, so let's make *this* life count. Big time. Triple-H today and every successive today. With health and wellbeing life is already tip-top; in such a state of mind and body, flowing with clarity and energy, we are fully motivated and enthused, and can do all kinds of things.

But back to our education and society, and our conditioning… always in the future, that's where the good life lies, they taught us as kids. As we set out in the adult world we are therefore oriented towards achieving that beautiful future. But then…

… 10, 20, 30 years pass and people get to their 40s and 50s, life is slipping by, ill-health and ailments are starting to kick in and stack up, friends or parents start to die and people begin to sense a mortality about their life, and now they start to hark back to the 'good old days'.

What?!

When young we look forward to the future good times, and when we get to the place and time where the good times were supposed to be happening, clearly they are not because now we're looking back at what we now kid ourselves were the better times of yore. It's not-now living, that's what it is.

Dear reader, whatever your age and station in life, it's never too late to focus on today living, making the 3Hs your daily objective. By ruing our past or wishing for a future time we literally turn our backs on life. Today is where we make our changes, nowhere else!

A central plank to the spiritualising of ourselves is connecting ourselves to life, and life is only to be found today, and so we make today living the main objective. This means most of us have to literally reprogram our minds and reorient our whole direction in life…

AN UNPALATABLE MESSAGE that comes with this book, the bad news if you like, is that we were all *conditioned into ignorance*, out of which arises nearly all our problems we encounter. We should not sugar-coat this and pretend otherwise, or say yes, maybe others are ignorant, but not me. We might want to do that because 'ignorant' itself is a horrible-sounding word. Yet, hardly anybody escaped its clutches (a few exceptions do exist) because we were all went through 12 years of de-education rather than education.

Our innate intelligence, skills and human essence, which we were all born with, were suppressed instead of encouraged and developed. Our education 'educated' us into ignorance, it conditioned us into a fraction of who we are, and so we don't know who we are, nor how life works. That we assume we do is neither here nor there. Unhappiness and sickness prove otherwise. More proof comes from clearly looking at all our relationships within the human family, and with the planet that gives us all our life. Not so much intelligence in evidence.

Education failed to teach us how to protect, promote and cherish life. As newly minted adults we then struggle from the off.

Really, it's such common sense when we stop and think about it: make the bedrock of our life good health and harmonious relationships, and then turn to other matters from a position of physiological and psychological strength. We need information, quality information, and we need to develop skills that were suppressed out of us, or left untriggered, during our formative years.

Education failed to teach us important and essential knowledge, and failed to develop in us essential life skills.

This leads us to the next bit of bad news, which again we will do best to face up to if we wish to overcome it.

It relates to matters of responsibility, trust and **external authority**. Our schooling trained us out of taking personal responsibility for our thoughts and actions, and into accepting almost unquestionably the idea and existence of *external authority* and its all-knowing centralised ways, values, knowledge, ideology. Trust the system, it has everything you need. It disconnected us from our own human nature, and from the ways of the natural world, disempowering us from looking after ourselves and our own health. It did not in any way teach us how to live a healthy, rewarding life. Instead, it trained us for a rat race and made us dependent upon the master rat, who itself depends upon all us minion rats. Nobody wins in a rat race. Compete against each other for scarce resources was the subconscious program installed in our psyche.

And then, once we are in the adult world, many experts exist who we can consult for information and answers, for fixing and building things, for telling us what to do and how to do it. But do the experts know how to live happy healthy lives, do they have harmonious relationships, eat good diets, treat Mother Earth with reverence? If they did, I logically reason to myself, our world would be in tip-top shape and we would not have hospitals and pharmacies doing a roaring trade in human misery, nor would we have doctors doing 80 hour working weeks. Nor would we have scientists trying to dominate and conquer nature instead of learning how to interact and work *with* it.

Our societies spend trillions on treating sickness and disease - this is indicative of failure in my mind. For example, for 50 years or more they have been always on the cusp of a cancer cure, but meanwhile it's still the same treatment as 50 years ago. This is hardly success. Instead, the stats now tell us that one in two of us will get cancer, up from one in twenty just a century ago. Something's gone badly wrong. Yet, if anybody does the research, they will find plenty of protocols for treating cancer which focus on building up the immune system to help patients overcome their disease. We think experts and doctors heal, they don't, they just treat; our own bodies heal, if we only know how to let them do their work. Cut yourself and you know what your body will do, in timely order, all by itself.

And when we call much of the food that much of the world's population eat, 'junk food', then we seem to be openly mocking ourselves. Why on earth would we put rubbish into our bodies?? Add in 'genetically modified' and 'processed' and 'refined' foods and one may wonder about our collective sanity here. Have you investigated or researched the animal factories that produce our so-called meat and dairy foods? They can barely be called animals, I call them MPOs, meat-producing organisms.

Since we have a top-down hierarchical system as the means for organising our human world, delivered through this notion of *external authority*, we can say this top-down system has failed. Through corruption and greed, it has enabled and created crimes against humanity and ecological disaster for Mother Earth. And it has stressed and diseased our bodies and minds.

Education has failed, and so has the law system failed... for time and again we see political and corporate corruption with nobody indicted or held liable for their actions; does this not just send a carte blanche message to continue on with these anti-life ways? Education is supposed to be the carrot to help us learn, but it's gone mouldy; law is the stick to help us behave opon fear of pain or loss of freedom, but it's bent and only hits certain people, missing others.

How can we any more trust our sciences, media, and the justice system?

According to my reflections I see food, medicine, education, law and media as the five pillars of a society or nation. If one or more of the pillars are crumbling, the foundations weaken and society weakens with it. It seems to me today that all five are broken. No wonder there is so much strife in our world today. We were taught to listen to and trust external authority, that it knows best, and that it is responsible for things, for fixing things, for everything.

Now, I'm not blaming anybody, and I'm not saying all our experts are wrong, just that we as citizens can no longer so easily trust them, just because they are the 'expert'. Failure is not a reason for me to continue giving my trust to those that brought about the failure! While I see *blame* as an impediment to solutions, its opposite counterpart, *taking responsibility*, is very much the start of such solutions.

And I'm not saying to get rid of the top-down nature of society, but I am saying we need to take more responsibility ourselves as individual citizens, and improve our lot from the ground up by attending to the grass roots of things. That's where human beings actually live, connected to the grass roots of our Earth and to our own local communities where life exists for real, not mediated from elsewhere via various forms of media. We need an optimal blend of effective intelligent leadership which creates, rather than corrupts, and responsible self-educated knowledgeable citizens who all actively play their role in the group's affairs.

A mix of top-down and bottom-up is always going to be the best way. But us citizens cannot change the top, so we must focus on ourselves and take up the reins of responsibility.

I think it's urgent for each of us to reflect upon such things: How is it that we, in our mainstream approaches to society, have a healthcare system which does not heal us or tell us how to prevent illness, rather just treats symptoms and teaches nothing of the causes of our ailments, so that we may change our habits to avoid a repeat?

We get the nastier diseases and die with pain, and before our time, because we keep on getting sick and stressed, ignorant of how we cause our own health woes.

How is it that we have an education system which does not cultivate learning, nor help us discover who we are or how life works, nor how to be autonomous humans?

How is it that we have foods which poison our bodies and minds? Why do we have factory farms? Factories are for making goods and material things. Why do we have the horrible-sounding genetically modified foods? Why do we think we are more intelligent and powerful than nature? Why do we use unimaginable amounts of toxic chemicals to grow our foods, and to use as ingredients in the foods made by corporations? Why do we have junk foods, processed foods, refined, toxic foods? Why do we poison and diminish our vegetables and fruits? Why does a banana grown in Queensland, Australia get flown down to Sydney, get sorted and packed, flown back up to Queensland and then put in the supermarket near where it grew to be sold to the customer? Why did it need to travel thousands of kilometres before it could be eaten?

Why is traditional mainstream media so full of negative news and views? Is this the diet of disempowering and depressing information we need in our lives? Always seeking to divide us by gender, colour, religion and any number of other pigeonholes. Is this the best humanity can do? Does this media tell us what is really going on, or is it conditioning, and psychologically destroying us?

I've researched stuff all my life, and it's an integral part of my work, and I have learned about so many things that I never see in this mainstream media. It's why I'm writing this book, to share what I've learned. There really is so much good stuff going on by so many human beings, but trying to find positive news and views from Mainstream Inc, from The System, is like trying to find a penguin in the North Pole.

Why do we never hear of all the magnificent things citizens and groups of people are doing to try and bring our world back into a state of health and abundance for all? Why is it that when we apply our trustworthiness meter to what we hear and read in the media we see its needle shoot to the wrong end?

Why is there a two-tiered justice system everywhere, one law for common citizens, and another law for the rich, famous and powerful? What the rich, famous and powerful may not have worked out yet is that as they corrupt others, as they enrich themselves at the expense of others, they are corrupting and destroying their own soul and spirit, negating any chance they have of finding happiness and peace of mind. Yes, their life is certainly better than being mired in poverty or being at the end of violence, brutality and terror, but this is hardly a claim for success.

To be human is *to be connected*, connected to each other, connected to the nature of our impossibly beautiful Mother Earth, and connected to the life force and cosmic consciousness of the universe. We are disconnected and disempowered. Until the experts get their act together we citizens will have to take responsibility for re-educating and reconnecting ourselves to the support grid of life.

To that end, the third bit of bad news, if you are feeling lazy, is that you will have to do all that work yourself! There is no magic pill or potion to infuse you and instantly move you into integrated intelligence, nor is there any guru who can bring health and harmony and happiness to you even if you pay them a billion dollars. Everybody will find they have to do all the hard yards themselves.

However, if you are fired up to bring health, harmony and happiness into your life today, and as a default forevermore until your final days, and you are inspired to actively contribute to helping Mother Earth heal herself from humanity's excesses and ignorance, then we move into the realms of good news. Because doing things for ourselves, and succeeding by our own endeavours, brings us multiple rewards which make being human a joyful experience.

You have found this book, I know you're from the second camp!

It's your life my friend, your learning, your revolution. The learning is all yours, finding your truth is all yours, finding understanding is all yours.

Let's further upgrade the good news...

Firstly, and despite resistance by orthodox thinking and the status quo, which never leave the scene quietly, is that understandings in science, modern medicine and healthcare modalities are finally catching up with how life really works. We have the exciting advances of quantum physics, and in the field of biology we have epigenetics, yet ironically both are only confirming what the ancients in India and China knew thousands of years ago: we are holistic beings, with mind body and spirit connected within, and all life interconnected with each other, with the world and with the universe.

For too long, western nations, where global power and influence lie, have told us we are separate, separate from each other, separate from nature and Mother Earth. They underlined this folly by separating science and religion, which has caused humanity no end of grief over the centuries. Now the two are converging and this meets truth and reality head-on. Later in the book we investigate the messages of epigenetics and Ayurveda, both of which understand and promote the holistic, interdependent nature of all of life.

But suffice to say for now, all the information, knowledge, and understandings that we need to help us navigate life with health and harmony are out there. Mainstream resists, but it's there if you want to find it. Anybody who tries to separate, is part of the old ignorant ways, anybody who promotes and speaks the holistic nature of all life, is part of the new spiritual understanding of life. Part of our spiritual odyssey is realising that we can find all this out for ourselves, that we don't have to rely upon any external authority. It's why I say it's your revolution, your life, your journey, because 'being taught' will no longer cut the mustard, we must learn and understand things for ourselves. Become and be the guru yourself.

Spirituality is the coming together of science and religiousness, making us whole once again. At which point, we can resonate with harmony within, conflicts will largely disappear, and life will be transformed. It's incredibly exciting. Politics cannot interfere with spirituality like it did with the religions and with the sciences. Politics as we've only ever known it is external authority, anti-life, anti-human, anti-love; spirituality is connectedness, internal autonomy, and it celebrates life by allowing love to flourish.

So, the good news is that none of us need reinvent the wheel, we just have to go beyond mainstream and orthodox thinking to find the good sources of information to help us on our journey.

The other majorly good news is that everything you need to get your revolution truly up and running, from wherever you personally are on your evolutionary journey today, is here in this book. My objective and intention is to leave no stone unturned…

As an unorthodox holistic educator, as a rebel teacher, the basis for my work is always to first create a classroom environment which supports and promotes optimal learning conditions for my students. They need to feel good, feel emotionally safe but cognitively challenged, and they want to get on with each other and share a mutual journey where the rewards just keep on coming, and mostly through their own work. Learning is an individual affair, nobody can do it for anybody else. It's a clumsy term, but I am a learner-enabler. When learning is fun and motivational, we humans absolutely thrive.

You will get plenty of information from me, and I will help you cultivate strategies and cognitive skills so you can verify what I say for yourself, and to put into practice what you learn. I only offer you my truth and understanding, but I do so to help and encourage you to find yours. Often, you will find, we share the same understandings, because we are talking about uncovering and reconnecting with our human nature.

The core message and objective I have for you in our book is learning for yourself and achieving autonomy, self-sovereignty, which gives you all the tools and understandings you need to achieve good health and much happiness.

Sometimes learning is memory, being reminded of what we have forgotten.

You get to become your own authority and guru, and you get to discern the real pros out there from the charlatans and pretend friends. And having warned about experts, there is certainly a growing and huge online fraternity, people from all over the world, at conferences and workshops and writing in books, who are revolutionising things spiritually and psychologically, and helping us all to enjoy good health. The best teachers and healers and authorities can be recognised because they encourage and empower you by getting you to do your learning for yourself. And they will talk togetherness and holism, not the loveless ways of separation and synthetic societies.

The good news is that you can get all the support you wish to be your very own spiritual pioneer and healthy human warrior. And in this book you get the best possible grounding because I'm a spiritual revolutionary myself and therefore write from my own first hand experiences and understandings. But I'm also an educator so I'm going to encourage, enable and empower you to become a super skilled learner for life.

To that end, I think it will be super useful for you to know a wee bit about me…

3

WHO AM I? WHO ARE YOU?

At any one time in our life, we are the sum total of all our previous experiences. We are a work in progress.

Observe others and learn about yourself, observe yourself and learn about others.

When we accept we carry ignorance, we begin to emerge from its darkness. When we learn for ourselves, we swiftly move into a beautiful energy field where love and light dance in the meadows, bringing joy to the heart and soul.

This chapter is about establishing common ground between you and me, and who we both are, so that together we can proceed through the rest of the book, navigating both the relatively easy bits and the more cognitively challenging bits with mutual confidence, trust and good intentions.

Who are you? Who am I? How do you know? In what ways are you and I similar and in what ways are we different? Have you resonated and connected with who you perceive me to be so far in the book? In what ways?

Do you even know who you are?! Of course, you have a good idea who you are today, but is it the real you? What's the difference between identity and character? Do we change, or are we fixed?

The very premise of this book is that until we do sufficient work on ourselves, until we go inside our own minds to discover what's in there, none of us really know who we are. And if we don't know who we are, how can we know how life works? There's no doubt about it, knowledge helps us empower ourselves, while ignorance disempowers us. Understanding who we are liberates and transforms us.

I think we should begin the book's main work in earnest, and have a bit of an exploration in this chapter about who we are as individual human beings, and who we are as members of the greater human family which is now nearly eight billion strong. There is who you are today, who you think you are today, and what kind of you will emerge out of your spiritual revolution.

In the next chapter I formally introduce you to doing awareness-raising tasks which will add to your reading and learning experience. However, it will be more than useful for you to do one now. So, to that end…

Task

I would like to invite you to return to the questions in the second and third paragraphs of this chapter, and spend a few minutes contemplating upon them. If you've not bought yourself a beautiful notebook yet, this is a gentle reminder to do so! Either way, write down your thoughts for referring back to later on down the track. Writing is also an excellent trigger for reflective thought, a great learning tool.

If you've never really done such reflecting, or even if you have, I hope you can really get into it and enjoy the fun of investigating who you are! When you've had a think, and a write, read on.

. . .

THERE IS who we think we are, who we can be, who we really are. There is also who others think we are, and what influence that has on our behaviour. When we understand who we *really* are then we can stop being who we *think* we are, or should be, and we can become the person we want to be, that feels natural to us.

At this point we 'come home' to ourselves.

My view is that without an active soul, we are not whole. I also say that when we reflect in this manner, we are doing so with the help of our soul…

The truly spiritual person, in my understanding, is an autonomous person, able to respect, trust and love themselves as the basis for respecting, trusting and loving this very life we have been invited to experience. And by life, I mean out there, in here, everywhere, all of it - the very heartbeat and innate beauty of it wherever it is to be found.

Everybody can be a spiritual person, but many are not. There is little spirituality to be found in Industrial Age society and so society does not teach it to us. Excessive materialism has caused an imbalance in us. We have become homogenous consumers and customers more than we are citizens and unique cosmic creations of consciousness. We live with objectives which do not support our wellbeing or ability to feel joy and love.

Becoming spiritual - that is, spiritualising ourselves - means acquiring for oneself useful cognitive skills, quality information, and personally formed understandings. The revolution bit is speeding up these acquisitions to make up for lost time. Trust in oneself, and one's ability to intelligently discern all incoming information, is crucial in this matter of achieving our autonomy.

For spiritual seekers, it's back to school for us! But this time it's your own personal school, and you will be both teacher and learner. *And it will never end.*

This autonomy we are speaking of pertains to the matter of gathering knowledge and developing pertinent skills to support one's quest to live a manner characterised by sound health, peace of mind, and a soulful connection with Mother Earth and our fellow planetary dwellers. We are talking becoming skilled navigators and livers of life. Primarily, we need life skills, communication skills, and various other cognitive skills, and we want to feel confident, worthy and intelligent. That is your autonomy and that is your spiritual living.

Underscoring all this is the essential, primary skill of learning. We didn't learn how to learn at school, not properly, and we have much we need to educate ourselves on. The best place to start is on ourselves.

I have said we were schooled into a conditioned ignorance. According to my observations, this ignorance lies at the root of just about all of our problems.

We have assumptions, beliefs and ideologies through which we interpret life, and which are triggered by all the situations and happenings that go on around us. This causes us a problem because such interpretations operate in our mind below the radar of our consciousness, whirring away in the background of our subconscious mind, where they masquerade as 'facts' and the 'correct' way of doing things. If you and me agree on things then no problem, but once we disagree we are likely to find conflict because we both assume ourselves to be correct, and therefore the other must logically be wrong.

It is this part of our mind which was conditioned and programmed into alarming levels of ignorance when we were being 'educated' in our schools and universities. Society, itself ignorant, repeats the problem generation after generation.

In short, it has led us to *believing* what is true, on account of what the external authority told us. Externally-supplied knowledge is king, and our own experiences are interpreted against the prevailing knowledge of the culture and society we were brought up in. We have been taught the knowledge and values of our society and culture, and we have been taught what to think. We have not *learned* for ourselves, nor *how to think* for ourselves. And why would we need to research things when we already know?!

We believe what we are told is true rather than seek out the truth by our own experiences and learnings. The books and experts have the knowledge, not we.

Clearly we *can* think for ourselves, at least to some degree, for it's instinctive and intuitive to a human being and hasn't been completely hammered out of us in our schooling, but we discover that various punishments or negative consequences will arise if we go against the mainstream view. Fear easily arises, which blocks us from functioning properly. And in this way, we lose touch with who we are as unique human beings. Very sad, and it's led to our global mess, and to me writing this book.

It is vitally necessary for all individuals, who care about life and our planet, and who desire good health for both, to decondition and re-educate themselves, to do inner work and to explore the meaning of things, using their own mind, heart and soul.

In doing this work - I call it **life inquiry** - we have to challenge almost everything we thought we knew, including who we are ourselves, and at times this can be a lonely process which brings about self-doubt and quite some mental tiredness. But many rewards keep us going, especially an underlying improvement in our health and ability to be happy and content. Because I've done the whole process myself, I'm going to do my professional best to make your inner journey a whole load easier.

You might like to consider your journey to this end as a process of guided discovery, with me to help navigate you through the terrain and challenges that come your way. How much help you would like from me is entirely up to you. I am a resource to fit your own needs, there is no one-size-fits-all here, not at all. The framework is the same for all, but the content will vary according to your own station in life.

Awareness and **conscious living** are your true friends to this end, my friend, and they will never let you down. Awareness exposes ignorance like the light of a torch shone into a dark room - darkness rules the roost until light shines upon it, whereupon darkness, the previous boss, has no chance, its power is gone because it cannot fight light. Same with awareness to ignorance, and the same with spirituality to politics. I have frequently observed in today's society what I call a *culture of certainty*, which I see as a last-ditch effort by ignorance to protect itself from being exposed.

Engaging in conscious awareness takes us from ignorance to knowledge to understanding to intelligence, and nothing can stop it.

It is through the process of **observation**, with the mind in a state of awareness (being alert and giving attention), that you can learn all you need to learn - about yourself, about others, about life. I can tell you, we all have abundant resources of innate intelligence within us - hitherto suppressed by society. You just need to trigger it all into action. Observing life, others and yourself with awareness does that, never fails.

Once you have learned how to learn - we have two chapters on learning, and seriously, very few people know how to *effectively* learn because nobody ever taught us - you will be up and away. Did you know that proper scientific process and rigour is to *observe* phenomena, take steps to *verify* what is seen, and then *replicate* it to augment, test out and double-check things? Well, on that basis any of us ordinary citizens who observe and reflect upon what we notice, can become our own mini-scientists. Knowledge and understanding is definitively not the sole preserve of the books and the educated experts, no matter what the external authority says.

With your newfound learning skills and conscious approach to things, it won't be a case of trusting or distrusting the information I bring to you here, it will be a case of you having the conscious wherewithal, intuition and impulse to verify and challenge it for yourself, and to apply it to your own unique context in life. I shall share my techniques on how to do that at various points in the coming chapters.

How DID you get on with the task in deciding who you are?!

There are various ways of looking at who we are, so different answers may have come to you. 'Who am I?' is the main question which has vexed philosophers and spiritual adventurers throughout the ages. I think an important part of our exploration is both finding out the bits which we all share as fellow human beings, and what marks us out as individual creations and unique expressions of the universal life force. We can only grow into what we consciously know and discover.

To learn who we really are, and how life works, introduces us to an interesting conundrum: we have to use our mind to learn about our mind. We look out at the world and universe through our mind. Yes, it all comes into us via our five sense organs, but all incoming information is processed and interpreted through our mind. And when we express ourselves through our words and deeds, we do so through our mind. Your mind is central to everything you are and do.

Thus to know who we are means we should know all about our mind and how it works.

I recall being interested in psychology at school, but when I studied it as an optional course it was confusing and they only talked about what famous past psychologists were saying. As usual, it was external knowledge coming my way to teach me about the world, instead of engaging me to use my own mind to think about things. I want to know about the world through my own mind, through my own explorations and experiences. I think we all do. And we must, if we are to become who we were meant to be.

Since that rather futile introduction to the inner workings of the human mind, I have, for my entire adult life, reflected deeply upon our psychology and human psyche, and on how life out there works. I have engaged in much discussion with willing friends, travellers, and lovers of existence over the years on 'the meaning of life' and who we all are. To me, life is part living it and part learning about it, and each enhances the other.

Without your mind there is no universe for you. And without the universe there is no you and no mind for you. We start to see the true nature of both our mind and the universe…

In my view, there is no realistic understanding of life, or ourselves, until we investigate our inner world, the outer world, *and* how the two worlds interrelate and connect together. Much of western thinking, science and medicine has been barking up the wrong psychological tree on account of their separation of the inner and outer worlds. It's why most of humanity is lost and messing up the health of everything it touches. It seems to me that they use the mind only as an instrument for investigating the external world, and not to investigate the mind itself, not to delve into our inner world, our inner being.

They also deny the soul, which is why so little of it is seen in society. I celebrate and nourish my soul, for it's my life force and my connection with the universe. Common sense alone tells us we are interconnected and interdependent on the planet which gave us our life. Luckily, cutting edge science is now recognising this.

I think our work is superficial, and our spiritual revolution not possible, until we explore our mind, and this is central to our whole enterprise. Everything we cover is, in some way, related to better understanding our mind and our inner world, and how our inner world interacts with the outer world. For be sure about it, my friend, the *out there* and the *in here* are intimately interconnected, and always the twain shall meet! Your mind is the bridge.

I'd like to tell you how it is that I managed to seriously advance my understandings of the mind in general and my own mind. My accidental new life that happened to me in 1991 instigated a whole chain of events, including my love of one particular activity, which is not your ordinary western human pastime. This activity blew my mind open and lit it up. I became a hopeless addict…

DURING THE ENTIRE 1990s living in Thailand, I became highly skilled and practised in the activity of *doing hammock time*, gaining hundreds if not thousands of hours of practice under my belt. If it were a martial art, I'd be a black belt. Said hammock would be on the veranda of my spartan eight bucks a night wooden bungalow, always right on the edge of the white sand beach of a beautiful bay or cozy cove, and looking straight out at the emerald green sea, sparkling under a deep blue sky and tropical sun. The waves were usually about two millimetres in height. Palm trees were everywhere, bulging with coconuts, and my bungalow would be set amidst a heavenly tropical garden within the resort's grounds. Back in the 90s the tourist explosion was yet to hit Thailand, there were no mobile phones or internet, and usually the beaches were empty, save the odd person walking along it, or an occasional fisherman in his longtail boat chugging his way across the bay.

Mostly speaking, *doing hammock time* involved four kinds of cognitive engagement. Two were more relaxing, taking-it-all-in receptive modes, and two were more reflective and productive modes…

I would observe the world of nature busy doing its stuff, doing what it does because that's what it does, and this was better than any movie to me. Picture each of the following, all vying for my attention: fluttering butterflies of all colours, gigantic bees buzzing all over, hovering and zooming dragonflies, scurrying red-headed green-bodied lizards on the sand, lots of birdsong, intermittent bursts of cacophonous cicada screeching, which would smash the silence to bits, a mesmerising ocean and sky view, and much else to dance its way into my senses; I was hypnotised… it was stamped 'heaven on earth'. I could watch it all day. And I did, day after day after day. Without knowing it at the time I was doing heaps of meditation on my hammock. I just marvelled at this scene, allowing the mind to wonder and wander as it so chose. Time stood still and I was absolutely connected to the grid of life; the only problem I used to have was what I would choose for my next meal.

Whenever the urge took me, I would reach for my Walkman (if you're a youthful reader, I hope you know this was the precursor to iPods and the like!) and listen to my reggae music. Reggae music in this peaceful mode of life further plugged me directly into the universe.

When I felt cognitively active and productive, I would take a break from the movie of the natural world and either concoct up new, exciting and challenging learning tasks and activities for my English students back in Bangkok (I still have my notebooks full of such stuff), or I would go deep into my mind, and investigate and reflect upon the nature of life and the human mind. It's where I did lots of inner work on myself, and certainly observing nature at close quarters, and for such long periods of time, helped me work things out for myself. I learned much from simply observing other creatures going about their business, all working and interrelating in a sort of giant web of harmony. The insect world and the singing birds didn't seem to have any problems, so why did we humans have so many?

Crucially, looking back, doing hammock time afforded me the time and space, in a very beautiful place, to reflect upon life, to explore it, to watch it, to learn from it. I used to think of it also as doing 'alone-time', not lonely, far from it - in this mode of living I absolutely did *not want* to talk to anybody!

And sometimes in my hammock reflections, I would explore why politics was like it is, why all the wars, inequity and corruption, and how things might be solved. Over the years, many answers and possible answers to this, and anything else I might ponder upon, came to me.

I was not yet investigating the spiritual books but, looking back, my island trips and doing hammock time were a deeply spiritual time for me. I looked outwards to a real-life heaven, and perhaps this helped me find the heaven within me. Which was the outside, within! I had always been taught that heaven was not in this world, not in this life, that one could get some pleasures along the way, but that deep happiness and contentment in one's life was not possible, not to be expected, just a dream… well, my scientific observations of my own life, and life going on around me, proved to me otherwise.

I might add that I tremendously loved my job teaching university students and working adults back in Bangkok, so I really was a deeply content person in that magical decade which preceded the explosion in technology and media. I lived in a one room apartment in Bangkok, had one key, one ATM bank card, and one bill per month, no TV, no computer. I was supremely happy with life, and only recall getting one cold and one other health ailment (which electrolyte salts solved in short order) throughout the 90s.

When I consciously began my spiritual investigations near the end of the decade and through into the early 00s, the spiritual books I was reading were telling me things I had learned on my hammock, and it was immensely exciting to realise others were writing about things I had been discovering for myself. Sometimes they were declaring this or that to be a truth, but my experiences ran counter to what I was reading, leading me to some challenges to solve. I especially saw the media talking about a world I was increasingly seeing for myself to be a different world, as if the media world was a parallel but opposite universe to the one I was in.

That is just a small glimpse into why it is I am writing a book like this. In fact, without me realising it, the 90s were me planting the seeds of this book.

Back to our questions, *Who am I? Who are you?* Related to them is... *How does life work?* For now, I'd like to offer you three possible variations and understandings. I offer them as a starting point for your own explorations, for as we progress through the book it is indeed the answers to these core questions that I think you will increasingly refine.

To make it clear and easy, and since it's you investigating who you are, I shall refer to 'you' most of the time, but it really just means all human beings.

The first **you** we shall refer to as the **'essence of human life'**. In this view of who you are, you are a body, a mind, and a soul/spirit which all merge and interconnect holistically in their inner workings, and are contained within the skin-covered body which houses you. This skin-covered body of yours - the blend of your body, mind and soul - marks you out as an individual and unique force of life within the whole human family.

Yet, you do not live in a black hole or a vacuum, you are intimately interconnected with Mother Earth who gave birth and life to you, and with the universe which is the supreme source of all cosmic consciousness and universal intelligence, which creates the force behind all expressions of life. You take in from the world food for your body, impressions and experiences for your mind, and from the universe, divine consciousness and the life force for your soul. Your body and mind are the unique essence of you; your soul is your interconnected essence of you - connected up with all other humans and everything else on our planet, and in our solar system too due to the influence of the sun, moon, planets and stars on us all.

Thus, you are *a holistic entity* with a blend of three identifiable dimensions who is interconnected with everybody and everything else beyond your skin. You are an amalgamated body, mind and soul entity, itself amalgamating with the external world. While you are a unique expression within the human world, in this *essence of human life* it's easy to see how we are all the same in one aspect, as in oneness of soul, full of consciousness and unity, in one big human family. We are an *essence of life* and the universe made us this way, and we are members of the human family who stand in contrast to other species and members of the animal and plant kingdoms.

Interaction, in this version of you, is the operative way of 'socialising'. We interact with life out there, and, within our skin-covered entity, physical matter and conscious energy interact and blend into a whole.

In the second view of who **you** are, you are **'your ID and ideology'**. In this view you have your *personal identity*, things like your name, passport number, nationality, religion; and then your *ideology* which provides you with a set of beliefs and values characteristic of your cultural, societal and national affiliations.

You can see that, to all intents and purposes, all of this was 'given' or 'taught' to you as a child by the human world, the *nurture* part of you if you like. We did not choose any of it for ourselves. Education and upbringing, media and government are the givers and the teachers. It is thought that if we all think and behave the same, or very similarly, then peace and order in society will exist and chaos and anarchy are avoided. Whether we have ironically created the opposite is for you to dwell upon.

So while your ID nominally differentiates you from other members of your nation, your thinking and behaviour is pretty much the same as all those around you within your society or country, and this has moulded you into a certain shape, or way of being. If you try to think or get outside of this 'box', you will likely find the going to be rough. In different nations you get different amounts of leeway for individual behaviour and thinking, and this itself is in flux, times change things. Nations with a strong literary heritage, where books are to the fore of everyday life, indicate to me greater leeway for the individual to explore life outside of the standard ideology of society. When censorship of books and in media rears its head one can logically assume that individual thinking is being suppressed or manipulated.

Again, as in the **essence of human life**, you have an individual persona and yet, again, it is easy to see how we are also all but the same as the other members of our identified group/s. But, unlike the **essence**, you were not born into who you are, instead you were taught, conditioned and moulded into who you are. Furthermore, the group to which you belong is not the human family, only a certain section of it, which first and foremost is your nationality, but also the societal and cultural influences which have arisen out of your country over the passage of time and history.

Everybody thus is labelled into this or that group, and in this way we are marked out as the same as other group members, but different to non-group members or 'outsiders', 'foreigners'. Even within the one nation and society many divisions are found and promoted by media and government, not least gender, colour and political persuasion. In this version of you, you are conflicted between being moulded by society and culture into the same as others, while being told you are different to others along group lines.

We are connected with other group members, yet we are disconnected from many people who are outside the group. In the past, and still, many crimes, much violence, and frequent wars have occurred within the same group or between groups, and for me this is due to a sense of disconnection with those we cause harm to. Whereas in the **essence of life** we are interconnected, in the **ID and ideology** mode we have a sense of disconnection from others despite the effort to mould us into a homogenous being.

Control - *controlling* or *being controlled*, and whether by persuasion or force - becomes the operative way of 'socialising' and relating to each other. After all, you have a fixed identity, and to ensure your group membership, you are expected to conform to the prevailing standard ideology of life, and if one resists then control is likely to bring you back into line.

The third answer to who **you** are is **'your unique essence'**, and in this view of life we are *intelligent interconnected individuals*. That is to say, a mix of *human nature* the same as all other humans, and *your personal nature* unique to yourself; the blend of which is your *natural self*, **your unique essence**. You will do human things because you are a human, and you will do things natural to your own unique self because of your unique creation and constitution you were born with.

By *human nature* we mean the instincts, impulses, and intuitions in our psyche as a human being, derived from the sum total of all that has ever happened to all of the humans, aggregated from all of time. The Stone Age or Medieval man and woman had rather different impulses than we generations alive today, but nevertheless, whatever they had remains within the code of what it is, and is possible, for us to be as a human being in this new Information Age that we all live in. Evolution, at least psychologically, doesn't get rid of things, it just moves along accumulating and adjusting.

If you ever get a feeling of just wanting to get back to a simple life, much more in tune with the rhythms of nature, then this is your Stone Age instinct kicking in!

By *your personal nature* we can say the instincts, impulses, and intuitions unique to you, arising out of such things as your parental genes and karmic influences from your immediate ancestors, astrological charts and planetary locations during your birth.

In *your personal nature* comes your innate likes and dislikes which predispose you to choosing particular foods, hobbies, colours, kinds of people for friends and so on. We also have natural skills (cognitive or motor) for particular activities we find easy to do, while in others we find we are not naturally adept; and we have typical traits and tendencies to kinds of behaviour, both positive and negative.

Reading your star sign or the Chinese horoscope, and other astrological sources of information, pertains to this view of who we are within our personal nature. You will also find out in the Ayurveda chapter about three major different kinds of constitution, along with a further four sub-types. All of this alludes to *your unique essence*, and helps you formulate your own understandings.

While you share the same aggregated *human nature* with all other human beings, *your personal nature* is unique just as your fingerprints, voice and face are, and thus you have *your unique essence.* In this way we are interconnected with each other, and with the universe, and we are innately intelligent and uniquely individual. We are intelligent integrated interconnected individuals.

Doing what seems and feels natural to you is the operative way of socialising in this way of being. Because being and feeling natural comes easily to us, we seek out friends of a similar manner, and often times good friends are a boon to us because we bond with them on the level, no hierarchy is implicit or explicit in such relationships.

This is your *nature* in contrast with the *nurture* aspect of you from your *ID and ideology*.

And so there you have it, three versions of who you are. In my understanding of life, nobody can tell you who you are, certainly not the government, nor even the master guru of all gurus, only you can work out an understanding for yourself, but it's always useful to get other people's ideas to help us, guide us, inspire us.

As we move through each chapter, the underlying current is to help you reflect upon life, your own life and yourself. The more we get to know ourselves the more we learn about life, and the more we learn about life, the more we learn about ourselves. And a big part of learning about life is learning about other people.

I WONDER if you've been to Thailand?

I live here and have done since 1991 when I left England to go travelling to the mystical and oriental Far East - and at that time it was surely a land little-known and little-visited by westerners, for this was years before the internet made our world seem smaller.

I loved the people and the country so much I never went home. It's another story which I will pick up on later.

Now, during this travel time I met and enjoyed talking with

many Thai people, and loads of other travellers from various countries and cultures. It wasn't so much tourism and suitcases in those days, it was still very much the haunt of travellers and backpacks. Getting to know each other and comparing life back in our home countries, and sharing our stories and adventures from our travels in Thailand (and some had been to other countries on their world adventure) was a huge part of the whole travel experience for me. What a buzz this travel game was. I think part of my own nature is to thoroughly enjoy newness, travel, and meeting people.

'Travel broadens the horizons', it is said, but with me it seemed my horizons were going galactic in expanse. I loved meeting the fun-loving Thai people, trying to use the Thai words I was picking up, but mostly communicating in English which many had enough to go on. The Thai girls were mesmerisingly beautiful to a twenty-seven-year-old single western man, and the men were super friendly and wanted to talk and get to know me. It turned out they all loved English football and my team Arsenal were champions at the time, but they all liked Liverpool or Man Utd. I was the winner!

It was a deep pleasure living every single day in this carefree atmosphere, and always the food, three times a day, sending the tongue into orgasmic orbit. It also *felt* like I was in Asia, far removed from developed and rule-bound Europe, and with the 'internet' not even a word yet, I felt suitably 'lost' in the world. Everything was raw, hot, happening, and all in stunning vistas and landscapes of nature.

It was during my travels that I became super familiar with an English language expression used by the Thais I met. It would go like this: we would meet, start by sharing names and where I'm from and (if a chap) what football team I supported, if I liked their food (I loved it beyond imagination, all the spicy coconut curries and banana fritters and pancakes for pudding, so delicious, 'aloy mak khrap'), and we'd then chat about other things, usually comparing our own lives and our own countries and cultures.

At some point, inevitably, the Thai person would laugh and smile and say, '*Same same… but different!*'. It was like a running joke, it was frequently said between people who were meeting each other for the first time. It spread also to being used between travellers. It was a mutual recognition that, despite our different countries and cultural backgrounds, we were basically the same people but… with some differences. We enjoyed the same things, had the same values and aspirations, wanted to get on with each other and did so with ease. We were indeed different in background, but in this slower-paced, stress-free environment, we all seemed same same in character, with the same basic desires for social harmony and mutual friendship. Same same but different. Neat!

As a side note, it was more than satisfying to be able to talk about oneself and one's own life and experiences and listen to others doing the same, with mutual interest in each other's stories and life; this was not at all what I was used to in my life in England where you're not really meant to talk about yourself much, which is a shame because we each live out our own unique life, and it's natural we should like to share it with others and hear them being interested in us, after all, you are you! Here in Thailand they wanted to meet you, hear about you, learn about you, and so did fellow travellers, and I wanted to hear all about the people I met. We are social animals after all, and here I could be me and was completely welcome as me. I felt natural and free, just the… **unique essence of me**!

Same same… but different. This is it in a nutshell for me, this is the heart of the human condition, and when we learn its truth we realise how deeply we are all interconnected, how we all cry together or laugh together. We each have our own destiny, but we also have a shared destiny, and the two destinies are intertwined. It is essential we care about ourselves and about others. In this way we learn and we empathise. The more we meet others, the more we speak and listen, the more we learn about each other and life.

Learning is the basis for discovery and liberation, to me this is a no-brainer. Since learning is the mainstay of this book, I'd now like to introduce you to the essential ingredient for effective and enjoyable learning. I have used it for over 25 years in my classrooms and any educational experience without it is unthinkable to me. All my teaching revolves around it.

I am talking about the humble but amazing **task**. Tasks ensure personalised learning, taking the focus off the teacher and putting it onto the students. Tasks have dozens of benefits, not the least they develop the mind's abilities and cognitive skills. Tasks enhance learning, and learning enhances life. Job done!

Just before you start the new chapter, have a think on this: what does 'task' mean to you from your experiences in life? Can you remember doing any during your schooldays?

4

A DOZEN TASKS

It was December 1991, and my spending money was shot. I came to Thailand on a one-way ticket (seems crazy now, but it meant more spending money and therefore more travel time), and I'd told friends and family I'd be on my travels for a year. I'd lasted not even four months, so much for budgets and best laid plans. Money never does what it's supposed to do.

Not only did I feel entirely unready to return home, so much fun was I having, but pride also kicked in about returning so soon with my tail between my legs, not to mention it being the middle of a, no doubt, freezing cold and grey British winter. I would be miserable and feeling sorry for myself and my grand adventure would have been cut horribly short.

I had reached decision time with no hiding place: take the easy but distasteful choice of bottling it and going home, or try and get that English teaching job I had read about before setting off to the Far East. Doubts surfaced, how would or could I get a job in a far-off land?? Was it really possible? Me, a teacher?! Never had I considered the idea in my 27 years of life so far.

And then there was the gut-wrenching realisation that my travels and my simple, zero-problem beach life were about to end, adding negative vibes to the mix.

At the start of my trip, chilling one day at a cafe in the warren of guest houses and eateries of the top end of Khao San Road in Bangkok, beyond the temple, I had met a fellow traveller and was talking about my idea of trying to get a teaching job when my money ran out. His words were now ringing in my ears loud and clear: 'If you really want to get an English teaching job, you will get one'. It made me feel good at the time, and now that time was here. I might add that I'm a person who is predisposed to take the easy path in life.

But I really really did not want to leave this amazing land called Thailand and her people which had grabbed my heart and mind during my time here. I was clear: no bottling it, put yourself out there man, just do it. *Do* it.

The bottom of my rucksack suitably ransacked, and with my pair of crumpled trousers, tie and shirt (put there months ago in England on the off chance they might be needed) now lovingly cleaned and ironed by the girl working at the Apple guest house in Khao San Road, I set off by bus early in the morning to the centre of Bangkok. I don't recall getting on the bus, nor the journey getting there except for the unbelievable traffic, but I do recall getting off the bus and out of the air-con, and being pitched into the middle of a bustling city with tall buildings everywhere, and the heat, oh man, the heat! As I got off the bus it whacked me fair and square, like I'd stepped into an oven. My three month uniform of shorts and t-shirt had given way to a long-sleeved shirt and a tie, which in this heat felt like I was in the hangman's noose. Within seconds of walking the sweat began, and once it's started it never ends.

Armed with my bit of paper with about six private language school addresses on it, which I'd written down back in England, I went looking for the first one, and presently found it. Excuse me, do you need any new English teachers? No, no vacancies. I tried the next one and, excitingly, they sat me down and started asking questions. But it seemed I wasn't qualified or experienced from my completely honest answers.

I was back on the steaming polluted streets, lost, and wandering around looking for the school which had several branches around the city and therefore seemed the most likely to have a job for me. The sweat was pouring down my back and drenching my forehead; thoughts of giving up were already getting louder in my head, and of getting onto an air-con bus to escape this boiling polluted madness so I could get back to the travellers' sanctuary of Khao San Road. Yes, this seemed the best option. Clearly, getting a job just wasn't that easy. And what was I thinking anyway, you can't just pick up a job halfway across the world.

Suddenly, with my internal chatter nattering on like a busy woodpecker, I noticed ahead of me a sort of square with many buildings and some trees which at least would afford me some shade to properly contemplate my next move.

As I turned the corner, I saw three huge letters on the side of one building, ECC - English and Computer College. Wow, that's the one I wanted to find, I thought to myself, feeling a most welcome surge of positive energy. Fancy that, just sort of bumping into it. I thought I was lost. As I headed over to it, I saw three or four westerners walking along together, and they were wearing shirts and ties, indicating to me they were English teachers (I think it was about lunch time by now). I thought to myself, they had got jobs, so why can't I? I felt a jolt of envy mixed with hope.

As I entered the building this blast of cool air enveloped my whole body, and the relief from the intense heat and sweat was instant. The very next thing my senses picked up on were four or five impossibly beautiful girls sitting behind the front desk in a pretty large room, and all wearing smiles. Not only had I found the school I was pinning my hopes on, but it had morphed immediately into cool heaven replete with angels.

They gave me two forms to fill in, an application form and a grammar test form. I filled in the first form and, learning from my previous experience, included a couple of, erm, white lies. I turned to the grammar test. Oh my Buddha, what on earth is a *present perfect?? The passive voice? A split infinitive?* I wracked my brains back a decade to learning French in school. I did the best I could, thinking I'd probably failed at the first hurdle.

The most mesmerisingly beautiful of the impossibly beautiful girls took my forms away upstairs somewhere, and then I was sitting down in a chair to the side, waiting. Students, teachers, secretaries came and went. I think I must have been there nearly an hour, still waiting, thinking they'd forgotten about me and considering just getting up and going back to my travel digs. All sweat had gone, but my Aries impatience was kicking in. Perhaps it wasn't meant to be, just face it, the British winter was looming large... Luckily I remained long enough, because suddenly one of the secretaries came over to me and led me upstairs. Now we're talking, action!

She sat me down in a sort of corridor right outside this huge solid teak or mahogany door with a brass plate on it declaring it to be the office of the 'Managing Director'. Opulence or what, and I thought this is it, this is your chance, be calm, make sure you smile - Thailand is the Land of Smiles after all. I think my dedicated desire for getting a job and not going back to England yet dominated my feelings: in more normal times in my life I would easily have given up by now, and I didn't feel particularly overwhelmed by this solid door and nameplate, or from the occasion I was now wrapped up in. I found myself easily sitting there nice and calm. Maybe three months of being a beach vagabond had helped too.

Presently, the solid door opened and this smallish, somewhat rotund, friendly-looking man bid me welcome into his office. It was a large room, and his desk was more resplendent and extravagant than anything I'd seen in my 27 years of life, more solid teak, but as I sat down opposite him I then noticed, leaning against the wall next to his desk, a large London A-Z road map. We said our hellos and before he could ask me any questions, I commented on his map, 'I see you've been to London before'. A broad grin enveloped his whole face and for the next ten minutes or so he regaled me with his travel stories of his visit to the great city of London. Clearly he was fond of England and English people, and once he'd finished telling me about my capital city, with me sitting there like a Cheshire cat, he said the 'interview' was over and he would take me to the Head Teacher now. Blimey, that was an easy interview!

Now I was sat opposite an affable smiling bespectacled man called Dave - it said so on his nameplate on his desk - who told me he was from Bolton. We small chatted for a while, and I told him I'd just been living in nearby Manchester for four years. We got on well, sharing our nation of birth, and I recall the lack of formality in him which was most agreeable with me and put me at ease. Then, as anticipated, he asked me if I had any teaching experience. Zilch of course, never had I even given an atom's thought to becoming a teacher before my big travel adventure.

My fellow traveller who had said I'd get a job if I really wanted one, had primed me to say no, but that I had taught some local villagers in Spain once. I trotted out this answer in absence of anything better to say, and I never forget his reply, word for word: 'Exactly how I started', he said, grinning and banging his desk with his fist in what seemed like an act of camaraderie and brotherhood to me!! Oh, bingo I thought, it seems to have worked. Maybe that's what everybody says, maybe it's some sort of code language which, if you had managed to come across it, showed resourcefulness (instead of lying) and would open the doors for a job.

But then I remembered the grammar test which I surely had failed.

Then, and again I can hear his exact words as time stood stock still, 'When can you start?'. I affected nonchalance as best I could (didn't want to appear desperate), and informed him tomorrow would be no good (as if my diary was too busy), how about the following day. He said great, told me I was assigned to the Lard Prao branch and to report to Glen, the Head Teacher there, first thing in the morning. I had an urge to hug him, but that felt improper.

I left the building, barely noticing the angels downstairs, virtually skipping into the gigantic hot oven with the utmost delight and excitement. I just could not contain myself and felt like screaming with joy, but somehow withheld myself; I had landed a job and didn't need to fly home to the super cold winter and the ridicule of my friends! I sat on the cool air-con bus for an hour or two going back to Khao San Road, marvelling at the idea I was about to be an English teacher, and that I was staying in Thailand for the foreseeable future. It felt like a dream too good to be true, but it was true. What a beautiful bus journey it was.

I burst into the guest house and told all my travel mates I'd got a job. They were all chuffed for me, and life seemed immensely sweet.

I think I had about 30 pounds worth of baht in my pocket… I had come right down to the wire.

And so began my new life. I'm still on that one-way ticket…

My tale of how, what turned out to be, my accidental emigration and accidental brand new line of work began, brings me nicely onto the matter at hand in this chapter: some one dozen **tasks** I have for you.

I immediately found out, right from my first day's work - on a Saturday morning for a three-hour class with three students, and an afternoon class for three hours with about ten students - that teaching was my vocation in life. I already knew how much I loved being in Thailand and meeting Thai people, and now I was 'teaching' young Thai adults, the majority of whom were female. It was all too good, *and* it was true! What a surprise to me to find that I loved teaching and was natural at it. Did the universe gently direct me to where I needed to go??

My head teacher Glen told me Thai students wanted to speak and they wanted fun and games in their learning. I took it to heart, making it my primary objective to become the best teacher I could be, and the main tool and strategy I had to help me through the initial months, while I built up some experience, was the humble but brilliant *task*.

In essence, in ordinary life, a task is a 'job to do', a bit of work that needs doing, a chore even. But in the educational context it gathers a life of its own, with so many guises and uses, and its major benefit is that it is a highly motivational tool to direct and facilitate learning. It makes learning a positive experience. And *that*, my friend, is priceless in human life, would you not agree?

The learning task is the central component around which all learning takes place. It drives the learning process. Well-set tasks motivate students, get them working together in pairs or small groups (without the teacher), in collaboration or competition or both; tasks make it clear what they have to do and achieve, provide experiential learning, develop their self-confidence, build trust between classmates, and last but not least, task-based learning gives the teacher opportunities to observe the students going about their learning, and to notice where they are struggling or succeeding, helping them out if requested.

Students love this kind of learning - they achieve results, they see they are learning useful stuff, they acquire a whole gamut of communicative and cognitive skills, they gain in self-esteem, and by the time the money and time has run out for their studies, they are well set up to learn for themselves out in the wider world context. They are learners for life because they are now skilled in learning, problem-solving, and communicating, and know how intrinsically satisfying it is to be a human being when learning something new or becoming more skilled at something.

A task has a process, an objective, and content. It engages one's brain, and being passive is not an option. After the learning episode is over, a reflective task can be set which gets the students thinking and talking about the task they have just done, what they learned, what they found hard or easy, if it was fun and so on. Strategies and techniques can be developed and practised.

To sum it up, the task personalises learning, allowing people to see how what they learn fits into the context of their own life. It brings them knowledge and develops their communication and life skills, and therefore puts them in charge of their own life. We are beautiful, unique, individual expressions of human beings who feel best when socially connected to our fellow humans with whom we can explore, collaborate, compete and enjoy life together. The task knits it all together, triggering the expression of our nature as *innately intelligent interconnected individual* human beings.

THE BOOK you are engaging with is a book of learning, and so I'd like to bring you into the world of *task-based learning.* I said at the outset you would have much 'work' to do since it's your life, your revolution, your spiritual quest, but that I would help and guide you along the way. My main method for doing that is to offer you tasks at regular intervals throughout the book, and in this way you can find your own answers and develop your own understandings and skills as you evolve. Often the tasks ask you to think about the issue at hand before I give you my ideas, triggering an awareness in you that you know a lot more than perhaps you previously thought you did. You ought, if I'm doing my job well, to then feel curious and motivated to find out what I'm saying about the topic matter, to compare it to your own ideas.

In this way you will find the more cognitively-challenging bits easier and more rewarding. So don't skimp on the tasks! They literally are integral to your spiritual revolution.

In essence, such tasks are opportunities for you to observe things, raise your awareness of issues and then reflect what it might all mean to you.

To that end, I have a nice round dozen of them for you to do over the coming week (but don't begin any of the tasks until you have finished reading this chapter). This will set you up nicely for the *Main Courses section* where most of the cognitive work and learning is to be done and where you'll find plenty of other tasks along the way.

If I'm about to sound overly like a teacher in a moment, please forgive me, but if one is new to learning through tasks, some important things need to be noted at the outset to ensure the tasks are fully effective. So read carefully!

The first thing to say is that you will need, if you've not got one yet, to buy a notebook, and might I suggest it's a beautiful one with good quality paper? Beauty and quality are motivating forces, and will help you to enjoy doing the tasks, recording your thoughts and ideas in your beautiful notebook. I don't want to stop you from using a computer if you prefer, but I heartily recommend acquainting yourself with the old-fashioned pen and paper writing skill - you will not regret it.

The second thing to say is that each task has two stages: *doing it,* and subsequently *reflecting upon it.* The second stage utilises your notebook. A more effective and deeper learning arises from going through a sort of playback, where you go through what you did, after the event, thus gaining a different perspective, and in this way the learning event is enhanced. If you find yourself reflecting *while* doing a task too, fantastic, go for it. Reflecting is recalling, inquiring, better understanding… and it develops within you a keener eye for observation, and promotes self-awareness, two essential learning tools for your spiritual mission.

The third thing to say is that if you have a friend reading the book too, you could do the tasks at the same time. Or, even if they don't have the book, you could persuade them to do the tasks, and then, once you've both completed them, you can compare and share your experiences in doing them. But if you're on your own that's fine.

Here are some of the **cognitive expressions of your mind** which will be triggered by doing the tasks: *noticing, observing, discerning, questioning, inquiring,* all of which lead to and enhance learning. They are essential mental skills for your spiritual revolution, and will be needed in spades once these foundational chapters give way to the rest of the book. All of them help you cultivate *conscious living.*

The dozen tasks are split into two groups: firstly there are six *one-off* tasks, one to be done each day; while the second group comprise of six *ongoing* tasks, all to be done every day for the six days. The seventh day is for a full reflection of the 12 tasks.

With my teacher's hat on, here are **your objectives** for the 12 tasks, and please let them really connect with your conscious attention:

i) to familiarise yourself with the interactive nature of this book whereby you will be an *active* reader and a *proactive* revolutionary, putting into action - mentally or practically - the information that I'm sharing with you, testing it out for yourself and not just accepting my word as true

ii) to familiarise yourself with the procedure of doing tasks, which will support you through this book and for your own lifelong learning thereafter

iii) to give you practice in observational and noticing skills, meaning you are engaging in self-awareness and conscious living

iv) to help you motivate yourself for the learning journey ahead of you

v) to enjoy the challenge of being a learner

vi) to learn about, and delve into, your own mind.

Would you like to add any objectives of your own?

Still with my teacher's hat on, please carefully read through the **task instructions:**

i) Do them only to the best of your ability, there is no such thing as failure here because there's nothing for you to pass; just put your full heart and mind into doing them.

ii) Each day for six days you will have a one-off task to attend to, and all six ongoing tasks to do. During each evening (after dinner is often a good choice), find a period of time to reflect upon the one-off task you did, writing down your thoughts, observations, ideas, discoveries, anything you think merits recording in your notebook. Writing is the perfect tool for encouraging reflective thinking, so be sure not to cut corners here. Make similar notes relating to your ongoing tasks too.

iii) In order to successfully carry out the first instruction make sure you won't be interrupted by anybody or by any kind of media, notification sounds, or phone calls - full attention and focus on the task at hand is required to make it successful.

iv) On the seventh day, after you have completed all 12 tasks, *return to this instruction* so you know what to do next. Conduct an overall reflection and note down any insights, questions, or thoughts that have come to you during the week or during this reflection.

Also write down how you felt while doing them, and how you feel today (day 7) in mind and body compared to your usual feelings. And, after you have finished this reflection period, sit comfortably and ask yourself, 'What have I learned about my mind and about life?'.

v) If a friend is doing the tasks too, get together on this seventh day to share your experiences and reflections; if you so desire, get together each evening to discuss and share what you've experienced and noticed so far.

This preamble ends with a couple of **notes** about doing the tasks:

i) Be the most attentive noticer and observer you can be of things going on outside of you *and within your own mind* while doing the tasks (and it will be good news for you if you apply this to the rest of your life during the whole week too). Keep away from media or other distractions.

ii) The one-off tasks need not be done in the order presented, so long as you do one each day. If for some logistical reason you find yourself unable to do a one-off task as planned, then do two of them the next day.

iii) Have fun doing them, and put your all into it.

iv) If you intend to continue reading the book during this week of tasks may I suggest you don't start the *Main Courses* yet. There are two more chapters in this section of the book to tide you over.

v) And finally, before you get started, I have a quick task for you, not to be skipped! Without looking, how many of the cognitive expressions, objectives and instructions can you recall? Then reread them and see how you got on!

One-off tasks

Day 1 task: Observing nature

Find a place in nature that you like, and is easy to get to. Could be your garden or anywhere in the great outdoors where nature is abundant. Sit comfortably, alone and without any potential for interruption from people you know; turn off your phone and all social media so you don't hear any pinging noises, and remain there for about an hour, longer if you wish, but ensure a minimum of half an hour. Your objective is to notice and observe everything going on around you which enters your senses, in particular the sights and sounds, but any smells too. Notice any feelings and thoughts that are triggered by what you see and hear or by your overall situation, and notice if your attention is distracted by random thoughts popping into your mind - if they are, just return your attention to the scene around you.

DAY 2 TASK: Observing people

Go to a busy place where people come and go, are constantly on the move - for example, a train station, a cafe, a market, the town centre, a beach, anywhere there are people coming and going. Again, make sure you won't be interrupted by others or by your phone. Sit down and (surreptitiously) observe them, do some people watching. Perhaps for an hour or so, but at least half an hour. Notice their facial expressions, body language, posture, actions, movement and pace. You can only see them as they are now, but for them they are in the middle of their life - they came from somewhere and they are going somewhere, things will have happened to them before you see them and things will happen after: try to imagine these before and after bits, let your imagination flow and decide if you think they are stressed or calm, happy or unhappy people, even what kind of life they've had.

As you observe them and think about them, notice your own judgements, thoughts, and general mind activity.

DAY 3 TASK: Random acts of kindness

Carry out an act of kindness to a stranger. Do it several times with different strangers throughout the day if you wish. For example, hold the door open for somebody and smile at them as you do so, give some money or food to a beggar or homeless person and talk to them for a while, help somebody across the road, go visit a person who is lonely and would love a chat, or find any kind of situation where somebody looks like they need, or will enjoy, help. You may pre-decide what you will do, or you may act spontaneously as the situation arises. If you feel shy or a bit silly, just notice the thought and ignore it. Notice how you feel after being kind, and recall how the person you helped responded to you.

Day 4 task: Listening to music

Choose a favourite album, cd, or playlist, half an hour to an hour should be about right. Get comfortable and listen to it with your full attention, and *do nothing else* until it's finished (breathing is a fair exception). Really *listen* to it, to the singing, and try to pick out all the individual instruments. If you find your mind wandering, and as soon as you notice its meanderings, just immediately return your focus to the music. And you know it by now, no interruptions and no phones, unless of course you're using it to listen to, in which case don't use it for anything else for the duration, and turn off any notifications.

Day 5 task: Slowing down

Choose a day (a day off or a work day, whichever you prefer) and make it a 'go-slow' day. Do everything more slowly than normal: having your shower or bath, cleaning your teeth, buying or cooking meals, eating (focus on fully chewing your food), drinking water, tea or coffee, breathing, walking, driving, cycling, speaking, reacting to somebody, work, decision-making, chores, everything. The objective is to not do things *too* slowly, rather to just consciously slow down from your usual subconscious pace of doing things, and to do them with as much focus and attention as you can muster and maintain. See if you find the little routine things enjoyable or laborious, and notice how your mind reacts to going slower than usual. Also notice if you somehow have sped up to your usual pace, and then return back to the slower pace.

DAY 6 TASK: Cooking and enjoying a healthy meal

Probably dinner is best, but any meal will do so long as you're not in a rush to go somewhere. Stir fry a mix of vegetables lightly in some herbs and spices, or make a vegetable curry. Focus your attention on the preparation and cutting up of your food, and on the cooking. Buy fresh local organic vegetables if possible. Do your best to avoid buying them from the supermarket unless they are organic. Eat with potatoes, or any whole grain such as brown rice or brown pasta. Use white if you cannot get any brown. Enjoy eating the meal at the table, with no TV, no smartphone, no reading and no conversation, just focus on enjoying the meal. Chew well every mouthful and carefully observe the tastes in your mouth, and the whole eating experience. If your mind starts thinking, wandering off at tangents, give it a reprimand and return your focus to your chewing and tasting of the food. If for whatever reason you can't cook your own meal, then buy the healthiest meal you can and follow the instructions for eating it.

WEEK-LONG TASKS

THE IDEA I have with this second set of tasks is that they take you out of your routines. Routines and habits, especially for some, are very hard to change for we like our patterns in life, we like an easy life, and comfort zones can be hard to get out of. And I mean thought routines as well as action ones. It's easy to get stuck in routines or thought patterns which no longer serve us, or to develop habits that are detrimental to our health, often without realising it. These six tasks will bring about changes and new mini-routines into your life for a week, and then you can see what rewards and insights come your way from making such changes.

Start all of them as soon as you can, on the same day, and *continue doing them every day for six days*. Be mindful that some of them may prove difficult to achieve at the beginning, just persevere each day the best you can, and notice if the going gets easier. Remember, there is no success or failure with these tasks, simply that you do them as well as you can - if you fall off the wagon one day, then pick yourself up and get back on track the next day. Don't use one day's 'failure' as an excuse to quit doing the task on the other days. If you fail to do one or two of them on a day, it's no big drama, but that said, do your very best to keep them all on track.

Task 1: Gaining an hour in the morning

Go to bed an hour earlier than your usual bedtime, and get up an hour earlier than usual. During the extra hour each morning (and after your usual ablutions):

i) Do some stretches, some yoga or tai chi, some running on the spot, go for a walk - whatever feels good and is easy for you. If your body is out of shape, then be gentle with yourself. Don't over-exert yourself. The aim is to just get the muscles moving and stretching. Maybe about 15 minutes.

ii) After your exercise, sit down in a comfortable upright position, make your back straight and focus on relaxing your muscles, especially the neck and shoulders, push your chest forwards and hold your shoulders and head upright, and then focus on your breathing. Breathe in and out as deeply as you can, feeling your chest expand and contract. Count to 30 breaths, if you lose count, start again. Notice why you lost count. Probably 10 minutes or so will be good here. If you get to 30, do another 30.

iii) Make yourself a nice breakfast and enjoy it without feeling rushed and without any media. If you can hear birdsong where you live, enjoy listening to it.

Then return to your normal day, albeit incorporating the rest of the tasks.

. . .

Task 2: Being proactively positive in a relationship

Pick a person - a family member, friend, neighbour, anyone you'll see most or all of the days during the week. Be extra nice towards them for the week. If you react negatively inside your mind, explore this feeling or emotion and try not to act on it, bite your tongue if need be. Decline to get involved in any typical arguments you may have. *Don't tell them what you're doing* until the six days are up. Being positive towards them, noticing how you feel about this, and noticing how they respond, is your focus and task objective here.

Task 3: Food and drink

Choose one of the following, but ideally do both.

i) Avoid eating any processed, refined or manufactured foods and drinks. Such foods are a) made by food corporations and in some kind of packaging, with a list of ingredients on them, many of which are strange words or number and letter codes; b) all corporation-made fast food and junk foods. This may mean no sauces you might normally use, unless home-made or with natural ingredients only.

ii) Avoid eating white sugar. Not only does this mean not adding white sugar directly to your food or drinks, it means no coke or similar soft drinks, no cakes or biscuits, no donuts, no chocolate bars, no crisps, no processed foods, no nothing that has white sugar in it. You may have to get used to looking at lists of ingredients. High-fructose corn syrup and artificial sweeteners are out too. Sticky unrefined brown sugar is okay. Be careful with bread, it often has a lot of sugar in it.

You may wonder what you can eat. Whole foods in their natural state is the answer - brown bread, brown rice, brown pasta or other unrefined grains, potatoes, vegetables, fruits, seeds, nuts, honey, eggs, dairy, meats, but with the last two items eat only minimal amounts, or even better, not at all. Drop dairy foods before meat. Eggs should be from free range chickens. The emphasis for this task is to eat wholesome, nutritious and natural foods only. Each evening during the week, note down how you felt in body and mind that day, whether you are sleeping better, and any other changes you notice in your body and mind.

Task 4: News-fast

Do the first of the two, and try very very very hard to do the second one as well.

i) Avoid exposure to the daily news. Don't watch the TV news, don't listen to the news on the radio, avoid talk radio, don't buy a newspaper, don't look at news sites on the web, avoid even seeing headlines if you can. No news at all.

ii) No social media. If you need to, just post up a message saying you're embarking upon a six-day experiment. If you're addicted to social media, just go cold turkey, you can do it! Only the first day will be hard.

Total news-fast is the objective. Just experience and enjoy relating to your own real, non-media-driven, world for a week.

Task 5: Alcohol, cigarettes, coffee, drugs, chocolate, sweets, cakes, snacks, comfort foods, other stimulants

Whatever you frequently have, or are addicted to, stop for the six days. If you feel you can't stop, then cut down as much as you possibly can. Don't increase another to make up for your loss.

Notice any cravings, and what your feelings are as you progress day by day. You might find it easier to resist your cravings by building on your new beginning to the day each morning - let it get you off to a good start, and this change in routine may well help you get through the day without succumbing. I can tell you from personal experience that changing our environment or routines helps us to drop harmful habits and neutralise addictions.

Task 6: Researching and learning

Think of a subject matter or process you are interested in, or would like to learn more about. The world is your oyster here, from making fermented foods to ancient Chinese history, from painting people to the geography and culture of Bhutan, from creating a podcast channel to the basics of permaculture. Set aside some time each day to do your research, and create a summary of what you learn either on your computer or in your beautiful notebook. A good objective is to learn enough so that after the six days you will be able to teach other people about it.

Optional extra: Create your own task

If you get into the mood, come up with one or two of your own tasks to add to the mix.

Day 7: Reflection time

Look at your notes from each day that followed each task, and now spend some time reflecting on them as a whole. Here is the fourth task instruction again, which I wanted you to reread when you get here after the six days is done: 'Conduct an overall reflection and note down any insights, questions, or thoughts that have come to you during the week or during this reflection. Also write down how you felt while doing them, and how you feel today (day 7) in mind and body compared to your usual feelings. And, after you have finished this reflection period, sit comfortably and ask yourself, 'What have I learned about my mind and about life?'.'

Find a place to reflect that makes you feel comfortable and content. The objective here is to look at the bigger picture, to take in a more macro view of the 12 tasks. I'm especially keen for you to notice, and be aware of, anything you have learned about your mind, consciousness and self-awareness.

It would be most useful for you to write a summary of your reflection of the whole week.

Now that you have arrived here you are ready to start doing all the tasks. Good luck, enjoy them, and just do your best. They are for your own learning and revelations, there are no 'answers' from me, although as we progress through the subsequent chapters I shall refer back to them when an issue triggers me to. Don't forget, once the six days are over, return to the 'Day 7 Reflection time' instructions just above.

5

THREE TALES

I have three tales from my life to share with you. Each have their own flavour and educational or entertainment value, which I leave for you to relate to based on your own experiences in life. In the spirit of the *Starters* section of this book, they are designed to trigger in you contemplations and reflections about what is important in life.

Task

I think it would be good to do a quick 'pre-reading' task. The three titles of my stories are 'A Spiritual Morning', 'War Bloody War', and 'My Introduction to Natural Healing'. Your task is to guess or predict what you might read about in each tale. Put your ideas down in your beautiful notebook. Once you've done that, read on to find out if your guesses were good.

A Spiritual Morning

I exit my bungalow, walk down the track of the resort and out onto the road, and begin my walk towards the temple. It's early morning, dawn is done, and the sunlight is just beginning to flicker through the trees and foliage, throwing the day's first shadows onto the road surface. As I walk along, breathing the fresh earthy-smelling morning air deeply into my lungs, there's not a vehicle or human being to be seen or heard. Lining either side of the road are impressively thick silvery-grey trunks of trees that reach bolt upright far into a clear blue sky. They are so tall I creak my neck trying to look at their tops. Such tremendous life forms, they inspire awe and delight in me as I put one foot in front of another. As always when I'm amongst trees, I feel calm and cool, joyful and alive. I think they engage my soul. I was into trees as a boy. I used to have a tree encyclopaedia, and the pictures and description of the giant redwoods of California used to blow my little boy's mind to bits, and these ones I am now in amongst remind me of them.

To my right, visible between the trunks and just beyond these immense life forms, is a forest dense with other trees of myriad shapes and sizes, and to my left in the near distance is the magnificent sight of several jagged mountain peaks soaring into the cloudless sky. In the foreground, between me and the mountains, is lush tropical jungle bush vying with open grassland. In glorious quadraphonic surround sound, and entering my whole being as if by osmosis, I hear the songs of a thousand newly-woken birds in playful mood, all alive and wise to the new day. The orchestra is in full flow, the conductor invisible. I keep walking slowly on towards the temple, drinking in this immensely pleasant scene. The morning is young and what a song to delight my soul. I feel at one with the universe, I'm feeling sweet, the vibes of life are real good and playing just the right tune for me.

I'm in northern Thailand and I'm heading along this winding deserted road towards a well-known mountain-top temple for the first time. (I think it's a monastery, for many monks live there and it's a big complex, but we'll call it a temple.)

After a couple of kilometres of this immensely pleasant scene, the road comes to a dead-end and I'm in the temple grounds. To my right there's a small car park area without any cars parked there. Just behind it is a large immaculate lawn hosting a resplendent

Buddha statue, and trees are all around. To my left are a couple of worn-looking buildings containing typical paraphernalia found in temple areas in Thailand. And then I espy ahead of me the beginning of the walk up to the temple on the mountain. My excitement builds, for I am now at the start of what I have been told are over 500 steps in a forest setting leading up the mountain to this temple. I live for these kinds of experiences.

The tall trees and flat terrain are finished, and now, as I start climbing, I am under the canopy of a new set of trees to behold, protecting me from the heat of the fast-climbing summer sun and keeping the air fresh and cool. To either side of the walkway is jungle growth. It's a riot of greens interspersed with bits of purples, yellows and pinks, each claiming their own space while beautifully enhancing the greens. Slithers and slices of sunlight, which have managed to penetrate the canopy of trees, flicker and dance in concert with the shaded bits. My internal vibrancy amplifies in its resonance to an awesome frequency - the sights and sounds around me have pitched me right into a heaven, and I feel light and fully alive: thank you Mother Earth.

I climb slowly, in no rush at all. Such an immensely pleasant scene.

Then, stuck on a tree trunk, I see a green sign with white writing on it, in Thai and in English. I stop to read it. It imparts a Buddhist wisdom of life on it: 'Look and contemplate within to see the truth. Looking out at others we are immersed in delusion'. I pause to let the message massage my mind and inner being.

Then as I resume my climb, and not many steps later, I come across another green sign: 'However kind or mean the hearts of others is their affair and not ours. We can't control the hearts and minds of others. Our duty is to work on our own heart. Work on the only heart we can truly feel - this heart here in this body and this mind'. The notions and experiences of *control* and *freedom* are close to my heart, which I have reflected upon at length during my life, especially in my hammock, and I love this message. I stick around, feeling the words imparting their wisdom in me, contemplating, in no rush to continue my upward journey.

But on I go, finding many more of these signs all along the journey towards the mountain-top temple. I stop at each one, imbibing their messages. The quiet wisdoms they offer, combined with the majestic jungle and monastic setting I'm in, offer a calming feeling for my body and mind, and I feel my soul engaged; my earlier volcanic-like excitement has quelled and given way to a feeling of serenity and inner stillness. Their messages in the natural peace and tranquility, punctuated by the birdsong from near and far, combine to further enhance my spiritual state of being.

After a particularly steep section it flattens out and I come to a sign that says I'm halfway, but that the going gets much easier now. Then, just a few yards along comes an opening in the trees to my left, and there, above and beyond in the near distance is a glorious golden pagoda, sunrays sparkling off it, sitting amidst a temple complex, all perched on a mountain ridge and surrounded by thousands of trees. Behind it is the towering presence of the main mountain which, framed by the deep blue sky, looks just so handsome; the blueness seems to be giving divine protection to the whole monastery. What an awesome sight. The sparkling golden pagoda, the mountain, all the trees and the deep blue sky all vie for my attention.

I sit down on the bench that is conveniently placed and admire this epic view, wondering how long it took to build this temple all the way up there on its mountain peak.

I stay sitting there, absorbed by my surroundings, not wanting to move. Then, almost as if on cue, a line of monks appear to my right dozens of steps away, coming down towards me. The first people of my morning. Their orange robes brilliantly add colour to the scene, giving relief to the green all around them. As they descend, sunlight flickers on and off their shaven heads and faces, and it seems the movie is playing out for me perfectly… I like the director's style and I love the script.

After what seems a long while sitting there, I decide I must pull myself away from this tranquil spot and head up towards the temple. It's a tough choice because I had completely lost sense of time, and I am so at ease just sitting there drinking in this immensely pleasant scene…

Anyway, I think I'll cut the story short there. Suffice to say I got to the top, which put me right in amongst the treetops and the songful birds, and whereupon I communed with the nature for quite some time. I also sat alone in the temple which was built into a sort of cave, offering cool air and some respite from the heat outside. In here were a whole assortment of Buddha ornaments, such as amulets, sculptures, huge candles, incense sticks and so on.

I literally was, and felt like I was, on top of the world.

Some time later I began wending my way down, ready to exit my spiritual experience and go get a *pad krapow*, the go-to chilli, basil and garlic-based dish in Thailand, and to cool myself down from the, by now, very hot day with a nice cold beer. My Buddhist bubble of serene spirituality had waned, and it was back to the more material-based pleasures of life. It was a beautiful spiritual morning indeed, but now for a spicy lunch washed down with some cold beer. What a grand day I was having!

However, the tale does not end without relating to you my very favourite message of all the green signs, and at which I stopped on the way down to reread and enjoy. It was the one that most resonated with my understanding of human life and, in my view, if all people lived by it, our world would indeed be magically transformed. In fact, it feels like it is central to the whole enterprise of one's spiritual revolution. See what you think:

To harass others is to harass yourself
To belittle others is to belittle yourself
To destroy others is to destroy yourself
And block the path to your prosperity.

War Bloody War

Bang at the start of this new millennium we had the second Iraq 'war' which followed the 911 attacks in New York, America. By now I knew the 'game' of global politics, I understood how it all worked, and that the mainstream English language media version of everything was mostly just a work of fiction.

Since I can remember, seeing ordinary people suffer from injustice and unfairness has affected me, and whenever I can intervene to help I do. I saw lots of it at the school I went to, and I hated it. I don't like bullies, nastiness or cruelty. Perhaps it's why I followed politics and geopolitics closely and always had done. Before I left England I knew of the crimes committed by those holding powerful jobs in powerful countries, but not the extent of it all, nor what the root causes were, or what the solutions might be.

For nearly a decade - pretty much since starting life afresh in Thailand - I had been reading books on 20th century history, politics and major events in our world. It made for brutal reading, and really messed with my human essence. The crimes powerful humans committed against the powerless were (still are) heartbreaking and outrageous in equal measure. So pointless.

This was still the pre-internet days. I carried on reading book after book, due to my penchant for learning and understanding madness in order that we may find solutions for our human fraternity. I found it impossible to avoid feelings of rage inside my whole body. It was these bouts of anger that actually pushed me towards my own spiritual expression, for I realised that my health and wellbeing were suffering. I had to do something about it. I did, and it showed me again that pain or discomfort can be the trigger for learning and evolving in one's life. Back in the 90s I held a terrible hatred for those who bombed, burned, and broke humanity. Nowadays there is none, no hatred. I realise those who act like this are themselves broken, no soul, no spirit, no essence of life in them.

We absolutely need solutions in our world, for all of us, every single member of the human family, both the transgressors and those transgressed against - to destroy others is to destroy oneself.

THE IRAQI CITIES and people were being bombed mercilessly by the 'allied' air forces of the US and the UK, with people and buildings alike being destroyed into rubble. Democracy by the ballot box? Not by this manner, no sir, in Iraq, democracy was coming by death and destruction. The media never asked the people orchestrating all the killing how a dead man was supposed to vote. Instead, they parroted the politicians' rhetoric, labelling Iraqi citizens 'insurgents' and 'militants' who were 'defending' their 'strongholds'. These 'rebels' and 'terrorists' were, of course, just ordinary citizens like you and me, trying to stop these powerful bully nations from smashing up their towns, their communities and their very lives.

We can see how language can be used to seed certain images and ideas into our minds, to 'persuade' us of the righteousness of those who were warring.

I personally was feeling sickened, as were no doubt millions of other American and British citizens in whose name this military aggression was being perpetrated, sickened by this naked violence, mayhem and death being delivered on a massive scale, and equally sickened at the misleading reporting of it in the main newspapers and on the TV news. And sickened that I could do nothing about it.

Did it not matter that thousands upon thousands of citizens were being killed, leaving distraught friends and family members behind? And did it not matter that if those spared death were lucky enough to keep all their body parts intact, then most certainly their minds would have been in trauma and turmoil, just ripped apart from losing loved ones, and in some cases having their whole families wiped out? And what about all their markets and schools and homes being converted into rubble by the American and British bombs smashing into their communities?

There were over a million people in the UK marching against this 'war', but that made no difference to the prime minister and his support for the US. Nor the media's. The whole thing would screw with my head every time I thought about it.

I went to my local paper shop on this particular day, and bought *The Bangkok Post.* Different media, different nation, not subject to all the war rhetoric and government propaganda back in my home nation. And there, on the front page, was a large photo to bring tears to my eyes, to bring the full horrors of what certain people in the corridors of power in the US and UK were doing to this proud, ancient and historical nation right into the heart of my mind and soul. Pictures have a resonance, an immediacy, that even the best writers cannot capture. Pictures do indeed tell a thousand words.

The image is still seared in my mind whenever I think about it. I'll copy and paste in here what I wrote at the time since it captures my raw feelings without the mists of time interfering with my memory...

Today's front page of the Bangkok Post carries a photo I doubt very much will appear anywhere in the British or American press (although I'd love to be wrong). In the background is a tank and in front of it is an Iraqi family fleeing along an otherwise empty highway lined with street lamps. The father, a little paunchy (maybe likes his beer?) is on the right and is holding his daughter's hand. She looks about nine or ten, as does her sister who's holding her hand. This smaller sister is close to tears. Holding her hand is her older brother, perhaps about 13 years old and good-looking. All are very smartly dressed, and all have bodies intact with no missing parts. Or at least they did at the time of the picture. They are clearly fleeing from something.

This poor poor family, it makes me weep in my heart, makes my eyes fill with tears. The father has a pained, anguished look on his face as he tries to find safety somewhere for his family. It is just so so sad. A father, his two daughters and his son, ordinary people like you and me, trying to live their life, but having it ripped upside down by this so-called war, this monstrous and insane invasion of their lives.

I then find I'm wondering where the mother is... blown up, killed?

It was such a sad image. And I recall an overriding thought as I looked at it, shaking my head at the stupid viciousness of man and his barbaric underside, that it could have been a British family fleeing for their lives on the M25 (the eight-lane motorway that circles London) as Iraqi bombs rained down on their homes, neighbourhoods, and cities. But we really shouldn't think too badly of the Iraqi bombers, because after all their government were doing this to bring democracy and freedom to the British people...

I looked everywhere on the net to see if such an image had made it to the US and UK papers, but nothing. Clearly not an accident, because the picture demanded a human response to a human suffering. Our so-called free media were doing their best to sanitise the war, as is their norm. This family were not insurgents or rebels, but they *were* the enemy... and the face of this 'enemy' was not to be seen by the people from the countries that were fighting this enemy.

In our name as ordinary citizens, powerful people attack and kill our fellow citizens, our brothers and sisters, in far away lands. One wonders if they will one day turn on their own.

Not many years after this imperial adventure, we learned that something like half a million Iraqi children had perished in the subsequent brutal sanctions against Iraq applied during the Clinton era. The female Secretary of State in Clinton's government, being questioned whether this was a price worth paying for having the sanctions, replied in the affirmative. She said it was 'regrettable' but 'worth it'. Half a million children dead (they never said how many adults had perished)… but that's okay.

Not a man who said this, a woman. Insanity clearly is gender-blind when stalking the corridors of Empire office.

Sorry for the negative vibes in that tale, my friend! But now a happier tale for you.

My Introduction to Natural Healing

A big big change to my life began in 2008. I was 44. I became acquainted with my own body…

While I had extensively explored politics, philosophy, spirituality, and all matters relating to human psychology, the mind and the soul, and their inner workings, for whatever reason it had never occurred to me to explore the inner workings of the body that housed them both. I was absolutely ignorant of the very thing which carried me and my life. Furthermore, I was pretty ignorant of how physical stress could impact negatively on my mind.

Physical pain, one time too many, made me change. For two or three years my body had been struggling with back pain, muscle problems and other associated 'tensions'. Doctors and treatments and pills were beginning to creep into my life.

When I look back now, I'm astounded that I neglected to take good care of my body. Not only that, but I had, frankly speaking, hammered my body with beer for over two decades, and, at this time, was still unable to quit my part-time smoking habit. However, not taking care of one's body is commonplace in most countries, and again I shall put it down to our skewed education system. It seems we treat our bodies like a garbage dump instead of the temple we ought to. After all, it carries us in our life, and such mistreatment is unlikely to end well. But here's something one can only learn by oneself: a bad diet and harmful habits don't punish you today, only at some point in the future. We think we are well, but we are brewing up trouble... we accumulate problems in the background, out of our sight, and then one day bam, pain, or worse arrives. Lack of information and understanding is the culprit. As always!

For a good two decades of adult life I'd enjoyed pretty good health - barely taken a pill in nigh on 40 years - and I'd led a very happy, rewarding life, much of it in Thailand. I used to covet good sleep, drink lots of water, and generally be good at avoiding mental stress, but these were the only things I proactively did in relation to my health. Until I took up golf in the late 90s, I basically did no exercise, although I do like to walk.

My diet in England had been woeful and I recall getting colds or the flu two or three times a year. It got much better in Thailand due to their focus on using fresh produce, plenty of herbs and spices, and all is available at markets on almost every corner of the nation. It was super cheap to eat out, and that's what I did all the time. Interestingly, I only got a cold once that I recall in the entire decade of the 90s while living and working in Bangkok. Undoubtedly I was living a very happy life.

But back to 2008, and the years of my free-wheeling life were clearly ending, for I had become a target of my own dietary and lifestyle choices. My bullet-proof youth was over!

One or two warnings had crossed my bows in my late 30s, but

upon getting better I paid little attention. However, now was different. My primary health complaint was lower back pain, which was striking me more and more often, most especially in the middle of the night when I would wake up with the pain. I could only get relief from the pain by sitting up, but then I struggled to get back to sleep. I think losing my precious sleep was what finally pushed me into action, good sleep being one of my few efforts to be healthy. My body was undoubtedly too tense and rigid, and I think this affected my mental and emotional outlook on life too.

At times I might have been bending over cleaning my teeth, washing the dishes or something innocuous, and my waist and lower back would suddenly seize up and convulse me in agony! One morning I resolved to myself that I needed to pay a visit to the hospital to get medical help.

An x-ray revealed no physical problem with my back, which I thought was good news, and after consulting with a doctor, a physio, a back specialist, a herbalist and other assorted avenues over the next few weeks, nothing and nobody could help alleviate the problem. My logical thinking told me that if there was no physical deformity there must be a solution somewhere.

As I was trying to work out my next move, I suddenly recalled an article I had read in the *Bangkok Post,* which was so interesting at the time I had cut it out and kept it. I managed to dig it up and reread it. It was an introduction to the health system of Ayurveda from India, and reading it got me excited. I sensed it would lead me to answers and a solution to my back hassles.

I did a search on the net and found three Ayurveda places in town; two were at five-star resorts and charging exorbitant prices for the financial means of a teacher, but the third one, in the old part of town, looked promising so I rang and booked an appointment.

On the 31st of October, at 5pm, I turned up at the Ayurveda Centre for my appointment. Revelations galore were about to unleash themselves upon me.

First thing I noticed was a lovely tropical garden, and upon entering the reception area I sensed a serene vibration to the place. The scent was good, not those sanitised smells you get in hospitals, it sort of felt like a home, and I was greeted by a smiling elder lady. I was given some kind of herbal drink and details were taken. The energy felt good, and I felt calm. So far so good.

Presently, two other younger ladies dressed in traditional northern Thailand style clothing beckoned me into a room. There, on a table, I saw a small machine which immediately provoked curiosity in me. Looking at it as I sat down next to it, I saw it had a dial ranging from 0 to 100 and a needle resting at zero. Out of it came two wires, one with a sort of copper rod which I had to hold in my left hand, and at the end of the other wire was a sort of metal pen-shaped thing. One assistant would then push this pen thing against the bottom of each finger and thumb of my right hand, on both sides, and then the same again on my toes of my right foot. This gave them 20 readings of my body. Each time the pen thing touched my skin it would provoke the needle into action and the other lady would note down each score. From memory, only two readings failed to reach 100, and for most of them the needle rapidly flew to the 100 mark, making a sort of screeching noise. I deduced 100 to be not a good score. I could see on the form where they recorded my measurements, different parts of the body listed, such as my liver, kidneys, stomach, nervous system, heart, blood, lymph and other parts I can't recall.

Now, I'd never come across any such machine in my life, nor knew of the existence of such things, but I was very interested to learn that a machine could measure the state of various parts of my body. I could not yet trust it, because it might be some gimmick, but I was curious for sure; I was good at physics at school and have a rather scientific bent to my mind.

I was led back to my original seat to wait for the lady doctor, and I contemplated upon this machine and its readings for me.

Shortly, one of the assistants led me into another room which was airy and nicely cool within the tropical heat, made so by a slowly whirring ceiling fan. It had one wall covered in books, and in the middle of the room was a rather large table. Sitting behind it was a smiling lady who was a bit older than me perhaps. She bid me to sit down. She had a kind face and a most serene manner which made me immediately feel super calm, and behind her was a large window revealing the beautiful tropical garden. Still smiling, she asked me to tell her a bit about myself. Now this was a surprise! 'Normal' doctors don't ask things like this.

Well, already I was fully at ease before we'd even got started.

I told her I was a teacher at one of the universities in town, and told her about my time in Thailand, how much I loved my life over here, that I was soon to get married, and a few other things, and only then did she ask me what my health complaint was. I told her about my back problems, that an x-ray had shown it was physically fine, and that I suspected my beer drinking might be causing my hassles, but it seemed to me she wasn't really concerned with my back or the beer. She looked at my 20 readings and I joked that I thought 100 was not a good score. I was right, and the nub of it was that this machine had revealed to her that my whole body was overheated, all the organs were being overworked, and my immune system was struggling.

She talked about many things, including giving me a basic introduction to Ayurveda and the three different body types (doshas), and that my type was prone to overheating and inflammation. She also talked about different diets for blood types, and about acid- and alkaline-forming foods. Lots of her talk was about diet. This was the first time in my life that I'd really been told about a direct link between diet and health. She mentioned the importance of sleep and a few other routines one should follow to promote good health. Everything she said was about promoting good health and preventing ill-health. Nothing was mentioned about my back! But from our chat it was clear she was focusing on my whole body, not any one part of it.

All this stuff about food and developing healthy habits was brand new to me, and a source of serious interest right away because I love learning new stuff. She was an amazing lady, speaking calmly with a lovely smile and, in my estimation, with great authority about health matters, and with that wonderful greenery outside her window and the sweet sound of birdsong, I almost felt like she was healing me as I was sat there. I felt super peaceful in that room with her, and over the hour I was with her she made me more and more optimistic I would be able to heal my long-standing back issues, explaining why and how we get ill. I'm into stuff like that, I'm always looking for causes of things as the means to a solution.

This was my first experience of speaking with a *health* professional who spoke about root causes of ailments, how the body worked in a holistic manner, and about the very concept of health itself - what a strange thing in this human world of ours! And very much so back in 2008. In fact, my whole time there was all based on this - hitherto revolutionary - concept of health and how, with her guidance, I was going to get it back. It generated in me a tangible anticipation and a feeling of positive energy, and she wasn't giving me a single pill, hooray!

I asked her about the machine and she said it was a bio-energetics machine she had got from Germany. In fact, I asked her lots of questions because she seemed to me the source of so much useful information. She patiently and willingly answered them, clearly explaining things to me. She gave me several sheets of paper with various bits of information pertaining to foods that complemented or antagonised my blood type, charts of acid- and alkaline-forming foods, and a list of healthy habits to build into my lifestyle for my specific Ayurveda constitution type. My 'treatment' was a mix of two spices (looking back I think turmeric was one of them), to eat over 60% alkaline-forming foods, and to avoid the 'bad' foods for my blood type, which mostly speaking meant all dairy foods, pork, white sugar and foods with sugar in them, processed foods, and one or two others. But in essence no dramatic change to my diet, although cheese and bacon would be two big losses for me, as would my shredded wheat with milk and sugar for breakfast. Oh, coffee had to go too, and I drank lots of that, but it would be revolting without sugar and milk. I also would think nothing of eating a whole big bag of crisps/chips before dinner with some pre-dinner beers, and that was now out due to them being processed foods.

One of the healthy habits she strongly suggested I include was to get to bed for 10pm. She also said I should make sure I don't get frustrated, impatient or angry with my girlfriend, or anybody for that matter.

This was not your usual visit to a doctor: in and out as if on a production line, you've got an '-itis', here take these pills and see if you get better, thank you and goodbye. What a difference.

She booked another appointment to see me again in two weeks. I asked her if I could continue to drink beer, and she said a few would be no big problem, but I don't think she understood how many beers an Englishman can drink, and in any case, I wanted to follow her diet properly and to test out this machine in two weeks time, and didn't want the beer messing up the readings, so I resolved to drink no booze until I saw her again.

I emerged out of her centre and into the twilight of the evening, my head buzzing with all this new information and understanding, climbed into my car and drove home, noticing a bit of a stupid grin on my face. I could not wait to get started.

As I drove home the only problem I could foresee was going to be my decision to not drink beer. It was Monday, and I knew I could fairly easily get by without until Friday, but the weekend was a different matter. Friday nights were pool league nights and going to the pub and not drinking beer, in those days, was surely impossible for me. I thus resolved to disappear from town after work on Friday and go to my favourite getaway up and over the mountains to another valley and small town for the weekend. I got home and told my wife about everything and that I would have to go away on my own for the weekend.

WELL, dear reader, my optimism proved well-founded indeed! By Thursday morning I had now had a full night's sleep without waking up to any back pain and, furthermore, I now realised from this rather strange, more flexible, *alive* version of my body, that I had got used to various other niggles and tensions because they had gone too. I also felt clear-headed, energetic and rather joyful. It felt like a miracle! Rewards coming to me so quickly.

The next day after work, I headed off on the three-hour journey to my favourite resort and favourite place in the whole of northern Thailand. My pool team would have to do without me!

I had a super healthy and tasty dinner at the resort, as always, cooked up by owner Orn, using ingredients from their garden. Her food was always to die for, and in my super healthy week it now seemed entirely appropriate. I wondered to myself when I had last gone a Friday evening without beer. I was unable to determine the answer. I went to bed early and slept beautifully.

After a super healthy and tasty breakfast in the garden, I walked into town through the paddy fields, about half an hour or so. I was feeling on top of the world, all this grand food and even grander tropical nature, and with a body that was flying with zest, and a new quest filling my mind.

Now, walking along the bottom road of the town, which is set against the river, I came across a familiar sight which in the past I always simply walked on by. It was called 'The Good Life and Herbal Restaurant', and previously, so I thought, it had nothing to offer me... what did I want with herbal drinks, I used to think somewhat derisively, beer was my tipple, beer gave me the good life. (Oh, how we can be so shaped by our set perspectives.)

But on this occasion as I got adjacent to it, I found that my body, by its own accord, turned left and I found myself entering this strange sanctum. My mind barely had a chance to imagine what I might find, but my body just took me in there.

I didn't emerge until nearly dinner time.

What an Aladdin's cave of foods, drinks, brews, potions, powders, herbs, plants and books it was! Just as its name suggested. It was a sort of bohemian design inside with chairs hanging from the roof, big shared tables to sit at, hundreds of books all related it seemed to health, nutrition and travel, and it sort of felt like somebody's large living room. Nice sweet herbal smells and home cooking permeated the place. The menu was packed with all kinds of healthy food options, and full of information. It also revealed dozens of different teas - black teas, green teas, white teas, oolongs - kefir and kombucha, which I'd never heard of, and other assorted concoctions. I saw lots of grass growing which turned out to be wheatgrass for making wheatgrass juice. Several people were in the restaurant and all clearly enjoying life.

I had never been anywhere like this and it was a heaven and a haven.

I ordered a vegetarian meal and the kombucha recommended to me by a chap in there, and dug into the books. I'm a book lover and knowledge junkie, and here were lots of books full of information on health and diet and so on. What I was reading in my skimming and scanning of several books was blowing my brain wide open. I was nearly a week into my own health journey, miracles were taking place in my body, and suddenly, here I was in a temple of health and good fun, with several other happy people in there, all looking the picture of good health and vitality. I got talking with some of them, mostly Americans, and I told them about my story, and my new efforts to live in a healthy manner. They were very generous with their time and patient explanations, and answers to all my questions. As with the books, what they had to say to me was super interesting.

I think the universe pushed me into that wonderful place that afternoon. I go back every time I'm in the town now.

I made lots of notes from the books I was looking at, agog at all the health information relating to diet and nutrition. This was not in mainstream media and had not been in any topic of conversation that I had ever known.

My head was really spinning now, what a week this had been. The next day I went right back to the health cave, and into those books again. A switch had gone off inside me, for sure. I do research in my job, am trained at it, and I do it very well. I had a new topic of interest to research, and I just could not get enough of it that weekend: diet and promoting good health.

THE FOLLOWING Friday I went out to the pub to play my pool league match and didn't have a single beer, it had now been 12 days and my momentum carried me through the evening without incident. I woke up early on Saturday morning feeling refreshed like never before on a Saturday morning.

On Monday I went back for my follow-up appointment. It was as if I'd had a body transplant since my previous visit, a man of verve, vim and vigour I was! My mind felt razor sharp and in fine spirits. No backaches, a full night's sleep each night, a flexible body, all bloody marvellous it was. How good life was!

The same two girls happily greeted me to put me on the machine again to measure my readings a second time. More miracles unfolded. I keenly watched the needle for each reading and guess what - just one reading went up to the 100 and it did so without any screeching sounds, while all the others were in the sort of 50-70 range. That did it for me, this machine was the real thing. Due to my teaching work at postgraduate level, which requires of me a scrupulous approach to avoid making any wrongful claims without supporting evidence, and my natural desire to see things in action for myself so I can speak from personal first-hand experience, I was overjoyed to see the machine was clearly a quite brilliant diagnostic tool for health problems. Why did they not have such machines in all hospitals I wondered.

It turned out my sole 100 reading was for my liver, and the lady doctor said the liver takes much longer to rejuvenate itself. But just two weeks of dietary changes, and I clearly had a body brimming with inner health.

And so thus began a new phase to my life, proactively seeking out healthy ways of living. It was a heady adventure for me, full of discoveries, and still is.

Since that final day of October 2008, and ongoing, I've done thousands upon thousands of hours of research into nutrition, healthcare modalities, 'alternative' natural medicines and treatments, the pharmaceutical and food corporations (it's hard to speak neutrally about them) and how they literally create ill-health in us citizens. I prefer books to the internet and have a whole library of them now, but I do also find many good quality websites. I've kept food diaries to investigate the links between foods and feelings in my own body, I've studied reiki, tai chi, and craniosacral therapy courses, done yoga programs, been to yoga festivals and investigated all kinds of healthy pursuits. Some I find not my cup of tea, many I really enjoy.

My very favourite research subject is Ayurveda and I have a good dozen books on this ancient but thoroughly modern and effective health care system. This puts your health care into your own hands. I devote a whole chapter to it later on.

I adopted a default diet from those early steps of mine, which I follow at home, but when I travel I'm not fussy and will generally eat what comes my way. In keeping my food diaries I have clearly seen for myself how diet can literally turn on and off my health. The link is undeniable to me, and of course there's a whole industry out there on it all nowadays. I didn't eat any dairy foods for about seven years, except for when I visited England or Australia, and I could always notice a downturn in my body's wellbeing after those trips. I could write a whole book on my experiences, but that's for another day.

I've increasingly investigated the link between thought and all mind activity and physiological responses, and I know very well that negative thoughts and patterns can impact negatively on our physical health.

All this time I've been battling with the beer, but the big victory is that when I do have some, I don't drink a lot. I successfully got rid of cigarettes a few years ago, and all in all, I do a good job of living in a healthy manner without being obsessive (perhaps in the early years I was a bit, but that was due to my tremendous excitement at learning how we can be in charge of our own health). I love eating healthy foods, and my focus is on whole foods. I never did eat fast foods and junk foods out of protest at these corporations and the damage they do to our planet. Out of ease I still eat a little meat, but wouldn't care if I never had any again. I do love eggs though, and won't give them up. I drink coffee again, with a bit of milk, but the thought of sugar in it is ghastly! Northern Thailand now grows outstanding coffees, and I enjoy a cup most days.

I will be the first to run straight back to the pub lifestyle and die early with a painful back if I ever find the healthy stuff boring or that it's taking the fun out of my life, but it does the opposite. I find good health in my body a brilliant basis for fully enjoying life now that I'm no longer protected by my youthful years. The amazing thing is how a happy, healthy body impacts so positively on my mental outlook on life. I also began to notice I became sharper in my teaching, and teaching topic matter like psycholinguistics, how the brain works, and how to do action research to my teacher students needs me to be on my cognitive toes.

THIS BOOK WAS BORN out of all this research. For years I had focused my attention on learning about our mind, yet now, finally, I had put the body into the mix. Now I had all the pieces of the puzzle, and just had to put them together. Back doing my hammock time a few years ago I hit upon a formula for who we are as individuals and a framework for understanding how life works... my trusty hammock strung up in beautiful nature always delivers! I think you'll love this formula and framework for life, and it neatly encapsulates the holistic and 'wholistic' nature of life.

My formula is '3DH5DL' and comes in the *Main Courses* section. The next chapter closes out this first section of the book, and gives you several short bursts of ideas and some good food for thought.

We then head into the main section of the book where I want to share my understandings of our body, and the mind and soul it contains. It is also a call to you, fellow citizen, to help our world by creating demand for whole foods and cleaner food production. Healthy food leads to a happy mind, leads to a desire for more healthy foods, leads to the dropping of harmful stuff, less stress, and bam, before we know it, we're in a virtuous cycle where life keeps on giving to us. Healthy people will demand a healthy planet, because they know how both are intimately linked.

6

FOOD FOR THOUGHT

The foundations to ensure the success of your spiritual odyssey and revolution are almost complete. By that I mean I hope you have been reflecting upon important issues of human health and life in your own mind, that your awareness of life around you and within you has been raised from your previous level, and that you are motivated and inspired to put in the dedicated effort needed to transform your own health and life. No doubt you're already on your journey, but it's a hard journey on your own, and the more help we can get from others the better.

In this chapter you will find various morsels to cognitively chew on and digest. They are fairly random and are from my notebooks I've kept over the years. If any of them prompt your own thoughts, or trigger memories, write them down in your notebook, or pause to allow your mind to do its work…

If the grass over there looks greener, water your own.

Knowing is fixed, understanding is fluid.

Living consciously allows us to choose and monitor our language so that we can avoid unintentionally hurting others. Using non-violent language creates a warm energetics within our own being, and will spread that energetics outwards for others to receive.

Either you're complaining and blaming, or you're living, but never at the same time.

First-hand experience >> confidence >> personal growth.

Pain and suffering is an opportunity for self-growth. Every problem is an opportunity in disguise; just look for the cause and take intelligent action.

Common sense, conscience, and compassion are excellent guides for us as we navigate the challenges of life.

Focusing on what we haven't got brings us suffering, focusing on what we have got brings us gratitude and contentment.

Change what you can't accept, accept what you can't change. Using violence or force as a means to effect change will always come back and bite you. Learning to accept the unacceptable in life is our greatest human challenge.

Don't give up, give.

All people love a good listener. And a problem shared is a problem halved, so let others share with you.

People who may do ill by you are only doing so out of their own hurt. Be gentle with them.

Harbour grudges and your boat will never sail.

It's your world and your life, so make it your world and your life.

Expectation is the mother of disappointment.

Don't expect respect. Don't expect, respect.

Use it or lose it; abuse it and lose it.

There are three kinds of energy in our human world: positive energy, negative energy and not-negative energy. Spiritual living is about cultivating the first and neutralising the second into the third.

I can't control what you do but I can control my reaction.

It's none of my business what you say about me, that's your responsibility.

Your greatest achievement is not to be somebody, it's to be you.

Scratch below the surface of society and you'll find a vipers' nest of egos destroying themselves and each other. Society is ego, and ego is society. Ego, untamed by soul, is complete suffering, and causes it.

Awareness, bravery, courage, dignity, empathy, fun, giving,

healing, intelligence, joy, karma, learning, mindfulness, nature, observation, peace, qi, reflecting, solutions, truth, understanding, valour, wisdom, x-factor, you, zest. Now create your own A-Z of positive vibes.

Spiritual nourishment is engaging and interacting with the world. Be loving, loveable and lovely.

Don't block love and happiness or think you don't deserve them, cultivate and celebrate them.

If not now, when? If not here, where? If not you, who?

Treasure yourself, for you are a living miracle. Discover your bad habits and replace them with good habits.

Ignore your prejudices, they're not yours anyway!

Learn to learn… learn to live and live to learn, learn to listen and listen to learn, learn to love and love to learn, learn to lead and lead to learn. Learning is your liberation!

Cultivate the 4Ps: being positive, productive, proactive and peaceful. Practice leads to skill.

Intelligence is living in harmony with the world.

Freedom requires boundaries; without boundaries there is no freedom.

It's your world, so look after it by looking after yourself.

Stop conforming to a mould, create your own and use the universe as your boundaries.

Don't be the person you think you should be, be the person the universe would like you to be.

We try to get rid of psychological or physical discomfort and pain any which way we can. We take alcohol, drugs, pills, comfort foods to numb ourselves from the pain. We try to ignore it, suppress it, pretend it's not there. We will try to control others who we blame for our pain, we will politically try to eradicate it, we will do anything at all so long as we don't have to change our habits and the thinking which led to the discomfort in the first place. Treat or suppress the symptoms, ignore the root causes. This is ignorant living, against nature, against intelligence, against harmony, against our soul.

Karma is absolutely clear: out of an action comes a related

reaction. Sow something today and you will reap the consequences in a future time. Any reaping you do today are those consequences playing out from your past actions, from your past sowing. Therefore if we reflect upon, and seek out, the causes of our problems we need not repeat our mistake. If we consider consequences before we act, then we can prevent future problems. Pain today suggests wrong action yesterday. Doing good things today suggests good results tomorrow. This is intelligent living.

Living consciously and spiritually means being aware of one's actions and reactions, and allows us to use free will in shaping our own life and managing our own health.

When somebody says or does something which you don't like, you may react with anger or resentment and you may blame them for your discomfort. Now, undeniably, they may have said or done something wrong or bad or unfair, but your problem lies in your reaction to that person, not what they did or said. If you blame them you are beholden to them, you allow yourself to be controlled by them, you accept their negative energy.

The purpose of one's spiritual revolution is not to change the world, it's to change yourself to create the person you would like to be. But since you are part of the world, part of the whole, by changing yourself positively you automatically change the whole positively too. The objective immediately goes from the undoable to the eminently achievable. Create the world you want by changing yourself.

Politics and political revolution is doomed to failure because it fails to address who we ourselves are. It's forever fixated on the external world as if it was separate to us, and we to each other. It is not and we are not. Everything is interconnected and interdependent, and therefore any politics or ideology which imposes itself on others against their will is hurting its adherent too.

Why would there be any higher objective than to seek health, harmony and happiness?

Pleasure is a momentary hit of sensory stimulation from something in the outside world. Happiness is a state of mind and heart which comes from within. It becomes possible when there's an absence of pain and problems.

Each moment of now - a 'now-moment' - carries a cause and a consequence. Therefore, present time contains past and future in each measurable segment of its perpetual infinite progress.

What is spiritual nourishment? Being in nature, being of service to others and the universe, giving and sharing, loving, nurturing life.

When you are ready to learn a teacher will appear. Sometimes that teacher is you.

Politics wants to know and control, philosophy wants to ask and learn, spirituality understands and appreciates.

Understanding something liberates you from it.

Anecdote is the voice of the citizen, a voice the 'experts' and powerful try to vilify.

Be a warrior not a worrier; be a wonderer and a wanderer.

Now is the bridge between cause and consequence. Learn the cause, shape the consequence.

Don't compare yourself to others, compare your today self with your yesterday self.

Being spiritual = respect and love for yourself, life, and others. In that order, and then once there, simultaneously.

If you're busy trying to be the same as everybody else, how can you ever be you? How can you even find out who you are?

Taking responsibility for one's health and life is the precursor to freedom.

It's always darkest in the hour before dawn.

The phoenix will arise from the ashes.

Don't beat your head against a brick wall. It hurts.

Nature is all intelligent, watch it and learn.

Spiritual living is you entering into a voluntary contract with Mother Earth to protect and enhance your life and hers, to the best of your ability. This requires you to forever push the boundaries of what your 'best' is. Thus you become a lifelong learner.

That's it my friend, the *Starters* are over. Now, time for the major part of the meal!

MAIN COURSES

This section is for feeding your mind and brain! It is for developing and enhancing your cognitive explorations and understandings.

Here, as you are imbibing information, you will simultaneously delve into the mechanics and sub-skills of learning. This will set you up for life. Learning is not a temporary activity for the spiritual warrior, it's a lifelong affair.

Plenty of tasks along the way will ease your path, help you get your head around the concepts and ideas, and to trigger you into uncovering your own, perhaps hitherto hidden, understandings and cognitive skills.

It's all about living consciously, with self-awareness, and reflecting upon your life and experiences. The *Main Courses* ask you to really extend yourself and push your boundaries, but in so doing you will experience many rewards and inner joys that come from discovering how intelligent you really are!

As you read through each chapter, bear in mind the two key questions which we seek to answer for ourselves during our spiritual revolution: *Who am I? How does life work?* It's an ongoing effort to answer them. And, I suggest, the answers are intimately linked, each leading to the other.

7

LEARNING: THE MOTHER OF ALL SKILLS

Fear of failure is our nemesis, the destroyer of the life force in us. We are subconsciously petrified of being seen to be ignorant or unhappy, and this primal energy blocks our evolution. Yet, most of us are ignorant or unhappy most of the time. Our fear is grounded in reality! We fear what we are, yet pretend we are not; and the greater fear is that we shall be found out for what and who we are. There is one glorious path out of this horror show: learn how to learn. And we're talking ***proper*** *learning.*

Which one is the odd one out: being taught, being told, being led, being educated, being learning?
The last one is conceptually, as well as grammatically, wrong; do you see the difference in practice? Learning is the greatest of all human endeavours and we have to do it ourselves, nobody else can do it for us.

Learning, and I specifically mean skilled and enjoyable learning, is the foundation for your transformation. Only you can do it for you. Teachers, gurus, self-help guides, books… all can offer you some help, but only you can do the learning. Committing to learning makes us responsible for our own life, it liberates us from dependency on others, and it enables and empowers us.

Learning is the bee's knees.

Welcome to the *Main Courses*, home of all the crucial stuff to be learned, so what better way to kick off than to focus on the mother of all skills: the skill of learning. But, what exactly is 'learning', and, how skilled at it are you? What are your previous experiences of it, and what feelings or thoughts does the word trigger in you?

Did you know that the system that spawned society handicapped us all when it comes to this super-useful, uber-essential skill in life? Read through this chapter to find out more. In it we must confront the dispiriting and shocking revelation that rather than being educated during our schooling we were *de*-educated. Ours was an anti-education.

In the chapter following this one I share with you various 'tricks of the trade' when it comes to becoming a skilled learner, because there's a simple equation in my view of things: the more skilled and proficient we are at learning, the more skilled and proficient we will be at living. And skilled living means loving, the giving and sharing kind of love. Yet when we have love inside us and share it out we can be sure it will find its way back to us. That is the law of nature. To love, and to love life, is the greatest beauty of being a human!

Skilled living also means enjoying optimal health, happiness and harmony as your default experience, from which you can lead a creative, productive and fulfilling life unhindered by negative self-talk and self-limiting beliefs.

And then, when the janitor from heaven arrives for your collection, you can look back on a long life well lived, have no regrets, and offer no resistance.

It's our personal responsibility for how well our body, mind and soul are working. We want a vital body, a sound mind, and an active soul, and it only happens through acquiring quality information, implementing what we learn, and practising our new habits to make them second nature.

Learning how to learn, becoming a *skilled* learner of learning, is the essential prerequisite for one's self-education, self-empowerment and transformation which underscores the spiritual revolution. It is good to learn knowledge, but it is even better to learn cognitive skills. For some extraordinary reason, the world's education systems in schools and universities fail to offer the subject matter of Life: how to skilfully live life and be a healthy human. We shall have to do the work ourselves.

I LOVE LEARNING, and I always have done, it seems I was born with a voracious appetite for it. I grew up very happily in a village in the green countryside of 1970s southern England. I engaged all the time with the great outdoors, loved nature, and it's still the same today albeit in the tropics. I recall being in awe of the moon and the black starlit night skies, I recall looking up at blue skies, wondering where the end of it was, I recall forests as places of magic. We had many family day trips down to the seaside, and did many walks around the fields and countryside where we lived. I spent time helping the local farmhand, playing in the woods with my mate, and cycling everywhere. Me and my friend made catapults, fished in streams with jam jars, never catching a thing, hung out in his dad's hay barn, and in general explored the living world around us. Our family had a black dog and two black and white cats throughout our childhood, and I loved them with all my heart. I learned so much about life from my relationships with these furry friends of ours.

I read lots of books, had a junior encyclopaedia, and my mum had a full set of the adult encyclopaedias, one book per letter. She bought it second-hand for me. This was the mecca, the Aladdin's cave of the book world, and I would happily and randomly dip into a letter of my fancy and learn something about the world and add it to my memory bank. I was always learning from books, always learning from nature, always learning from doing stuff. I knew everything about every football club in England, and I knew all the flags and names of the capital cities of the world's nations, and heaps more besides. I was your serious book and knowledge junkie.

As a young boy I was glued to the TV to watch *Star Trek* on Monday nights because I also wanted to explore other worlds and planets; in fact, as a young boy during the Apollo moon missions, I definitely wanted to be an astronaut.

A few years later we had *Whicker's World* on the TV, probably the late 70s, with Alan Whicker, an erudite, well-dressed Englishman with a moustache and a posh but terribly exciting and awe-inspiring voice, who travelled all around the world to many exotic destinations, meeting ordinary and famous people alike. His weekly travel reports used to be an hour long or so, they were absolutely essential viewing for me, and I sat riveted to the TV screen dreaming of going to such places and exploring our world, just like Alan.

This was the era before mass plane travel began when it was still super expensive to go abroad, but we were very lucky in our family for my dad worked for Air Spain and so we were able to fly at 10% cost, on stand-by. Before I was two months old I was in Kenya, the country of my mum's birth and upbringing. Before adulthood I had been to Kenya several times, America, Canada, France, the Canary Islands, Austria, Dubai, Sharjah, Bahrain and a couple of other African countries I can't recall. Airports and aeroplanes infused me with serious boyhood excitement, and seeing the world was utterly mind-blowing for me.

It seems entirely unsurprising, therefore, that I ended up travelling, and ended up as a teacher. Both my teaching and travelling help me to never stop learning. I'm still learning, it helps keep me biologically young!

I can tell you after more than 25 years' experience in teaching, the number one quality a good teacher should have is being a skilled learner themselves. There are two kinds of teacher: *transactional* teachers who give you but a fish, and *transformational* teachers who give you a fish, a fishing rod, train you how to use it, and motivate you to love fishing.

The sad thing is that transformational teachers are a rare breed. Teacher training courses and curriculums revolve around the transmission and transaction of knowledge, so the teachers themselves are sold out from the start.

We immediately recognise a transformational teacher when we experience them because they inspire us to learn. We find it enjoyable, they make us feel like we are intelligent and can do things, and they teach us how to learn skilfully by constantly cultivating and developing our learning skills. Learning becomes super-rewarding and life sparkles into action. Such teachers don't *teach* so much as *make learning happen*. A gift for life has been shared by the teacher: she or he passes on the love and joy of learning. The transformational teacher is the teacher who gradually makes themselves redundant as the students blossom into autonomous learners, able now to teach themselves.

If liberation is the path to a happy heart, a joyful mind and an active soul, learning is the path to your liberation.

Unfortunately, society has, to put it politely, really messed up on learning and teaching. Whether by accident, ignorance or by design, no matter, education systems nearly everywhere are in a parlous and precipitous state. In this chapter I would like to appraise you of this dark stark situation through my eyes, the eyes of a classroom teacher who bases his whole approach on motivating and inspiring students to love learning. Love learning, love life: engage, express, enable, empower.

I will also show you the way out of this mess. I mean you personally, and for society too, if they are listening. Nothing less than a re-education will do it.

Since I follow a *task-based learning* approach in my classroom, and this is a chapter on learning, we had better have a task. Please avail yourself of your beautiful notebook.

Task

Recalling your own experiences in learning/teaching situations in your life, and thinking about your own ideas, what do you think *learning* is? How does it happen? What is *teaching*? What makes *a good learner* and *a good teacher* in your view? What kind of experience did you have at school? What was the teaching like? What did you learn at school? Take some time to write down your thoughts and ideas for referring back to.

Read on when you have had a think. Keep your notebook handy.

My computer's software dictionary says that learning is 'the acquisition of knowledge or skills through study, experience, or being taught'. This is a useful starting point, telling us what learning is, and giving us three sources for acquiring the knowledge or skill. I also like the focus being on the person doing the learning, as per 'acquisition of'. We see that we can study, have experiences, or engage another person to help us. The first two are by our own efforts, the third brings in another person, and at best they only have a certain facilitative and enabling role to play; ultimately, we still have to do the learning with our own mind and heart. We can of course teach ourselves.

However, this definition says nothing of why we might learn nor, most importantly, how we can make this 'acquisition' happen in cognitive terms, nor how we might do it skilfully. Learning, whether knowledge or skills, requires us to engage the mind and do things with it to make acquisition happen. And as with all skills, we can do it well or not so well. We need to explore much more.

Task

Look at the list of 22 activities below which one can learn and practise, and in your notebook split them into two groups according to type, giving each group your own title which you feel describes the two different types. Just to be sure my task instructions are unambiguous, let's do a dummy run. Here are six foods, put them into two groups of three and give each group a name: *cabbage, carrot, apple, broccoli, melon, strawberry*.

Okay, I'm sure you succeeded nicely!

Here is the list of activities which one can learn and practise, see how you get on. Be careful to not see my own answers before you've done the task yourself.

Cooking, playing a guitar, learning a foreign language, asking questions, solving problems, predicting, playing golf, observing, teaching, reflecting, gardening, making new friends, listening, deducing, painting, inferring, being a good person, driving a car, expressing gratitude, understanding, fixing engines, thinking outside the box. (Keep your eyes in this paragraph to avoid seeing my answers until you are finished.)

THERE IS no one correct answer, you may have a different and completely valid one to mine. However, here are my two lists:

i) cooking, playing a guitar, playing golf, gardening, painting, driving a car, fixing engines;

ii) learning a foreign language, asking questions, solving problems, predicting, observing, teaching, reflecting, making new friends, listening, deducing, inferring, being a good person, expressing gratitude, understanding, thinking outside the box.

And the names for my two groups are i) 'motor skills'; ii) 'cognitive skills'. Things we do with our hands and body, things we do with our minds.

There are some crossovers which could be in both groups, *teaching* and *solving problems* come to mind, and in fact all the motor skills still require some cognitive and thinking skills in order to learn necessary information and to make decisions in order to carry them out.

This leads us to my main first point for the chapter. *Your mind is central to everything you do in life*, even when you're doing things with your body. We had better learn how to use our mind properly, and we had better learn all about it because if we don't, it will use us.

To learn well we must learn what our mind can do, what we can do with it, and then practise using it to become a skilled learner, and we do all that actually using the mind. We use the very thing which we are learning about to learn about it!

Why did we not learn about our mind, or how to use it in

school? This mind can do millions of things, yet we received almost no training in using it.

Many people feel they are not good at learning - 'I'm not academic', 'I don't like theory' - when it comes to the cognitive stuff, thanks to their experiences of the schooling system; suffice to say that the perception we're not good at something tends to become a self-fulfilling prophecy because we fail to try it out for fear of failing at it, or simply that we don't like to do things we think we're no good at. And because of that we never get the practice and so we never will be good at it, thereby confirming to ourselves that we were correct all along!

When my students tell me 'I can't do that, I'm not creative', I just say to them 'You mean to say you *won't* do it'. When an adult says 'I can't', it just means 'I won't'. It's not an ability thing, it's a fear thing, fear of being seen to be no good, fear of failure, of embarrassment. Later the class will do some tasks which indeed require them to be creative, and when we're reflecting upon the task after it's done, I refer them back to their claim they were not creative. This is experiential learning clearly in action and proof of it to the learner. The learner does it because that was the task, they do it well and in collaboration with friends, they don't fail, and now they know they can do it well because I reflect upon it all with them. Job done.

We are humans, we can do a million things if we put our mind to it. But often we have self-limiting beliefs, negative self-talk, and have blocked ourselves by saying we're not good enough at this, that or the other. Again, this is thanks to an education which thoroughly failed to encourage and enable us. Whether you think you're a good cognitive learner or not, you *are* one! By nature all human beings are cognitively blessed. It's all about practice and confidence.

And this is *precisely* our focus: learning about learning itself, learning how to learn, learning how to use the mind, which is our cognitive instrument of learning, finding out what it can do, what we can do with it, and then putting our newfound knowledge, understandings and skills into practice. Most people know more about their smart phones or computers than their own mind, and hardly anybody knows about their body. This is not good for our health and wellbeing, my friend, not good at all!

Why did we not learn about our body and how it works in school?

Our work, if we seek to become spiritual warriors, soul adventurers, and skilled livers of life, is to proactively create health and wellbeing in both body and mind, and if we don't know how either works, we are seriously handicapped in our task.

We need information, and we need learning, discerning, clarifying, verifying skills to determine its usefulness and truthfulness. And we need to put what we learn into practice.

That is our job at hand for the rest of the book.

To do the above task you made use of various learning sub-skills, including deducing, problem-solving (task, challenge), clarifying (rereading, going back, why are there not an equal number in each group, have I got some wrong?) and so on. You were learning, and practising learning, entirely by use of innate cognitive skills you have, triggered by the task. We all have these innate skills, but without tasks and triggers to use them, they likely lay dormant.

This is why *task-based learning* is so successful in the classroom because students are constantly using their minds, and in multiple ways, to solve challenges.

If kids practised this for 12 years, well, just imagine yourself how they'd be set up for adult life…

Doing tasks is a learning activity, and learning happens by doing, experiencing, questioning, reflecting and so on. Learning to become skilled at something means lots of practice, including in the cognitive activity of learning itself. Loads of successes along the way instil confidence and self-esteem in us, and this inner satisfaction sustains our motivation to continue. As we practise more, become more confident, we become more skilled. It's a virtuous circle. Self-limiting beliefs melt away. Time and again I've had young adult students come up to me and say how amazed they are at their learning abilities; they never knew they could do such things.

Let's do a speedier version of the above task.

Task

Here are two lists relating to things we can learn about, already separated into their type. You just need to give each group a name by what you think they share in common. Again, you may find there are some crossovers which seem to belong in both groups.

i) diet and nutrition, herbs and superfoods, natural healing, healthy lifestyle, illness and disease, the body, the mind, the soul, the ego, life, ecology and ecosystems, time and space, the nature of energy and energetics, consciousness and awareness, relationships, nurture and nature, learning, leadership, problems, solutions, conscious living, motivation, Ayurveda, epigenetics, karma

ii) reading critically, listening carefully, being attentive, noticing, observing, being aware, living consciously, being alert, discerning, thinking creatively, being imaginative, contemplating, reflecting, conceiving, exploring, inquiring, questioning, investigating, analysing, deducing, inferring, making sense of, clarifying, comparing, memorising, remembering, recalling, problem-solving, expressing oneself, understanding one's fears and desires, experiencing, sharing, giving, keeping a food diary, eating a healthy diet, having faith.

THE FIRST LIST is learning *about* things, and I'm calling it 'information' or 'informational input'. These are topics or issues which carry information to be discerned, utilised, practised and learned. When we have such information at our disposal, then we can do many things with it. For example, we can learn information about healthy foods, and then practise eating them and giving up the harmful ones our tongue just loves to get hold of. Or, in the other direction, we can learn to read critically and then read some information and ideas about what makes for good leadership, and really get to grips with the heart of the matter.

This brings us to the second list, and these items are learning *to do* things, and I'm calling it 'skills', mind skills.

The more cognitive skills we are practised in, the easier it is for us to learn and understand new information; the more new information we learn and understand, the more cognitively skilled we become. It's a two-way thing. Learn to read carefully and listen attentively, read and listen to learn. Learn to think and think to learn.

But they didn't teach us this stuff at school.

There is much upcoming information in this section of the book, and it will be for you to discern it for yourself. My tasks will trigger you into practising various sub-skills of thinking, and thus hone your cognitive skills while acquiring the useful information. If you reflect upon the tasks after you have done them, you will consciously see in what ways you used your mind to do the task.

When we play a game or sport, we will do well to learn the rules, learn some strategies, learn how to overcome the lows, learn how to enjoy the highs, and to practise practise practise. Well, in the game of life it's just the same.

Learn to discern, and discern to learn. The discerning mind navigates life with the minimum of fuss and suffering.

My purpose in this book is to bring you valuable information while triggering your mind into using various cognitive skills to read, challenge, and make sense of it for your own context in life. In my classrooms, students don't just learn knowledge and information, they get to practise various skills in the learning of the knowledge at the same time. It's a win-win - they get knowledge *and* cognitive skills, and always at the same time. In short order they can teach themselves with great aplomb.

There's something special about those two lists just above, I wonder if you can think what?! It's this: you will be reading and learning about all such information, and engaging in all such cognitive activities for the duration of this book, and already have been. And then it will automatically continue for the rest of your life.

At this point, dear reader, we have to pause and step backwards for a while, and take a look at what passes for education systems around the world. Please excuse me in advance because I'm not going to beat about the bush in my sentiments. I painted a rather bleak picture at the outset of the first chapter, and now we discover just why humanity is struggling, and we learn how to overcome our obstacles and then flourish.

It is absolutely tragic that as kids we spent a dozen years at school and we never learned how to learn.

They didn't teach us. They didn't teach us because they weren't taught either.

Just think about that for a minute, 12 years and thousands of lessons and, at the end of it all, we don't know how to learn… and I mean doing things for ourselves: how to think, how to question, how to read critically, how to listen attentively, how to express oneself, just actually *how to learn*. They don't teach us how to learn. Just to memorise things. You couldn't make it up.

In fact, my friend, it's even worse than that, because many of the innate skills, attributes and desires we humans are born with are not only not developed and honed, they are actively discouraged and stunted in us by the utter homogeneity, mediocrity and mundanity of the whole humdrum educational experience. We are, in effect, *nurtured out of our nature,* making healthy and harmonious living as adults virtually impossible.

Look at this list of what should be in the learning experience, and for each of them reflect upon whether they were an integral part of your own schooling: we're talking about things like *curiosity to learn, listening to stories, exploring things, asking questions, doing stuff, being creative, working things out for oneself, solving problems, being inspired, having fun, feeling joy, expressing oneself, collaborating with classmates and* so on. Might be quite useful for adults too; excuse my sarcasm.

All, more or less, knocked out of us. Most people can't wait to leave school, and were long since demotivated by the so-called 'learning' years. This is heartbreaking, and in no way conducive to creating intelligent, healthy and well-functioning societies.

At 18 the schooling is over, adulthood is reached, the bosom and security blanket of our parents is shorn, and we enter the big wide world out there. And we are miserably and woefully underprepared, handicapped and hindered right from the off… such a lack of useful skills to our bow, and... what do we even know, what useful knowledge do we have? What can we recall from all those years?

What do you suppose are the two most important abilities a human being needs to be skilled in, and navigate life with? Without which we are certain to struggle and find it very hard to live in harmony with others and our Mother Earth?

The **ability to learn** and the **ability to communicate**. They are the very foundation of human life. And we come out of the education system, effectively and practically speaking, illiterate in both. 12 years... and we can't speak or listen, write or read beyond a basic level! It's the most scandalous thing I can conceive of!

Think about it this way, we can *learn to listen and listen to learn, learn to read and read to learn, learn to express ourselves and express ourselves to learn.* We can say 'learn to do and do to learn'; it's a hand in glove thing, a two-way street. This is real learning in action.

In this manner we learn for ourselves, we can learn anything we want to learn, and we can communicate with others, doing so in a confident and clear manner. With these two skills in their toolbox a human being can do anything. If you know how to learn, and you are a confident skilled communicator, you can easily turn dreams and ideas into reality, you can much more easily manage your health and life, and you can proactively shape the social, economic and ecological environment around you. You become your own expert, guru, healer. You become the real you. We're not designed to be ignorant, fearful, and lacking in self-esteem.

But the education system did its best to make us this way.

People who discover how to learn never stop learning - new knowledge, new skills, new perspectives etc etc. I think it's because new stuff keeps us alert, energetic, motivated, young... there are many benefits. And a skilled learner solves their own problems.

Developing the skills of learning and communicating should be the central core to all educational curriculums, without any exceptions that I can think of. Living with confidence, autonomy and harmony are the natural consequences.

The truly incredible and sad situation is that our education systems and schools all around the world, with a few noble and notable exceptions, fail dismally to teach either skill.

And yet…

… they have the temerity to both fail, and threaten to fail, the kids before they've even reached adulthood. Imagine, you enter adulthood already labelled a failure, and fear not love is the dominant feeling towards doing new things, and your life has only just begun. You were only a kid and they have made you feel not good enough, they didn't enable you to flower and flourish, they cut you down. Even if you passed, the fear of the stick has been inculcated in you. And what did you 'pass' anyway?

And, you can be sure, if you don't come up to the adults' expectations, they will blame you, the useless new generation, not realising it was they who taught you and brought you up!

The system itself gets a capital F grade from me, and I'm an educator of over 25 years.

What we got instead was being 'taught' - aka being told and being tested - all the while sitting quietly, desperately trying to pay attention; no speaking, no doing, no collaborating, just non-stop listening. We learned - yes, we did 'learn' something - to memorise the knowledge given to us, to keep our head down to avoid being made to look stupid, and to do what we're told.

And to fear failing the tests, hundreds of the things.

We learned that external authority was king, and we should get our knowledge from it and comply with it. It knows best, we know nothing, we just remember it.

And so it is that we emerge blinking into adulthood without vital life skills. Many of us are lacking in confidence, and fearful of expressing ourselves or taking something on lest we fail and be seen to fail. And we have not a blind clue about how our body and mind work, nor how to take care of our own health, nor how to relate and connect with mother nature. We are ignorant and unskilled. This is the state of play nearly everywhere.

Instead of being inspired and empowered in our formative years, it is much more a case of being demotivated, discouraged and de-educated. Heartbreaking, shocking, nobody's a winner.

Here is a personal account of her schooling from one of my American students. She and her classmates were in my class in their first year of university, studying to be teachers. I always ask my students to share their prior learning experiences in group discussions in the class, and then in their learner logs. New teachers need to reflect upon what not to do! I will let her words speak for themselves, suffice to say I've heard so many stories of a similar message from multiple nationalities over two generations of time. She was writing in 2008.

> 'Every day I would come to class and find myself simply copying from the textbook. During exams, the information that was previously forced down my throat had to be repeated verbatim from the textbook for it to be correct. If I did something wrong, I would get physically punished (stress positions and various punishments aimed at humiliating the student). Overall, we had to conform to a traditional way of thinking, looking, and talking. I felt that no one had a sense of individuality. Furthermore I never had the sense that the teachers truly cared about me. Good students would be placed on a golden pedestal while poor students were continually ridiculed. I had no motivation to learn at all.'

No learning going on there then. And from more recent accounts from America, it's only got worse since then. Sad.

Because we, a whole generation, are handicapped in this way, never really recovering, when it's our turn to have kids and educate them, we inflict upon them what was inflicted upon us because we don't know any better. And so it goes on, generation after generation, in what has become a sort of macabre intergenerational relay race where the baton of ignorance is passed on every 25 years as we head towards our oblivion - spiritually if not physically. It's a vicious cycle, and I think we have to get out of it fast.

This is not to fail the teachers themselves, nor the administrators, nor the political leaders, no, my issue is with *the system*, I am giving an F to the system. That said, only people working in and under the system can break free from it, so we need courageous individuals and leaders to rapidly bring about some answers to this mess.

The system is, to be brutally frank, completely broken. And it breaks us, most especially those who work in powerful positions of society, protecting the system. You can only protect negative energy by becoming negative.

Over centuries or longer, humanity has somehow contrived to create a utilitarian, functional and ideological system more powerful than the force of its own human spirit and adventure, more powerful than our innate desire to be free, to love, and to dwell together in unity. Ideology, beliefs and rules trump consciousness, truth and expression of the individual.

Do you know, when I set out on my accidental teaching career I focused always on making learning fun and enjoyable, including many games, quizzes and role plays in my lessons. Many people, but not my students, all thought that if you played games and enjoyed yourself then 'real' learning was not taking place. Just such baloney.

Only by reconnecting with our soul can we escape from this tyranny within. It is way past time to rescue ourselves from the mess our species has inflicted upon itself.

Education is the foundational pillar upon which everything else in society is built, and if that pillar is crumbling or broken, then the whole of society will face serious problems.

And that is what we see in our world today. Personally speaking, I feel I've been watching the state of our humanity decaying my whole life. Yet I am optimistic because since the turn of the century perhaps, and below the radar of mainstream media and society, I can see so many good things arising, but the system itself hates change, hates any attempt at reform, so it digs in and resists. The face of the system is technocracy, bureaucracy, rules and regulations. Necessary to a small level perhaps, but not when it's eating humanity from the inside out.

If we can somehow overcome the system, and the pillar of education is made strong and stable, so society and humanity will follow suit. We know where the solution lies then. Education. The proper kind.

Since our education systems are not equipped to deliver, kept down by the system which keeps everybody down, it is up to the adults alive today to decondition and self-educate ourselves first. In this way we can avoid inflicting upon the next generation our own conditioned ignorance, rather we will liberate them by helping them develop their learning and communication skills in the schools. We must urgently put love and truth above ideology and beliefs, get shot of this destructive anti-fun anti-life system, and reclaim our innate human essence from past humans who gave it away to a monstrous creation of their own minds.

We do this through our *life inquiry* and our *spiritual revolution.* Nothing can change without skilled learning, nor without knowledge and understanding of our body and our mind. Luckily, that body of knowledge has been growing exponentially in recent years, just that the system is trying to suppress it, keeping it out of the schools and media. Millions of spiritual revolutions will hasten the demise of this increasingly totalitarian system which will only destroy everybody if we let it, and then of course it will have destroyed itself.

WHILE YOU ARE on your own on your learning journey and spiritual odyssey with this book, you will still be in your usual life, mixing with and relating to people in your various environments at home, work and online. I think if I describe some elements and features of my teaching practice and management of my classrooms, you may derive important insights which you can put into practice yourself. My classrooms are all about learning, and your spiritual revolution is all about learning, and so many features are shared and will be most useful to you. It will help navigate you through any external resistance.

If you are a leader of any kind, you can apply them to your work too. And family life. This is an exposition of group life, which definitely includes the family home. Just to reiterate the context of my work, I only teach adolescents and adults.

As you read through my account, see how you can apply things to yourself, your own environments and your own context in life. The environment around us is really important for our wellbeing and ability to learn and evolve, and if it's not conducive to happy living then you either have to leave it for another environment, or proactively set about changing it yourself, by making it a happier, more productive place for others in the community. In so doing you will amply reward yourself.

Two simple examples: if your local town has little to offer by way of after-work activities, set up a laughter yoga club somewhere; if you and your friends use your phones too much, set up a games night. Anything can be done, so long as we come up with the idea and then put it into action.

You might also consider the wider society and culture in your nation as you read my account.

As a teacher, my major areas of consideration are: i) the learners, the learning environment, the learning materials, the learning process; ii) myself as the teacher and how I relate to my students (my behaviour, temperament, language), my teaching methodology and philosophy; iii) classroom management; iv) the institution I work for, usually universities; and v) how that all comes together to help prepare everybody for life back out in their communities, cultures, nations.

I start, always, with one fundamental psychological consideration about human motivation and activity: *we want to feel good.* My students will learn best if they feel good.

This is my underlying objective all the time, and I never forget it. Creating a supportive classroom environment conducive to feeling good, and learning good, is my first and ongoing consideration in new groups and new classes. Group harmony is essential, it means the members are set up for learning, enjoying learning and enjoying working together.

The classroom becomes a mini-environment and a micro-universe consisting of the students as group members, and the teacher as group leader. For the duration of the course this group forms its own community with my guidance and leadership. Through my classroom management of the aforementioned considerations, I ensure they are learning in a supportive and compassionate environment.

We call it *positive group dynamics* in the trade. They feel good about being there, about their learning, about their community. They come to realise their personal progress is tied in with the whole group's progress. Their satisfaction is my reward, my yardstick for my success. I exist to do my very best for my students and inspire them to do their best. I cannot see any other point in being a teacher or a leader. When they are happy and learning, I feel fantastic inside myself.

Students learn best in a classroom when they feel supported, confident and important. Learning, they find, is interesting and rewarding.

My students feel emotionally secure yet cognitively challenged, and they find lessons motivating and enjoyable. I encourage them to reach for their boundaries. They feel at ease with me as their teacher, especially females who often tell me they like my classes because I don't make them feel stupid or powerless - I listen to them, and I treat everybody with equal respect and trust. Many students tell me too, that I never tell them they are wrong, that I don't favour anybody, and that I never lose my temper. I have heard some horrendous stories of their previous educational experiences in this regard!

It's quite simple, if we feel good, we can perform to our best abilities, we will *want* to perform, and we will thrive working with our peers and classmates.

My students sit in a U shape with me at the front of the room, but off to the side a bit and near my whiteboard. Everybody can see everybody. I may be talking to the whole class from time to time, usually sitting down myself to stay at their level, but much of the time they are working together in pairs or small groups, collaborating, carrying out various tasks, having discussions, doing role plays and so on. Often I have groups compete with each other, as it pushes everybody to do their best. They are communicating nearly all the time.

I frequently change the groupings so everybody gets to work

with everybody, avoiding destructive cliques from forming. Many times there are texts to read which I've selected, and I give them tasks to help them get maximum meaning out of the text and to develop their reading sub-skills. While they read alone, they will work in pairs to compare their answers to the tasks. The same goes for video or audio input, always questions and tasks to guide their reading or listening.

After input of some kind, then they get new tasks to do something with what they read about, to enhance their understanding of it, and to contextualise it for their own lives. For example, they might read about deforestation in the Amazon, and then talk about environmental damage being done in their own communities and environments, investigating and brainstorming causes and consequences, and looking for solutions. Input leads to output.

They might read about different herbs and their properties and then have to teach each other in their group about the herb they read about. They might role-play a local council meeting with each student representing a different stakeholder. They might brainstorm ways to develop a small business in town, and so it goes on, the purpose always being to replicate and practise real life stuff. At the heart of everything is communication, learning to communicate in productive and respectful ways; and often I ensure situations occur when they find they disagree, thereby giving them valuable compromising skills to maintain respect and consideration for each other. I might engineer things to go wrong, to trigger their problem-solving skills. Taking on challenges and succeeding builds up confidence and self-esteem.

We usually reflect upon the tasks and work they have done during the lesson, or from the homework they did. Reflection is replaying an event or task or situation in our mind, giving us a fresh, post-event perspective of it, and helps us go into a deeper learning and understanding. It offers additional insights which otherwise may have lain dormant. If they don't have the language to disagree politely, or struggle with making suggestions, then I will teach useful phrases to use for the next time. We can also share strategies and any other techniques the students used to work their way through the task.

Because everybody is learning, and the environment is positive and harmonious, there is hardly ever any issue with discipline. Prevention is the cure. When I'm teaching adolescents, in the second or third lesson I'll get them into small groups to brainstorm five class rules themselves, with the objective that their rules will support their learning and prevent laziness. Their rules, their class, their collaboration; by exercising their responsibility they feel tangible ownership and they thrive together. Show people respect and trust, and they always return it. It's up to the leader or 'more powerful' person to initiate this, and then the community will all benefit. All must have their roles to play, and responsibilities to each other, and then all will reap the rewards. Nobody is left out, everybody contributes.

Students enjoy their learning because they do lots of collaborating; they have discussions and debates, problems and challenges to solve, and role plays, all to mirror real-life situations. I also get them to conduct interviews, write quizzes, test each other, and so it all goes on. Mistakes are used to learn from, I never put them on the spot in front of the class, never make them feel stupid or embarrassed, and never tell them they are wrong (I'll let them know, if need be, in friendly indirect ways, though).

They become super comfortable asking and answering questions, they get preparation time, they watch videos, read websites, listen to audio and so on. I bring the outside world into the classroom since they are learning in the classroom to function better in the outside world.

I choose and write many of my learning materials, use bits out of official course books and other educational books; I utilise authentic materials, meaning real life stuff from the internet, books, magazines and so on. I develop their reading and listening skills, their speaking and conversational skills, and their writing skills. I use materials and topics which are interesting, useful and thought-provoking for them and their lives. I get them to help choose the topics and issues for is to work on.

As the students become more skilled from doing so many tasks several times, I start getting the students to teach lessons themselves, usually in groups of three who take it in turns to prepare and then teach a lesson.

I ensure, as the leader, that I am a good model: friendly but firm, I don't lose my temper, I treat everybody with respect, and I inspire them to maximise their learning opportunities while with me. A positive environment leads to a positive group dynamic, and being human is royally rewarding. After all, we are social animals, and do best when working and succeeding together.

I get loads of feedback on my own teaching because I have students write learner logs as part of their evaluation process, and encourage them to write how they felt during each lesson, and if they'd like me to change anything.

Whatever I do, and can do, in my work is because I never stopped learning myself, always driving myself to become a better teacher for my students. I think this is human nature, so long as the environment one works in doesn't oppress us.

To me, everything is about motivation, and either the learning experience will be motivating or demotivating. Sadly, all too often it's the latter, and I think it comes down to many reasons (for example, just take the opposite of all the above conditions), but there is one underlying demotivating force in particular: *control.* People don't want to be controlled against their will. If there's a perceived punishment to avoid, tests to be passed, authority to fear, then they will reluctantly be controlled, but when a human being feels respected and trusted, their very essence comes alive, their spirit is activated, and their minds and hearts are free to create, produce and dance.

Control unfortunately is the predominant feature of most relationships in our society, arising out of a schooling system which is all predicated upon conformity, compliance, and looking to the authority for knowledge and for what to do. We must find a way to replace *control* with *interaction, fear* with *love, and boredom with curiosity* in our classrooms, and this will, in turn, manifest into our societies.

This is our natural instinct; to work together, not to control each other.

I've seen it time and time and time again: give people the learning skills and a positive environment, and they always flourish and transform themselves. But, sister or brother, with your schooling behind you, it's now down to you to do it all yourself!

Decondition, re-educate, and empower yourself. Flower and flourish. To help you I will now share a few strategies and tools to promote skilled learning, which will carry you through your revolution from whatever stage in your life you're at. Learning how to learn means learning!

Learn to do it, be it, live it, love it.

8

A LEARNING TOOLBOX FOR THE SPIRITUAL REVOLUTIONARY

A ***proper*** *education is when we learn how to explore, think, express ourselves, overcome challenges, and manage our own life.*

Learning is your responsibility. Learning enables your evolution to unfold unhindered; your evolution is your responsibility.

Knowledge is transactional, learning is transformational, understanding is liberation.

Observe others and learn about yourself, observe yourself and learn about others.

The greatest achievement in life is not to be a somebody, it is to be ***you****.*

Learning relates to two things: i) converting the unknown or undoable into the known and doable; ii) improving oneself by becoming more knowledgeable and more skilled. Learning is acquiring *and* using information, and it is acquiring *and* applying skills.

While the 'doable' refers to both motor skills and cognitive skills, the main focus in our spiritual work is the cognitive stuff, the stuff of our mind. We learn new information, apply it to seek understanding for ourselves, and reflect upon it to gain a deeper learning. Many cognitive skills are practised along the way.

The more we practise the more skilled we become. The more we learn the more we can teach. The more we listen and read, the more we can confidently express ourselves.

Players of musical instruments, or sports and games, seek to constantly improve their playing skills through practice and playing. They are always practising and playing, and becoming more skilled. Learning and improving oneself is the essence of being a human being, striving to do one's best is our ultimate expression and reward for being human. If we strive, invariably we thrive.

Players of the game of life should do the same. Play the game, learn the game, practise the game, get better at the game, become skilled at the game. Enjoy life more, and help others enjoy life more. Be a pro.

Learning is the name of my game, and it's the central and essential skill needed by a third millennium citizen, and certainly by all spiritual revolutionaries who seek to be confident contributors to the collective pot of human affairs. The activity of learning chases fear and control out of town, replacing them with love and freedom.

Yet even then, things can and will go 'wrong' in our life, but having life skills at our disposal will help us to solve whatever problems or challenges come our way, and in an expeditious manner.

Learning, so stunted while we were in our formative years of schooling, is our primary means for navigating and enjoying our life, so we really had better overcome this handicap.

So far as we know, we only get the one life, there are no second goes, no dummy runs, no dress rehearsals, no reruns, this is it, this is your lot my friend, there's no going back. To live in accordance with nature and universal intelligence, learning is your best friend, bar none. Be a skilled learner and only your imagination will be your limit.

Learning very much relates to improving our mind - discovering and using its full range of cognitive abilities, reevaluating its attitude towards life, and using it with intelligence, sensitivity, and positivity. The amazing thing is, we use it to learn how to use it better. If we don't use it, it will use us.

To me, learning is synonymous with living and loving, and loving living. The more I learn the more I live, the more I live the more I learn, the more I live the more I love, the more I love the more I live... round and round one goes in this virtuous circle of the 3Ls. If you live and love well, you evolve well.

The mind is always the instrument of learning, even when you kick a ball, combine ingredients, or play a chord. Doing things uses the mind just as thinking does. And just as there are a thousand varieties of things to do, so there are a thousand ways to think, and we want more of them!

When I observe people in life doing their work and going about their business, and it might be a waiter or a plumber, a teacher or a doctor, whoever, I notice those that put their full effort and heart into their work are more at peace with life, more fulfilled. My experience tells me it's exactly the same for life in general. Our attitude and outlook towards life absolutely shapes our experiences - what happens to us, and how we feel within.

In the previous paragraph are three key words found in every skilled learner's toolbox: *observe, notice* and *attitude*, and all come from our mind. Everything comes from our mind, goes into the mind, is remembered by the mind, is interpreted by the mind, is produced by our mind - our mind is our central processor and storage of information. Your whole life goes through it and comes out of it.

What I'd like to do in this chapter is share my experiences from teaching the skill of learning, offer a few of my *tricks of the trade* as it were, and how I cultivate and develop this essential skill in my students. The underlying principle is to use a variety of tasks which require students to use their minds in various ways, and in this way I can encourage, enable and empower them to become super learners. Then they are set up for life.

The second half of my teaching life has been mainly teaching teachers - new, or experienced - who are learning their master's degree in teaching English. This means I have been developing the learning skill in them so that they can then do the same thing with their students. It's simple to me: the more learning going on in our human world, the better it will be for all of us and our planet. It's why I love being a teacher trainer. And why I'm now writing this book.

Let's open this toolbox then.

I HAVE three main tools to share with you: one of which you can use to give yourself the right foundations, thereby setting yourself up in a solid manner, one of which improves one's *experiential* learning, and the third which will help with the *study* means for learning. Each tool will pop up again in the coming chapters as practical means for helping you in advancing your spiritual quest, but for now we will focus on what the tools are, what they can do for you, and how to use them. Then you just need practice.

Strong foundations are essential because we notice that, at the start of doing work on ourselves, many things out there trigger in us negative emotions, thoughts and reactions. We also find that we have harmful thought patterns and harmful habits which, incredibly, will resist your efforts to remove them. Just about everybody has to contend with destructive self-talk whirring away inside their mind.

Unless we set the foundations properly from the outset, such inner talk will return to haunt us. I believe this is why affirmations, while they sound wonderful and appeal to our common sense in calmer times, don't properly protect us from reacting with negative emotions to life's situations and happenings. We must strengthen that which our schooling weakened in us, and I refer to the *conditioned ignorance* that was programmed into our subconscious, autopilot mind. My first tool will emphatically help you do that. It addresses our outlook on life. First, though, another task.

Task

Ask yourself what your *outlook* on life is. Many have never really consciously thought about it. If, upon reflection, you find yours is negative, if you think you're no good at learning, no good at this that or the other, then you're already set up for failure. You are a human being, dear reader, you can do *any*thing you put your mind to, but only if your outlook is favourable. To do that you simply need to consciously set yourself up for success. You do that by *reprogramming your subconscious soundtrack.*

Welcome to my **'OOAAI outlook reset' tool** to ensure your mind is open, willing to learn skilfully and live harmoniously, and not in a position to let self-doubt put the kibosh on you. *You* consciously choose an outlook which will serve *you* positively, and avoid negative distractions derailing you from your journey of empowerment and transformation. And, then, you just keep on reminding yourself of it over the coming weeks and months (using my second tool), and in this way you install it into your autopilot mind. Bingo, your outlook is now reset, job done!

OOAAI adds up to your **outlook** and stands for **orientation, objectives, attitude, approach** and **intention**. You can choose your own OOAAI, use mine, or concoct a mix, whatever works for you. Let me show you the idea.

Orientation is like a 'posture' of the mind, it points you in the right direction. A slumped body posture doesn't mean business or support your health, nor does a stressed or feeling-sorry-for-itself kind of mind. If you want polar bears don't point yourself towards the south pole, and if you want penguins don't be looking to the north pole.

A good orientation is committing yourself to being open-minded, ready and willing to learn now, and forevermore. 'I am a skilled learner', you tell yourself… believe it, do it, become it. Your orientation sets you up for your ongoing journey. Being open-minded means not rejecting or resisting that which you disagree with, and it emphasises learning and understanding over knowing.

Setting **objectives** is a top motivational force, but only if they are achievable, if not they become counterproductive. Our schooling conditions us into being future-oriented people, and so we think of objectives as something to strive for and achieve in the future. That is fine, but not if it's at the expense of today. Since I had my own transformative life experience in fixing my back problems, my objective for life has been simple, and it is for now, today, every day, not some future point in time: *to be healthy and happy, and living in harmony with other people and the world about me.*

With it necessarily being an ongoing commitment (it's a journey, not a destination), recalling this objective makes life so much easier when faced with decisions and choices - I just choose the best or least worst option, always based on the 3Hs. They become a lifestyle choice. Any other specific objectives one may have for the future become so much more achievable - and exciting - if you are in a harmonious, healthy and happy state of being. Health first, my friend, everything else next.

Attitude is a mental and emotional frame of mind looking out, from within our whole being, towards the world at large, and which forms the default view and perspective through which we see everything out there. You can think of it as a filter, or a pair of glasses if you like. What you see depends on your attitude.

Pause for reflection: if you change your attitude, do you change the world?

Complaining and blaming will ensure the world continues to look blameworthy and not good enough. Being and feeling unhappy and discontent about everything will confirm to you that the world is an unhappy and disagreeable place. The world and how it looks, to a very great extent, mirrors your attitude.

I like to have an *attitude of gratitude* for my life, in part because I like rhymes. But really, it works beautifully for me. In bad moments or times of stress I may temporarily forget and have a good moan and groan, feel sorry for myself, and seek out some sympathy, but I can quickly return to the norm just by remembering my default view. It always helps me in bad moments - as my Mum taught me to do - to recall so many people who are worse off than me.

As one gets used to this attitude, reasons for being unhappy and miserable, for blaming and complaining, drop away. Feeling and expressing gratitude for one's life dramatically alters one's view, one's actions and one's language! Less and less one succumbs to negative energy. Such an attitude encourages a proactive and liberated stance towards life.

Your **approach** reflects, and leads to, the actions you take in life. It will be guided by your attitude and objectives. One idea, which suits me perfectly, is cultivating an approach to life which seeks to receive and produce *positive energy*. This acts as a great guide to decision-making, and to avoid being hamstrung by choices. Just take the option which produces positive energy and/or avoids negative energy. In the *Problems and Solutions* chapter we will investigate how we can convert incoming negative energy into 'not-negative' energy. The trick for me is viewing all of life as energy flow, and then choosing the good vibes and frequencies while doing my level best to avoid or neutralise the bad vibes. Harmony and sweet melodies are the order of the day!

Apply this approach to everything that comes your way, and to help yourself proactively shape and manage your environment, especially if it's a rather negative one. Positive vibes soon mute the negative noises. Don't wait for harmony, create it yourself using this approach to life.

Intention is perhaps the mother of them all, for if the intention is sound, then it helps keep all the others in line. Your intention towards life should be such that you don't have to keep remembering or recalling it. Set it, and then install it, in your subconscious mind to let it do its work and influence everything else you do in life. It is an excellent reconditioning technique. Your intention will, automatically, help you handle negative situations as and when they come to you, and it will help you avoid producing any of your own. Again, nothing works 100% of the time, but a top-notch *intention* will do sterling work for you in the background of your mind.

Mine is *ahimsa*. It is a Sanskrit word meaning *'to proactively practise non-violence'*. It is brilliant, especially in relation to verbal violence since anybody spiritually inclined is most unlikely to be using physical violence. Thanks to our conditioning and the nastiness of 'the system' which brought us all up in its anti-human ways, it can be rather easy to use harmful words in the emotional heat of situations, albeit unintentionally and often without realising, and usually aimed at the very people we love and cherish.

We may also discover - using the next tool - that we can, and do, harbour thoughts of hatred or bitterness towards other people, desires for retribution, or to punish them for past happenings, and any other kind of negative feelings of ill will towards those we view as transgressors. In so doing, we are producing negative energy which afflicts our mind and body, our entire being. That we may not physically act upon such thoughts is immaterial, we are already damaging ourselves.

We also can easily harm ourselves with our own negative thoughts and self-limiting beliefs, and may blame ourselves for past actions, or we feel shame, guilt, unworthy and the like. We certainly harm ourselves if we eat corporation-made lifeless foods.

The absolute beauty of *ahimsa* is that it's not about not doing something, it's about actively practising to not do something, you are doing a not-doing!

Cultivating this intention will help us be mindful and improve our temper and temperament. *Ahimsa* develops our conscious living, and living consciously enables us to become skilled practitioners of *ahimsa*. I have found it to be transformative in its own right. I learned about it from reading my Ayurveda books.

One's **outlook** on life is in effect a *state of mind*, through which one will act towards, and react to, the world out there. A positive outlook and state of mind is likely to lead to positive actions, and in turn positive actions will reaffirm and strengthen the positive state of mind.

By my reckoning, just consciously thinking about your OOAAI, and selecting each of the five components, will motivate you.

To sum up my personal outlook, then: I am open-minded and a lifelong learner, I feel gratitude for my life and all that I have and can do, I take care of the language I use and do my level best to not harm others or myself, I seek out positive energy and good vibrations, and I make choices which lead to, and support, good health and happiness, and a harmonious relationship with life. I consider that I navigate and make my way through my journey of life on my own personal wellness wagon, and if I fall off it, as is the unavoidable experience of being human, no big worries, I just clamber back on as soon as I can.

And practice makes everything so much easier. Difficult at the outset perhaps, but momentum builds and your spiritual transformation manifests.

With such strong foundations in place we can build strong and live long.

Task

Before we move onto the next tool, a wee task for you. Can you think about the following words and see what they mean to you? I mean in a practical sense as they apply to the living of life; if you were 'doing' them, what would your mind be doing? When you've had a think read on. The words are: *observing, being aware, paying attention, reflecting, judging, noticing, self-observation, self-awareness*. It will be good to write down your definitions.

If you want to really learn *about* life and learn *from* life, then, so far as I know, the best way bar none is to *observe* it in action. This is first-hand learning through your own experiences in life, and it develops your own instincts, gut feelings, and discernments from your own engagements with the world around you. You connect with the world out there through your own mind and sense organs, and you have to carry your own body and life using your own will and abilities, so you had better study it yourself, and the best way to study it is to observe, notice, hear, be aware of it. It? Your body, your mind, life out there, the whole galactic caboodle of everything.

When you observe something, you may not fully understand or be able to explain what is coming into your mind, but you will absolutely know that you have observed and experienced it. You can then talk with other people to see if they can help you make sense of it, or reflect upon matters yourself by contemplating the nature of life, inferring, doing more observations, or by thinking of comparable or similar past experiences which may help you derive meaning or insights into what you noticed or observed.

By practising paying attention and observing life with full awareness, you learn to trust yourself and develop a keener instinct and intuition; you can pack some serious intelligence into that gut of yours! Observing helps you uncover all your innate intelligence hidden from you during your school years. It also brings common sense back to the table, a commodity fast disappearing in this modern, technological and politically correct world of ours.

Direct observation of life stands in contrast to formal study and book learning, which is information and knowledge coming from others, as opposed to our own first-hand experiences. Both have their merits, especially when we build both into our life, for they can - not always but the possibility is there - perfectly complement each other.

To become practised and skilled in observation you can avail yourself of my **'OAR' tool**.

It stands for **observation, awareness** and **reflection**. Just as learning is the mother of all skills, so **OAR** is the mother of all learning tools. It is the tool of all tools to empower yourself and transform your life, and accordingly we should investigate it in a thorough manner. It is very very powerful! And I mean in a positive beneficial way for oneself, and humanity as a whole. Many of the tasks you've carried out during the book so far have required you to use this tool, and most of the rest of the tasks will do likewise. It works like this...

One *observes* something happening in life with full *awareness*. This happening may be out there in the world, or inside of yourself. Then, usually later but sometimes alongside the observing itself, one *reflects* upon what one observed, and what it might mean or what we might learn. *Reflecting* is the making sense, the discerning and interpreting part of the process, where our intention is understanding and learning. Using the OAR process means we avoid imposing our own judgements on people or situations which automatically arise out of our previously derived beliefs and values. We are seeking to learn, understand, and expand our horizons, not shut them down according to what we already 'know'.

This, in the shell of a nut, is *experiential learning*. In the field of cutting-edge education, we make the distinction between *reflection-on-action* (after the event) and *reflection-in-action* (during). The former might be a project team looking back on the work they've done and reflecting upon the challenges they faced and how they overcame them, with the intention of seeing how things could be done better the next time, or perhaps to learn more about the project from a fresh perspective, now that one is no longer needing to fully focus and concentrate on the task at hand. *Reflection-in-action* might be during a conversation discussing some kind of issue or problem to solve.

You may have heard the term 'cognitive dissonance' in recent times. This happens when we directly observe and experience something in life that runs counter to our beliefs of what is true, or our pre-existing 'knowledge'. Because of our conditioning by the system when we were young and defenceless against such 'teachings', we are likely to reject that which we see with our own eyes because the external authority of government, media, and assorted experts must be correct, so we must be wrong. Even though we have seen it run counter to their 'truth'! When people say 'learn to trust yourself', it means learning to overcome our subconscious impulse that tells us the external authority knows best.

You may surmise, then, that the OAR tool is a brilliant way to help us decondition and re-educate ourselves. No longer do we need to depend upon beliefs, values, and so-called 'truths' anymore, we can learn for ourselves.

Awareness is a **state of mind**, putting you in alert and attentive mode. It opens up your mind to receiving information (visual, auditory, smell) from the outside world, or from within yourself. Then, in this open aware state of mind you can give your attention to whatever it is you wish to observe. *Observing* is an **activity of your mind** which involves paying conscious attention to something. Awareness opens your mind, opens the door, to receive; observation does the receiving, allows stuff in through the door. Thus, they work hand in hand.

It's so important, I'd like to summarise it: *awareness* is a state of mind, and that state is open for the business of observation. *Observation* is an activity of the mind, and is the conscious noticing of what the senses are letting through the gates of our mind. Awareness and observation working in tandem mean our mind is 'tuned into' the happenings of life around, or within, us. *Reflection*, usually done afterwards, is using our mind to interpret and discern what it received.

There are the usual five sense organs, and their sensory channels, leading to our brain, namely: the eyes and seeing, ears and hearing, nose and smelling, tongue and tasting, and skin/hands/feet and touching. There is a sixth sense organ to consider, *a part of the mind itself* which produces your active thoughts and feelings - the autopilot conditioned part of your mind. Yes, you will need to practise observing your own mind's activity, and this is self-awareness in action.

It means we use our mind to observe our mind... hah! Think about that for a minute. We shall increasingly investigate this phenomenon during this section of the book, and return to it directly in the *3DH5DL* chapter. Yet, if you recall the nature, urban setting, and music tasks you did in the last section, then you were actively doing this very thing.

When you can do this at will, you will have liberated yourself from the emotional and mental enslavement that all humans are spellbound by thanks to, yes, that schooling system.

What you will find, when you start using the OAR tool frequently is that your sixth sense organ, the mind itself, interrupts what your other sense organs are observing from the outside world. And that, my friend, is where all our troubles in life arise!

Now, what I'd like to do is share an experience I had many years ago, which I subsequently typed up and used as learning material for my teacher students. I have slightly adapted it for our purposes. It will bring into reality the above academic discussion.

A major course that I developed and teach, *Classroom Inquiry*, requires my students throughout the whole term to investigate their own teaching practice, in order to bridge the gap between *assuming* what goes on in their classroom and what *actually* goes on. Often the two do not coincide, and it's exactly the same in our own lives as citizens in the world at large. We make many assumptions in life, carry many beliefs about things, and we take both to be true. By the very nature of teaching work, teachers are particularly prone to this (so are doctors). It's not always bad, but unless we are conscious of it, then that's when the bad stuff comes about. For, assumptions and beliefs are just that; facts and truth are different words and different kettles of fish in the world of information flow.

It becomes essential therefore to become skilled in observing, being aware, and reflecting upon what we see and hear in life. Through observing we can see things exactly as they are. And don't run from cognitive dissonance, use it as the basis for your evolution!

In this tale I think you'll find it becomes super clear what the cognitive activities of *observing, noticing, being aware of, and reflecting* actually look like in real life. Once you are clear, you can set about consciously bringing OAR into your daily life. After you've read my tale, you might like to return to your own definitions of the key words which I asked you to do in the task above, and compare.

Many years ago, I used to go to a massage place in a small valley town in northern Thailand. It was in an old teak building set in a nice tropical garden area, replete with the sounds of nature and, one quickly noticed as one entered the grounds, the sound of running water. The source of this water noise couldn't be seen, but it sounded just like a waterfall.

Having a massage is an interesting activity because we are (supposedly) in a fully receptive and passive mode for two hours while the masseur is doing all the work, with nothing for us to proactively do for that time period. It is with this receptivity in mind that this particular massage place becomes interesting to anyone who might wish to improve their awareness and observation skills.

Here is what I *reflected* on and learned about *noticing, observing, becoming aware,* and *losing attention* while having my first massage there. I do this kind of thing, not because I'm a freak, but because I teach my students about such matters. These are essential skills if we are to inquire about ourselves and about our work and our life.

I was lying there, muscles and tendons being worked on, and I suddenly *noticed* and *became aware* of the noise of the falling water. I felt startled at this observation because…

… clearly the water hadn't stopped falling but, equally clearly, I had stopped hearing it because how else could I have suddenly started hearing it again? This meant that, at some point, unbeknownst to me, my ears had effectively ceased being open for business. Something had closed them from hearing the water for a while, and yet now my hearing sense organ had suddenly reopened, whereupon I was *hearing* and *noticing* and *being aware of* the sound of the falling water again.

Some time later during the massage the same thing happened again! I suddenly could hear the noise of the water falling again. My ears had stopped hearing, again without me noticing when the hearing had stopped, but now that I was hearing the water again, they were open for business again. And this happened a few times, and now I was getting curious. As the masseur continued her work, I was *reflecting* upon it all and *realised* what I *wasn't noticing* was when I stopped hearing this water noise, the point at which my hearing channels became somehow blocked.

Clearly my *awareness* and my *noticing* of the falling water was intermittent. So what was it that was removing my awareness and noticing of the falling water noise? It was as if something within me was acting as a tap to the waterfall, turning it on and off several times during the time that I was lying down receiving my massage. But I would only be aware of the 'tap' turning the water on, and not of the tap turning the water off.

What do you think? What was turning the 'tap' off?

My explanation was this…

I'd be aware of the falling water noise. Then my mind would wander off, would start to think of things, either past memories or future projections. At this point my mind was now preoccupied with its own internal thought patterns and thinking, and this inner mind activity would shut down my access to external sounds and therefore block my noticing of the falling water noise. After a while perhaps my thinking would take a short break, at which point my hearing sensory channel would be accessible to my consciousness again, and would inform me of the falling water noise, which had of course never stopped. And so it went on!

So there was this sort of ping pong game between noticing the water noise on one side of the net, and the mind wandering off on its own journey of thinking on the other side of the net; when one started the other stopped, when one stopped the other started. If my mind was producing thoughts, I was unable to notice the water noise. If I was noticing the water noise, my mind was not lost in thought. They did not happen at the same time. I did not notice my mind's thoughts interrupting the water noise, nor did I notice the water noise interrupting my mind's thoughts.

Subsequently, upon making these realisations, and while still receiving my massage, I then resolved to *consciously observe* the falling water noise, rather than just noticing it. My aim was to continuously hear the falling water noise, and to avoid losing the sound of it which had been happening every time my mind became preoccupied with thinking.

And guess what!

I found that, even with this intention, I would still, without noticing, lose the sound of the falling water noise, but, most likely due to my new intention, I *was* able to quickly notice that my mind had wandered off into its own thinking, and therefore could stop this train of thought by returning to the falling water noise. So, it still had the power to disobey my intention!

I then moved it up another gear. Now I began practising the deliberate act of holding my attention onto the falling water noise in an effort to block the mind's thought patterns interrupting me. Amazingly, the mind would still try to do its thinking but by now, and being fully focused on the water noise, I could spot this immediately when it began, and therefore with minimal interruption I was able to continue to observe the water noise.

What in effect ensued was that I was alternately observing the water noise and observing my mind wanting to start thinking about something.

I was observing my mind, presumably using my mind to observe itself.

Interesting; I had to use my mind to focus on the external world's happenings, but the mind also had its own ideas and clearly preferred to be thinking about its own preoccupations rather than listening to some falling water. Yet, with practice I was able to fend off its efforts to take over my field of attention.

Try it out for yourself. Use the OAR tool, set yourself the objective of observing and noticing stuff going on around you, and then see if your inner mind's voice chooses to override you and create its own thought activity. We fully explore this phenomenon in the *3DH5DL chapter*. For now, I would ask you to practise learning to notice this inner mind activity, either as it starts up or while it's in the middle of its thought stream. It is central to all the problems we ever have! Being able to observe the goings-on in the world around us is a great skill in itself, but to also practise observing our own internal mental goings-on is where the real key to escaping our suffering and problems lies.

Incidentally, all this stuff we've been discussing is the preserve of meditation and mindfulness - noticing, being aware, self-aware, observing out there, observing in here.

WE NOW TURN to my third tool, which is a technique you can use to improve your reading and listening skills, and consequently, your speaking and writing skills - the more you learn about our world the more you can communicate about it.

It's the pre-eminent learning technique and approach to becoming a better all-round communicator, while simultaneously becoming more knowledgeable and informed. It forms the bedrock of my teaching of the four language skills (listening, speaking, reading and writing) so that my students can research anything or discuss any issue with confidence and ease. It is the main means for learning to learn. It is truly liberating.

While, primarily, we are talking about reading or listening for more educational or informational purposes, it still can apply to entertainment reasons for reading. The purpose is to become a more motivated, critical and skilled reader, and a more attentive and skilled listener. And then out of good listening and reading skills come good speaking and writing skills.

Only the sky is the limit for a skilled communicator. He or she can achieve virtually anything they put their mind to.

Part of the problem people unknowingly face (until they become aware of it), is when their pre-existing beliefs and understandings of what is correct or good become 'threatened', or are called into question, by hearing alternative viewpoints or knowledge. If we are to become the skilled learners in our *life inquiry* and *spiritual revolution*, we must remain open-minded, and so we have to train ourselves to avoid succumbing to judgements during our reading or listening.

Sticking rigidly to what we already 'know' invites decay and a closed mind, which in turn invites blocked energy. Seeking always to improve our understanding about life invites alertness, freshness, attention and an open mind, and in this way we can naturally evolve and continuously improve our life, and our enjoyment of it. You fulfil your potential instead of taking it to your deathbed!

It has no formal name in my teaching, so we'll call it the **'four stages to learning' technique**. While you can take the stages in any order you like, I'll present them to you in the usual sequence in which I use them in my classroom. I would suggest using this sequence until you become dialled in and skilled, and then mix them up as you see fit for a bit of variety.

In school we are typically given something to read, and then have to answer some comprehension questions, and that's your learning experience: read it, be tested on it. Few if any reading techniques or sub-skills are taught to help you be a more confident and skilled reader. As for listening skills… I'm sorry, I wasn't listening, did you say something?? No, school offered superficial learning at the very best on both counts. Read this. Listen to me for twelve years. No, not good enough by any yardstick.

To help you develop the four skills, and all the sub-skills, strategies, tips, techniques and put it all into practice would require a whole book of learning in itself, and it takes me at least a term with my students. However, by the time you are reading this I may well have finished creating an online learning course to do precisely this, so if you're interested visit my website or send me an email. Go to aspiritualrevolution.com

So here, I'd like to just concentrate on the procedure and some basic tips, and to show you how the brain works best when learning or taking in any kind of information. Then you can still train yourself very well through practice and diligence.

The four cognitive stages of effective learning, that is, what the brain is doing to make learning happen, are the **attentive, receptive, productive, reflective** modes. In terms of information flow, we can say **input, intake, output, reflection**. *Input* is the ideas from the other person in the text, while *intake* is your particular understanding of it which is tied in with the level of attention you are able to give.

Being attentive means your mind is open and focused; being receptive means you are receiving information from a source, aiming to understand it and not to judge it; being productive means doing something with what you read or heard to better understand it, to personalise its meaning for you; and being reflective is then replaying the whole experience, giving you a fresh angle and perspective. Put another way, you give your *attention*, you *receive* incoming language, you *produce* a response through speaking or writing about it, or thinking it over in your own head, and then you *recall and replay* the previous three stages and what it is you think you have learned. The last stage reflects upon both the content of the information and your experience in learning about it.

Each stage provides a learning experience in itself while enhancing the learning experience in each subsequent stage. Doing all four stages of learning leads to an easier memory recall, a fuller understanding, and greater communicative skills.

When you systematically apply all four stages to all the articles, videos and podcasts that you read and listen to, you very much improve the quality of your attention, your ability to discern and understand, and your open-mindedness towards alternative viewpoints, values. Once you are practised in using this four-stages technique, you will be a naturally skilled reader and listener, and find your ability to articulate things so much more rewarding.

The external authority approach to education claimed full knowledge and full ownership of morals, values and views, and it was merely for us as compliant kids to 'learn' their stuff and then we would 'know' about things and how to be 'good' citizens. We were conditioned to see things as black or white, right or wrong, good or bad, with no nuances or shades or degrees within. This is why we struggle with our health and relationships because it has divorced us from the full spectrum of life and the natural world. Political views and beliefs are polarising with both sides claiming they are correct and know best. Same with religions. It's how we have become so divided amongst ourselves.

I say forget the importance of being right or wrong, virtuous or vagabond, and instead focus on learning and understanding, and on being the best we can. Then let life meander as it meanders!

Use my *four stages to learning technique* for advancing and expanding your repertoire of information, know-how and cognitive skills. Don't protect and rigidly stick to what you already 'know' - challenge it, explore it, build upon it, expand it. If you think it's wrong or bad then okay, file it away in your memory bank as just that. You never know, when you get a bit older, or you read or experience something else you might decide it's not wrong anymore, that you were wrong before and now you have come to see things differently. Don't reject anything, just let it sit with you for future use if need be. Don't run from discomfort or unease, embrace it and usually it disappears, just by your acceptance.

There are 7.8 billion individual human beings as I write, and each person is a unique expression of life, we don't want to allow ourselves to any more be boxed in by rigid views of what is true, and how to behave, which came to us when we were kids. Not a day longer; system, be gone! Did you know that up to a certain age (I think it's about six or seven) our brain is wired to learning through the mode of hypnosis?! In effect the system hypnotised us during our formative years. Spiritual revolution is our way of escaping from any harmful hypnosis.

I think the last word goes to the first stage. Unless you can give your full attention to what you read or listen to, all the input, intake and output will suffer and be degraded. Attention is vital for learning! Think how hard it was to pay attention in your schooldays. Why was that? Yes, we need to be interested, curious, challenged in some way to choose to read or listen to something. But we also need to *stay* that way for the duration of the article or video. We need to give our attention and then maintain it. If something is boring or irrelevant or too difficult to comprehend, we're likely to lose interest and our attention falls on something else.

Here are a couple of ideas for becoming more attentive… when you have something you want to read or listen to, ask yourself what you would like to learn from it, look at the headline or title, the preamble or any pictures, and predict what might be spoken or written about. Write down two to five questions you'd like answering on the topic and then see if you can find the answers when you're reading or listening. Remind yourself to read carefully or listen attentively without disagreeing or disapproving of it, leave all that to your reflection time. In my classes the norm is for my students to read or listen to something at least two times.

Oh, the real final word is to return to the OAR tool. We have just talked about learning from the input from what other people have written or talked about, well, when we observe life out there, or inside ourselves, we are receiving input in the same way, except it's from our own direct experience. If we observe with full awareness then our attention level is at its maximum and then with our intake we can apply it to some output in some way, and then reflect upon it.

Thus: **input** is reading, listening to, or watching something in some media or book, *and* it is observing things happening. **Intake** is what we cognise, which depends on our alertness, attention, awareness. **Output** is thinking about the intake, questioning it, discussing it with others, acting upon it in some way. **Reflection** is replaying everything at the end to refine your understanding.

And then wisdom arrives.

Let's add a couple more tools to the toolbox.

First is the **pain tool**. When we feel pain, discomfort, or any kind of general suffering, whether in mind or body or both, we can try to numb the pain with drugs or pills, suppress it and pretend it's not there, or get rid of it in some way. Nobody likes pain and this is the common approach for dealing with it. But no learning takes place, we have not addressed the root causes of our suffering or discomfort. Only when we do this can we hope to overcome the problem.

Don't run from problems because, like a bully, they'll just come back to give you more hassle. Use pain or any kind of discomfort as an indicator that you're doing something in your life that needs attention, work it out using the next tool, and make that change. The way we are conditioned is to dislike change. This is how cancer comes, because we constantly refused to change our harmful habits, despite so many warning signs from our body and mind.

Second is my **ignorance-busting 10Is>>3Is tool**. Pain, suffering, fear, anger, resentment, all these expressions of negative energy in my view can be traced back to ignorance, especially in matters relating to how our body and mind work.

We were born to be the **3Is**, namely to be **intelligent interconnected individuals**, but the system screwed us up during our schooling. The **10Is** is a process to get from ignorance to the **3Is**. They are: **ignorance >> impotence >> illness >>**

inquiry >> investigation >> information >> instigation >> insights >> integration >> intelligence. We move along the continuum of ignorant living to intelligent living, which means harmonising your inner relationship between mind, body and spirit, and harmonising your inner relationship with the external world. The shorter version of my **10Is**, for recall purposes, is from *ignorance* to *inquiry* to *intelligence*. This is your life inquiry in a nutshell.

Whether we need to focus more on studying or observing, or pay equal attention to both, is decided on a case-by-case basis. Personally, I am always doing lots of both.

By 'illness', we mean any kind of discomfort or disharmony in mind or body. Read all about it in the upcoming chapter. A feeling of impotence can be recognised when we realise we are in fear or anger, we have self-doubt, or a sense of hopelessness has taken over. Feeling like this is being a victim of circumstance or happenstance, and is our innate intelligence trying to guide us into finding answers and solutions. Use this tool to just that.

Ultimately speaking, the seeds of all solutions and problem-busters sprout from learning the art of observing with full awareness. I mean observing life out there, and observing the goings-on inside your skin. When you can observe your own reactions in your own mind, observe the happenings within your body, then you are listening, and from that basis you can find out what you need to find out. Information is everywhere!

Let's get to the health stuff.

9

FROM ILLNESS TO WELLNESS: A LIFESTYLE

If you want a bully to go away, stand up to him, challenge him, don't run from him, don't give into him (could be a her, but we'll stick with him). Give him a buck and he'll be back for ten, give him an inch and he'll be back for a yard. If you run from him, he'll find you, if you feed him, he'll want more; but if you find courage to confront him, he goes somewhere else.
It works just the same way with illness and pain.

Be who you want to be, do what you want to do, say what you want to say. Just follow one rule: don't harm others. Seeking peer approval, and worrying about their disapproval, promotes illness and blocks wellness.

Wellness is a way of life: either you're on it or you're not. It's your choice.

'An ounce of prevention is worth a pound of cure.' ~ my Mum!

We humans have a tendency to only appreciate something when we've lost it. The spiritual revolutionary must eliminate this tendency! If you lose your health…

In the spirit of our journey together, let's start with a task for you. One of the ongoing requirements of a spiritual revolutionary is to check in with what they already know and understand to be true about something, and from that basis to explore and learn more, to adjust and fine-tune one's existing understandings, or to simply tear them up and radically overhaul them.

Some questions then for your rumination, and as ever, I recommend you write down your thoughts in your notebook.

Task

i) What do you think the dictionary definitions for **illness** and **wellness** are? Then follow that up by writing down your own understandings of them, based on your own experiences in life.

ii) What factors cause illness? What health problems typically afflict you? Do you know why they happen? What do you do when you fall sick or have a malfunctioning?

iii) Are your genes fixed from birth? Do they determine how long you will live and what diseases you will get? What do you think? Where did you get your understandings from?

iv) What proactive measures do you take in your life to avoid stress and support healthy living?

v) Do you view your body and mind as two separate entities or as an interconnected holistic whole? Why?

When you're done, read on.

Now, it would not be an unreasonable expectation to think that humankind - through all its societies, organisations, and knowledge - would set itself up to enable all its members to enjoy good health and vitality, thereby ensuring the collective wellbeing of humanity to which we all belong. What human being in their right mind wants ill-health, pain, misery??

Yet when I look at life in our human world, and I've been looking for a long time, it seems to me like humankind has decided to aim for the exact opposite. I see a humanity apparently doing its level best to make itself sick and unhappy, as if ill-health, stress, and suffering were the measurement of success in human life. Oh how I yearn to be miserable and sick, how happy I am when I am in pain and misery!

How could this be? Have I got it wildly wrong? Come with me on my journey, as I share with you my discoveries and understandings relating to *illness* and *wellness*, and see what you think for yourself.

My view is that our collective human family has been at the receiving end of a toxic cocktail of ignorance, professional egos, and resistance to change. Everybody's wellness has been compromised, including those who do the damage to the rest of us and our planet.

If society, by its default, has made it easy for us to be sick and unhappy, then it is up to the individual members to reverse this stupidity by their own efforts. We should embark upon a course of actions and develop a lifestyle which focuses on creating well-being for our own body and mind. This, in turn, will allow our downtrodden souls to awaken and flourish. Each spiritual revolutionary will add growing momentum to the collective pot of wellness, until such a time as humanity goes through a paradigm shift for the better. I like to think we are nearly there.

The direction our societies have taken, for however long I know not, has disconnected us from our souls, and thus from the very roots of our relationship with Mother Earth, the universe, and the living consciousness of the whole galactic caboodle of Life. Without an active soul we are not whole; we have become detached and separated from each other. We are lost, know not who we are, nor how life works (I mean collectively speaking).

Reconnection and re-education at the individual level is essential.

. . .

LET'S look at some dictionary definitions of our two protagonists. I have emphasised some bits in italics, you might like to wonder why I've done this.

From my large Penguin dictionary, version 2001, is this definition for **illness**: '1 a disease, period of sickness, or other indisposition; 2 an unhealthy condition of the body *or mind'*. There is no entry for **wellness**.

By right-clicking on **illness** the software definition on my computer is: '1 a disease or period of sickness affecting the body *or mind*; 2 ailment, disease, complaint, disorder, malady, affliction, ill-health, poor health, virus, infection'.

For **wellness** we get: '1 the state of being in good health, especially as an *actively pursued goal*; 2 a healthcare system *focused on wellness*, not sickness'.

Wellness, according to one of the biggest publishers in the book world, clearly only came into being some time in the 21st century! I think this is an important thing to investigate, because I think it reflects poorly on our times and on the collective direction that humanity is taking.

My view on this new word is simple: we humans have been creating an increasingly toxic world, and because we are intimately interlinked with the very world which we are poisoning, we are poisoning ourselves. We eat toxic foods, take toxic medicines; we live in a rat race where we try to outdo, rather than look out for, each other; and our mantra in life is 'enough is never enough'. We've lost touch with our roots, and become disconnected from each other and from Mother Earth herself.

We are out of whack and lacking any kind of coherent harmony.

I put it down to the system and the corporate juggernaut it has spawned, which eats up everybody, including those who protect the system.

Our cultures and institutions have become toxic and injurious to our wellbeing in body and mind. The harsh reality now is that if we just follow the norm, live by the default mainstream ways, we will become unhappy, stressed, burnt out.

This is not conjecture, the evidence is all over the place.

Our societies need to create for all of us a humane and life-enhancing healthcare system *'focused on wellness not illness'*, as the definition says. What we have at the moment is simply not fit for purpose, and it serves mainly to generate gargantuan profits for the sickness industry out of our suffering. The system thrives on sickness; billions of well people will decimate our mainstream healthcare (sic) system. But society is only the sum of its individuals, so it's individuals who need to step up to the plate. What each of us does, by our own actions, connects back into society. What you as one individual human being does, counts; and don't let anybody persuade you otherwise. You are an important cog in the wheel, my friend!

Ironically, but very excitingly in my view, we have at least two ancient, yet thoroughly fit for purpose, systems of *total* healthcare (no sic), based on i) promoting wellness, ii) preventing illness, and iii) treating symptoms by addressing their root causes in a holistic manner when they appear. Now that is a sensational and revolutionary concept, wouldn't you say!

Both *Ayurveda* from India and *TCM* (traditional Chinese medicine) are magnificent bodies of knowledge, understandings and wisdoms that have stood the test of time… thousands of years. In my view they have never been more appropriate and relevant to people's lives than today. We will investigate Ayurveda in the *Desserts* section because that's the one I picked to learn most from, and which is more comprehensively covered in the English language.

Let's explore and expand on the definitions so we can relate them to our own experiences and life. It said that **illness** is, 'an unhealthy condition of the body or mind'. Such conditions are usually referred to as symptoms, and it's these symptoms a doctor is focused on and will treat you for.

Relating to the body, I have read before there are thousands of conditions and symptoms, and we'll sample some to get the picture.

As you read through them decide if you are ever afflicted by them. My aim here is to give you a sampling of just what illness can entail!

In the world of *pain* we have the five aches of headache, stomachache, toothache, earache, backache, a sore throat, stiffness in the neck or shoulders or back; there are various *conditions* of varying severity which can afflict us, such as nausea, coughs, blocked nose, dizziness, migraines, gout, arthritis, fibromyalgia, kidney stones, tumours and lumps (benign or malignant), fungal outbreaks, cramp, dandruff, acne, skin afflictions, swellings, nosebleed, food poisoning, intestinal gas, obesity, diabetes, cancer; there are various kinds of *malfunctioning* which occur with the body's processes and systems, such as constipation, diarrhoea, poor digestion, acid reflux, metabolic issues, tremors, flatulence, heart attack, stroke and all diseases; and there are germ-type issues like fevers, colds, the flu, viruses, bacterial conditions, worms.

Then there is the world of unseen problems going on, such as overworked and overheated organs, as in your stomach, liver, kidneys, adrenal glands, pancreas, lungs, heart and brain. This is your 'engine room' so to speak. They, along with your glands, are responsible for all the bodily processes and systems, such as your metabolic, digestion, nervous, lymphatic, excretory, and reproductive systems. Take care of your organs and glands and they will take care of you. This is so essential.

But nobody teaches us this kind of stuff, we must learn for ourselves.

When it comes to the mind, officially speaking there are nowhere near as many symptoms, and only a few seem to be recognised, like depression, mania, schizophrenia, Alzheimer's, psychopathy, being suicidal… all pretty bleak advanced conditions of illness in the mind. And again, mainstream medicine will only look at the problem, not the underlying issues and causes. Pills are prescribed as usual, which may alleviate things somewhat for a while, but merely serve to mask the problem. Good for business though especially as these kinds of pills usually breed dependency and addiction.

If we want health and harmony in our lives, we must learn by ourselves what the root causes are of our problems.

For our purposes we are going to view unhappiness, stress, and any form of negative thoughts and feelings in the mind as 'illness', inasmuch as they steal our wellness from us. We can call them 'psychological disorders' if you like. We'll identify several later on when we look at impediments to wellness, but being the kindly chap I am, I'll offer you four for now: anger, resentment, bitterness, unworthiness.

Our purpose is to recognise when we are out of balance and to then get ourselves back to it. Pain, or discomfort of any kind, is our warning sign.

Now, all we've done so far is give examples of what illness looks like, in the body and in the mind. We have not looked at *causes*. Illness is a problem for us in that, at best, it detracts from our wellbeing and comfort, and at worst, brings us great physical and psychological pain, leading to disease and degeneration… but what brought about the problem? Why are we getting these symptoms and ailments? Why are we experiencing negative mindsets so easily, where does all this unhappiness, misery and powerlessness come from?

It's at this point we have to depart from the standard offerings of medicines and medical treatments, because the mainstream healthcare system of allopathy is focused only on identifying symptoms, and then prescribing specific pills for specific symptoms and ailments. The doctor gives your problem a name, and then you get the pills that are listed for that name. Preventing a recurrence and promoting healing and wellness are barely on their radar. Illness and disease is the focus; wellness and harmony… well, maybe they're still following 20th century dictionaries.

This is third millennium healthcare at its best: open the stable doors, let all the horses bolt, and then try and round them up and get them back into the stable. Mind-blowing. I read the other day if we don't make time for our wellness, we'll be forced to make time for our illness. I know that to be true.

An ounce of prevention is worth a pound of cure. Let that be your guide!

If you seek health, harmony, wellness then now you are pretty much on your own my friend, because you can't go to a hospital or doctor to get it. But let this book and other sources help you along the way. Luckily for you and me there is a whole wellness industry, and a massive body of knowledge and understanding out there to tap into. You just have to seek it out. Wellness is not an accident, it's the result of doing work to achieve it.

The purpose of my book is to cover all the fundamentals pertaining to achieving your physical, mental, emotional and spiritual health, to staking your personal claim to a life of wellness. Yet, you can research so many health modalities and treatment protocols which help our body heal naturally, with or without the help of others. Examples include: Ayurveda, traditional Chinese medicine, homeopathy, reflexology, acupuncture, acupressure, herbs, superfoods, reiki, craniosacral therapy, massage, aromatherapy, chiropractic, orthomolecular medicine, meditation, yoga, tai chi, qi gong, and others. I've used them all at some time or other, many as preventative means.

Let's now explore and expand on the *wellness* definition given, and then we can address causes of illness, as well as factors which promote wellness.

For me, **wellness** refers to a *default* state of being whereby one's body, mind and soul function harmoniously as one holistic entity, and where that entity itself has a harmonious relationship with the outside world. Harmony within you, and harmony between you and me, you and the world.

Wellness arises from interacting intelligently with all else that makes up the totality of Mother Earth and the universe. With it, one feels glorious, alive, full of beans old boy! I see it as the holy grail of human endeavours, the very basis for our life. We need nourishment for the body, for the mind and for the soul. Mother

Earth and the Universe has everything we need, she just invites us to use our innate intelligence and skills and she will give.

I emphasised 'default' because living with wellness doesn't mean no more health problems ever again, but it does mean a dramatic reduction in ailments in body and negativity in mind, because to achieve wellness means you will have already cultivated new habits which support good health, by removing the conditions in your body and mind which allow illness and stress to flourish.

A key ingredient of wellness is that we got there by our own research and understandings, and our own endeavours and efforts. It means this state of being includes developing sufficient autonomy and life skills to manage our own health and wellness. If we then feel down or stressed, or we notice our body is struggling with this or that ailment, we have the resources and skills to non-invasively fix ourselves using natural means. We will also know how and where to get help if need be.

I'd like to stress then, that the process of achieving and maintaining wellness is several things amalgamated. It is variously: *a state of being, a skill to be acquired, a never-ending journey, a vehicle,* and it comes to us by using *self-awareness*. One must become aware of health and sickness matters, learn essential information, and develop new habits to support our mission for health, harmony and happiness. Living with wellness is becoming skilled and creative in the art and science of life. As it happens, Ayurveda translates from Sanskrit into 'science of life'.

However, fret ye not my friend, in case it all sounds daunting, it is not. From my experience it's a thoroughly enjoyable and rewarding way to journey through life. In any case, the rest of the book is here to make it all nicely doable for you. When I feel healthy and happy this feels like the ultimate achievement to me. It is a purpose for living itself.

The journey of wellness is also unique to you and reflects your own constitution of body and mind, your genetic and karmic heritage, and your own bank of life experiences and choices. All is changeable with free will and determination, never be a prisoner to your past. I tell my students that, 'at any one time in life we are the sum total of all our previous experiences'; we absolutely are not fixed beings.

Just do your best according to yourself and your own nature. Don't compare yourself with others, compare your today self with yesterday's self, and keep on doing this.

Do be sure about it though, wellness is a way of life, a lifelong commitment to oneself. Past habits, moments of weakness, and factors beyond your control will continue to strike, for sure. However, that's because we're human. It's why I stress that wellness is a default way of life, subject to natural ups and downs. But *you* have to drive the process.

LET's be more specific about wellness, and look at it in terms of health, harmony and happiness.

By *health* I mean to the fullest extent possible for each of us: i) being free from physical pain, ailments or malfunctioning; being absent of any illness or disease, ii) enjoying noticeable levels of high energy and vitality, and a body that feels flexible and 'alive'. We're talking the body part of our being here, but a healthy body is a sound basis for a sound mind - pain is such a drain on our mental wellbeing.

A state of *happiness* can mean various things: content, happy, trouble-free, floating along on cloud 9, these kinds of feelings in our mind. We have no ill-health to think about, we have sound relationships, and most likely we enjoy our job, or at the very least we don't dislike it. We are largely free from various material desires, and instead we are content with what we've already got. We can be super happy aiming for more, but only if we are enjoying the effort to get more. If we 'fail', so what, we are already happy.

Happiness is felt only in the moment, today, now, because past happiness or any possible future happiness are only thoughts. This means that living with wellness means *living consciously* and making today the most important day. When you wake up the next morning it's a new today, a new most important day, and so it goes on. I experience happiness when there is an absence of physical pain, emotional stress and material desires. Such desires, and fears of loss, are killers of all three Hs because they steal our todays from us.

I don't think happiness is very easy to achieve unless we have a default attitude of gratitude for our life. Happiness is what comes to us when we have removed things like envies, entitlements, expectations. The foundations must be in place. This is part of your spiritual revolution work.

We are happy just being, or we are happy doing something creative or productive to our liking. I like the word 'contentment', because we don't have to be constantly walking around with this insane grin on our face all the time, just that within our mind we feel good, tuned in with life... we feel the vibrational frequency of resonance.

Many times on the really good days, I go off to work or into town for a coffee or tea and I feel like imploding with joy. It helps of course that I love my teaching and research work. I may think of my wife, and feel a tremendous love and affection for her, and I can be out in nature watching the animals, listening to the birdsong, taking in the views, and just enjoying seeing everything going about its natural business. I feel irie doing my photography, listening to my reggae, playing golf with friends, so many things. I am happy sweeping the floor, cutting the grass, having a cold shower, and just walking anywhere when I stay in the present moment.

In the zone of happiness or contentment we have good levels of protection against the challenges of life, and are able to bat off most problems that previously may have derailed us.

Harmony is achieved when mind and body are both in good shape and are working in sync with each other, just as nature means them to be. You will be used to a healthy diet of food for both body and mind, feeding on life-affirming offerings from the outside world and avoiding toxic input. Such a diet promotes within you a vital energy force, and triggers your innate creativity and motivation to do things which bring you contentment.

Harmony arises in you when you are intelligently blending with, and relating, to the external world. In harmony you are psychologically and physiologically at peace, your inner being is vibrating melodically. When mind and body are in good shape, the soul is activated and you can really begin to experience joys in life, where doing even routine things becomes rewarding - the small things bring you inner joys. You feel whole, and you feel connected.

Any kind of stress you notice within your mind or body is your innate intelligence telling you you have fallen out of balance. Just seek out the causes, make any necessary changes and return yourself to harmony. Inevitably you will find you have been consuming toxic foods or toxic input for the mind. Or perhaps past, unresolved mental toxins are surfacing.

As I said at the outset, our modern world does not allow us to live with wellness by accident, we must work hard for it. That, at its essence, means learning how to live intelligently, and then doing so. This is the mission and central business of one's spiritual revolution. Choosing wellness and the Triple-H lifestyle is a lifelong commitment. If at any time we lose that ongoing commitment we will have to take what comes. If the resultant pain or discomfort is too much we will have to recommit!

To summarise then, illness and wellness result from the kind of relationship we have with the outside world. We have physical, mental and spiritual relationships within the overall holistic relationship. Nature and the divine universal intelligence designed us to live in harmony, but also gave us the means to return to harmony as and when we somehow lose balance, go out of whack, become derailed. As humans we must tune into, and use, our innate intelligence, intuition and common sense to interact positively and harmoniously with the world around us, and to learn what to do when we fall out of tune.

Take full care of both your body and your mind.

Task

Time to get a bit more practical and look at the all-important causes of illness and contributors towards wellness. We shall begin with Philip's **Five Illness Busters** and **Five Wellness Boosters**! Each will have a substitute too. These busters and boosters are all practical things you can implement right away, today, no further delay. If you already practise them, then all well and good. If not, work out what you have to do to bring them into your life.

Then you'll be up and running and dancing with the 3Hs in no time at all.

My Illness Busters in no order of importance are:

- get corporate-made foods and drinks out of your diet, and whole foods into it
- drop peer fear (seeking peer approval, worrying about their disapproval)
- practise using the OAR tool every day to become a skilled operator of conscious living
- learn how the body works; learn to listen to your body, it has innate intelligence
- do morning stretches and breathing exercises, like a DIY yoga
- substitute: slow down

My Wellness Boosters are:

- eat lots of fruits and vegetables, get superfoods into your life
- get quality sleep (get to bed before 11)
- visit and embrace nature regularly: soul makes you whole
- cultivate an attitude of gratitude for your life
- live to enjoy today the best you can
- substitute: do things - hobbies, projects, sports, games, art, music, photography; just *do* stuff!

Okay, I think we need to address the commonly experienced phenomenon of trying to give things up, and trying to think more positively, yet, after some initial success using our willpower, we find we fall back into our old ways. Why is it we often struggle to maintain our efforts?

I say it's because we don't have the foundations in place, and therefore willpower and good intentions alone are usually not enough to keep us going. A building without stability is easily blown over in a storm.

Willpower belongs to our conscious mind, but if our subconscious mind is programmed in such a way to sabotage our efforts, we will most likely fail to make lasting changes because any old ill wind may come along and blow us over.

We come back to our running theme, our education system failed us miserably. Quite simply we don't have any foundations for wellness.

It's no wonder we struggle like we do. Because of this, and through no fault of our own, we get in our own way. In addition, most of us live in a society that also gets in our way, unsurprisingly since it's made up of millions of others floundering too. We're all blocking each other.

To flourish instead, to give our willpower greater strength and steel, we must first attend to our foundations. We need to know what subconsciously blocks us from wellness. Our mission is to consciously overcome the blockages and then put strong foundations into place, and success will come to us. Foundations first, actions second; learning and understanding first, implementation second.

To truly succeed in our revolution we must be fully cognisant of our programming. Let's revisit my five pillars of society (I first mentioned them in chapter 2).

The five pillars of society are *education, food, medicine, media,* and *law*. In most nations all five pillars are crumbling. Our ability to live with wellness is being busted and our susceptibility to illness is being boosted. It's completely the wrong way round. We, the citizens alive today, are tasked with building new pillars.

Our *schooling* we have talked much about already, but to remind ourselves here, it fails to teach us how our body and mind work, we know next to nothing about how our inner ecology works, how the ecology of our world works, nor how the two are intimately interconnected. This is criminal! It fails to develop in us key life skills such as learning, communicating, collaborating, and parenting. Research, and our own experiences, clearly tell us we enjoy life more when we work and play together.

Furthermore, the system actually represses our very nature and essence of what it is to be human… crushing our curiosity and creativity, and stifling our innate intelligence and sense of awe and adventure. We emerge into adulthood unskilled, unknowledgeable and lacking in confidence. We were not educated, we were de-educated.

Verdict: education system unfit for purpose in the third millennium - woeful, antisocial, anti-life.

What we have done to our *foods* in the last two generations can only be described as deeply criminal and against life. We investigate this crucial aspect of life in the next section of the book, but here, let's just look at the language that is associated with the so-called foods we eat, and it's a horrible list: junk foods, fast foods, processed foods, refined foods, pesticides, herbicides, fungicides, genetically modified foods, high fructose corn syrup, and lots of strange words in the ingredients.

None of these foods are as nature intended. Chemicals and toxins for the most part. Have you investigated the lives of the animals from which meat and dairy foods come? And what they are fed? These are all sick animals, and from them comes our food. Have you seen the health-attacking foods fed to patients in most hospitals? Have you looked properly in the supermarkets? Most of the foods in these gleaming shops cause harm to our health. GM corn, sugar and oil are in most processed foods.

It's a ghoulish nightmare, the whole food industry. I've just touched upon the litany of problems. So much illness arises from the modern diet, and be sure about it, that includes attacks on our mental wellbeing.

Verdict: most food is toxic and injurious to our health and

wellbeing, and to the planet. Her ecosystems and our inner ecosystems are being attacked left right and centre. If you eat any of those listed foods you are taxing and overworking your liver, kidneys, pancreas, heart, the whole engine of your body that's tasked with looking after you.

Any conscious examination of *mainstream media* reveals a diet of news and views just as toxic to our mind as most food is to our body. It's untrustworthy, carries much misinformation, and it consistently triggers negative energy within our minds. It peddles fear, engineers envy and division, and loves to build people up so it can knock them down. And if we poison your mind, our body will not be happy.

For me, while it has well-documented drawbacks, *social media* on the internet is a welcome evolutionary advance in our media world. In time I think the negatives can be ironed out - it's still brand new to humans and we will adapt just fine if allowed to. Suddenly we ordinary citizens can communicate with each other all over the world. People from Israel can meet those from Kenya, Peruvians can meet Spaniards, Thais can meet Japanese. We can find out that we all face the same common struggles, namely our poor education, corruption in power, injustice and health issues, while we can discover that we all share the same basic desires for our life, namely good health, happiness, hope, a family and friends. We can also learn from and be inspired by each other.

However, whether the toxic news and views of old media, or the addictive nature of social media, both are detracting from our ability to live with good health and in harmony. In particular we should be wise to the censorship in both. One brilliant new addition to our lives is the advent of citizen journalism thanks to the internet. This is really promising, putting power back into our own hands and into our local communities. Yet, many brave new reporters are running into the ire and muscle of those working in big corporations.

Verdict: toxic content and addictive nature damaging to our health in both, but much promise in social media. Perhaps old media is on its last legs?

Recall: how did you feel during your weeklong news fast in the

Dozen Tasks chapter?!

What of the *justice system* in your country? Two-tiered? Corrupted? Broken? It should exist to serve all citizens equally, with its laws put in place to protect everybody from harm done to them by others. Another problem is that more and more rules and laws keep on coming our way, further suppressing our spirit, and stifling our ability to express ourselves freely. In ten years of leadership in Britain, Tony Blair's government passed over ten thousand new laws and rules, that was three every day for ten years. This is brutal and against the human spirit.

Verdict: until there is one law for all, regardless of one's station in life, there will never be peace in our world. It must be that corrupt officials are made liable for their crimes. Corruption is the cancer of our societies. Our world has suffered since the 1980s when huge corporations were deregulated, while we citizens were more and more regulated. We cannot allow the monolithic corporate mindset to ruin us all.

You may wonder why I've left politics out of it. Well for me, politics and government simply reflect the state of the five pillars. Politicians come from the same communities as us, eat the same foods, had the same schooling and are prone to the same conditioned ignorance. Trouble comes once they get power and money, and if they are without love in their hearts… and without being made liable for their actions while in office…

I teach leadership, and when it comes from people with love and fairness in their hearts, it will be inspiring and beneficial to everybody, but when there's an absence of love or equity, then such 'leaders' will succumb to temptations if they find there is no comeback for their actions. Everybody loses out, including the leader who now has to live a lie every day of their lives.

Each of us, by our own actions, behaviour and intention can help rebuild all five pillars by becoming love-infused leaders of our own lives. Awareness of the issues and problems is our foundational block for escaping the stranglehold of our schooled ignorance. Demand, and seek out, the best foods you can get, only take in positive media, seek out positive people for friends, cause no harm *and accept no harm.* Through your own self-education, liberate your intelligence and reconnect yourself to nature and Mother Earth. Ills, spills and pills become a thing of the past.

Task

We shall deepen our awareness of the factors that provoke illness and promote wellness to finish off the chapter.

I'd like to end on a positive note, so illness provokers come first. Write down in your notebook about half a dozen of the ones which you'd like to consciously work on in the coming days and weeks:

- negative self-talk and self-limiting beliefs
- pretending to be okay and 'fine' when you're not
- seeking peer approval, worrying about their disapproval
- maintaining toxic relationships, being toxic yourself
- fears, worries, anxiety
- resentment, envy, bitterness
- hatred and intolerance, anger and frustration
- expectations, self-entitlement, greed
- no exercise, too much exercise
- cravings and addictions
- consuming toxic or violent media, movies, social media, video games
- rigid adherence to (political) ideology
- processed foods, junk foods and fizzy drinks
- refined oils, sugars and salts
- personal care products, shampoos, cosmetics, and household cleaners containing lots of toxic chemicals
- cheating and being dishonest, including white lies
- not honouring yourself, lacking courage to be the authentic you
- complaining and blaming
- harming others or allowing others to harm you
- using forceful or violent language, gossiping and putting people down.

I wonder if you noticed how many are mind-related?

All bring negative energy to our mind and body, and remember, a hurt mind hurts your body and a hurt body hurts your mind. Only you can make the required changes, we cannot expect others to do our work.

One catch-all, foundational remedy? Take responsibility for your own life and stop blaming others, however seductive the latter is. This really is the end of 90% or more of our negative energy. You can't control what other people do, but you can always control your reaction.

Now the wellness promoters. As you read through the list select the ones you'd like to incorporate into your life and write them in your notebook:

- make your diet predominantly whole foods, and drastically cut your intake of corporate-made foods
- cut down on animal foods, especially from factory-farmed animals
- reduce or quit alcohol consumption and quit smoking
- become aware of the widespread use of toxic chemicals and reduce your exposure and consumption as much as you can, step by step
- get into good sleep habits
- manage your media consumption by choosing life affirmative input
- find books and websites for improving one's health
- become conscious of, and improve, your sitting and walking posture
- slow down
- create regular periods of 'alone-time' to enjoy nature and reflect upon life
- train yourself to stop judging others
- speak honestly and never lie, which is being true to yourself and respecting yourself
- cause no harm, accept no shit (the latter is particularly important)

- if others speak ill of you that's their problem, don't retaliate
- use your body, or lose it; abuse it and lose it
- get those muscles moving, and get your blood and oxygen circulating
- don't feel a need to virtue signal to others, just be virtuous to feel good within yourself
- notice you can see, hear, taste, feel, touch, smell and be in awe of the miracles of your sense organs
- treat your body like a temple
- be kind to others, help them, give your time to them, become a good listener
- feel compassion for their efforts to navigate their own life - being human can be hard

Use conscious living and the OAR tool to practise making them a reality, until such time as you have brand new habits that will deliver you optimal health, harmony and happiness, bingo, job done! It's all about practice and creating life-supporting habits to decondition us out of our harmful ways.

Create and cultivate your own REALITY: live with **r**espect, **e**mpathy, **a**wareness, **l**ove, **i**ntelligence, **t**ruth and all for ***y**ou*. If you do that for yourself, you will automatically afford others the same. Listen to your intuition and conscience, and hear what your mind and body are saying to you. Use common sense, take responsibility for your health, and satisfy yourself in this life of yours, not your peers. If you love yourself you will love life, and others will love you. If they don't, that's their negative energy. Start with you, go inside and discover yourself and your mind, then look outwards. Stop letting the external authority out there determine your life. It's *your* life, live it well and live it long.

Our silly system got it all 180 degrees wrong. By overturning it all we will achieve wellbeing for ourselves. But always remember, wellness is an ongoing commitment. It is a journey that only ends when you are ready to transition to the next incarnation. Speaking of journeys, come this-away >>>

10

JOURNEY AND DESTINATION: TIME, SPACE, CONSCIOUSNESS

'It is good to have an end to journey toward, but it is the journey that matters in the end.' ~ Ernest Hemingway

Travel broadens the horizons.

Are you the master of your time, or is time your master? If your life is a train journey, who's in the driver's seat?

Leave the rat race to rats; stop trying to get somewhere, you're already there.

You've only got one life, there are no dress rehearsals, no dummy runs, no second goes, this is it, this is your lot. Don't take your potential to your deathbed, make it happen on your journey.

A few years ago, I was chatting to a most interesting young German couple. We were in the wonderfully-named

'Rebellious Art Gallery' for an evening of Indian curry, spiced-up chai tea, and some fine Indian music, including the magical sounds of the sitar... and the paintings were really good too, the owner of the gallery being a top local artist. It turned out to be tip-top art and a tip-top evening.

This couple had got my ear for sure because, it turned out, they had been on the road non-stop for quite some time and were now taking a two week break here in Thailand, and being a seasoned traveller myself, I love hearing travel stories. Their travel story was monumental, their means of transport cycling. They'd left Germany a few months previously, and had cycled through countries like Turkey, Iran, one or two of the Stans from the old Soviet Union (nobody can spell those countries), Russia, Mongolia, China, Laos, and were now in northern Thailand. They were taking it easy and really slowly, doing just about 50 kms each day.

I loved listening to their tales from these countries, especially Iran and Turkey which have always interested me for their tremendous history, architecture and stunning landscapes. I have also taught students from both countries, so their stories deepened my desire to one day get to them.

As is always the case with people's travel tales, I heard about the really friendly locals they kept on coming across (in contrast to all the beasts and terrorists our media keep on throwing at us). One amazing thing was that neither of them had had a puncture yet - from Germany to Thailand without a blowout, wow! What an adventure for them and not even over yet, for after their break they were off to Malaysia, Indonesia, Australia and finally New Zealand.

Now this was what you could call a proper journey. I loved the 50 kilometres a day bit, just my kind of pace; it reminded me of a sign in one of my favourite resorts: 'Slow is beautiful'. They were very happy buzzing people, which is what travel does to the human spirit, and certainly their horizons at times must have been broad and breathtaking.

The point of my tale, though, is that we chatted on about life itself, our thoughts on what makes it all worthwhile and meaningful, and I told them that I was writing this book. We hit upon the subject of 'success' and our western view of what represents success, and we agreed it was always the material dream, money, possessions. We talked about health and wealth, and agreed health was the most important. They told me about some graffiti wall art they had passed by in Berlin, right at the start of their journey.

The art depicted the story, through a series of cartoon-like captions, of the lives of two, now dead, competing businessmen and all their major acquisitions and successes over the years - mansions, beautiful wives, holiday villas, club memberships, bundles of cash and all the rest of it. The final caption, marking the end of their lives, was represented by pictures of their tombstones. One tombstone was bigger than the other, and etched onto this bigger tombstone were the German words for 'I won'.

The two of them on their own spirited adventure, along with this story of theirs about two competing businessmen, could not have provided a starker contrast in how we humans can approach life in two different ways.

I THINK the two tales neatly encapsulate the differences between what we can think of as *destination-focused* and *journey-oriented* living, between *material* and *spiritual* approaches to life, between a *time-dominated lifestyle* and a more *timeless-based experience*.

One approach is always focused on tomorrow, chasing the fruits of one's desires, seeking to be successful and to be seen as successful; while the other approach is focused on enjoying today and whatever experiences it will send our way, and what others think is of little importance. One is *future-oriented living* and always trying to get somewhere else, even to be someone else; the other is *today-oriented living* where one is content with where they are and who they are. One pits us as rats against each other in a race, the other harmonises the human spirit with the world to which we are intimately connected.

At this early stage of the chapter, you might consider which approach best describes your own life's journey thus far. Which do you focus on more, enjoying today or seeking a better future?

Typically speaking, as kids we are educated and brought up by the adults in society to seek financial, work and material success as the path to achieving happiness and freedom. The objective inculcated in us is to 'make it', and be lauded for doing so. Certainly, if it delivers happiness and success then this will be great, but once one makes it, then what? There's still lots more life to be lived - how long does the 'making it' last? Do we have to keep on making it? And what if we don't make it? How do we feel? A failure, not good enough?

This kind of success, then, simultaneously requires us to be recognised and acknowledged by others as being a 'worthy', 'important', or 'acceptable' kind of person. You will see how this makes us dependent upon others for our own perceived self-worth, and, from my observations, this seeking of recognition spreads out into all areas of our life, dominating our subconscious decision-making in life. We are set up to seek praise and approval, and fear blame or disapproval. We lose autonomy, we lose touch with our roots, our soul.

The main basis for receiving the plaudits in a materialistic society is to have wealth, status or celebrity. Money is the currency of success in our programmed subconscious mind, and being well known and envied is a solid second.

Until we inquire into our life, do inner work, we are unlikely to be aware of this subconscious impulse. But if you observe, you will see it everywhere.

In this way we are 'externalised' in our approach to life. We are acquisitive and we seek to be seen by our contemporaries as important and successful, and the stuff we need is external to us. Gaining both the stuff and recognition, we were led to believe, would deliver us the happiness and freedom we all innately yearn for. Many will attest to the illusory nature of this expectation. When it doesn't work, though, we get greedy for more and cravings become commonplace.

The stuff we want is out there - peer recognition and praise is out there, blame and disapproval is out there, all the good things in life are out there, as are the bad things. Everything is out there. This externalised living means the yardsticks for our success and worth as a person are measured by others.

By this approach we cede control of our own lives, we become driven and riven by desires and fears, become dependent on what others think of us, and it keeps on being like this year after year. We desperately try to control our lives in such a way that others will see we are doing well and that all is fine and dandy in our life. Even when it's anything but; externalised living leads to pretend living.

An inherent part of the measurement of this kind of success is that we are seen to outdo and outperform others in order to get that recognition. The two wealthy German barons killed themselves trying to win all the time! Beating and competing against others becomes the norm. Out of this way of life come phrases like 'it's a dog-eat-dog world' and, 'business is business', as if one has carte blanche to act in any way with little regard for the welfare of others: if I don't overpower you, you will do it to me. Of course, that is precisely what we see in the political, media and corporate worlds as a default.

Being the one who doesn't make it carries stigma; we will do anything to not be seen as stupid. Embarrassment and humiliation are to be avoided at all costs. Pretence, lies and deceit arise as defence mechanisms to avoid this nightmare. This has a tremendous impact on our psyche and emotional wellbeing, putting huge stress on us because in effect we are living a lie. And we're talking a way of life here, not just an odd incident we can quickly recover from.

Externalised living fairly and squarely orients our perspective and attention on the future, for we are constantly looking for more or for better. Today's not good enough. Today is barely noticed. Here is hardly seen, over there yonder is our focus. The mind spends most of its time preoccupied, distracted. This hijacks our sense of inner harmony and wellbeing.

If we willy-nilly follow this approach, we fail to address our own deep-rooted needs for social connection, love and self-worth, and to feel like we are contributing to society and the greater good.

In this way we lose much of our ability to be free and authentic human beings. We are not contributors to the collective pot of the human family, we are subtractors, takers. But it takes from us, from our spirit and psychological wellbeing.

We diminish ourselves and reduce our capacity to be happy and content. The law of life says if you take, it will take, if you give, it will give. As with almost everything in life, it seems to me, the system taught us the non-natural non-loving way.

In this approach to life we enslave ourselves to the altar of public opinion. We are constantly trying to fit into a preconceived mould and model of life, to be who we should be, do what we should do and think how we should think. This is our subconscious programming directing us, and if we succumb we can never find out who we really are, because we're too busy trying to be somebody else. We have to break out of this mould, and only conscious living can do this for us, and that means focusing on the journey of our life, which is only and always today.

What we would like to discover, through inner inquiry, is another approach to life which will *really* bring us happiness and freedom. We would like to feel a sense of fulfilment for what we do on our own personal journey until such time as the janitor from heaven is knocking on our door. I think we all want to be healthy and happy within ourselves, feeling like we are contributing to the greater good of the human family, and of course to cherish and revere Mother Earth herself, source of all life. We would like to live in a REAL manner, with respect, empathy, awareness and love.

The key to it all lies in today. Life only exists today…

We can think of life as having past and future along with the present, that is, yesterday and tomorrow divided and bridged by today, which is the usual time-based way of looking at life. We experience things today, we carry memories of past experiences, and we can imagine future experiences.

Notice carefully, however, that the remembering and imagining of experiences not happening now, is happening now. Get it?! Either we are experiencing the unfoldment of life now, or we are experiencing thoughts of past or future life now; experiencing or thinking, both happen in the now. There is only now. There is the *idea* of past and future time, contained in thought form, and we can make it seem real simply by remembering the past or projecting into the future. Our mind is a stunning creation!

These experiences of ours, happening now, or the ones we are thinking about from another time, can be good or bad, interesting or boring, adventurous or routine. This means that we have our experiences in life, and we attach a value to them too. You might like to reflect: upon what basis do you decide if something is positive or negative…?

In a rather more novel view of things, we can see life as consisting of a whole bunch of todays, which arrive one after the other, ad infinitum, until we reach our final today. We could further narrow this view to even smaller increments, whereby even within one today - just the *today* today - we can think of so many hours or moments, or quite simply a whole bunch of successive 'now-moments'. Life, seen this way, becomes a perpetually regenerating small unit of time, and our mind has the power to conceive that unit as one second, one minute, one hour, or one today, or even longer.

In this way we can view and experience life moment by moment, happening by happening, day by day, and in fact 'time' as we know it sort of melts away into something more akin to a timelessness, where there is only ever now, just only today. You may think there is 'tomorrow', and that's fine, the thinking of it, but as soon as you actually wake up the next morning it's not tomorrow at all, it's simply today again. And one more day added to your past, gone forever.

I've seen it in a pub in England, and in a restaurant in Thailand, a sign on the wall promising 'Free beer tomorrow'. I went back the next day, but… I had to pay.

In the world of life and the life of the world, in the happenings of the universe and in the universe of happenings, in the whole grand galactic scheme of things, there is only ever now, perpetually manifesting itself. Life simply keeps on happening. It is we humans who were granted the capability through our minds to project backwards or forwards in time, and we can call it thought. Thought liberates us or enslaves us. Only conscious living can give us the levers of control over our thoughts.

When we connect ourselves to this timelessness zone, it's as if we've become the water of a river, just gently making progress without any kind of measurement, just flowing along with the natural currents of life happily enough, content, taking in one's journey with no particular expectation, certainly in no rush. When we meet the estuary it's the end of our journey and we find the heavenly ocean ready to embrace us... so why rush to meet it?? If the river of life is good, fulfilling, slow down to experience and enjoy it more. If the river of life is not good for some reason, you are human, you can use free will to make changes, but only today!

Thus we can view ourselves as having one life, or we can view ourselves as having thousands of todays or millions of now-moments; one long macro-journey of life with many other separate micro-journeys of today. From this perspective, focusing on the micro-journey is a tremendous start to escape from the full-on acquisitive, future-oriented, peer-judged, mould-fitting rat race we described above.

Either one life, perhaps divided into a few stages, like youth, young adult, middle-aged, old-aged, gone; or 36,525 todays, assuming you live to 100.

We certainly get more value for our money through this perspective, and if one micro-journey goes wrong, we have many more opportunities to make the next one better; not really possible if we view life as just one long journey - get that one wrong and you better be hoping reincarnation will save your bacon.

There is thinking about life in the past or future, or experiencing life in the now; *thinking* about it or *living* it. But bear in mind, whether you are thinking about life, or experiencing, seeing and living it, it all takes place in the now-moment.

There is only ever now, life = now. And forevermore. Let that be your guide.

THE MATERIALISTIC WAY of humans - the *destination-focused, future-oriented approach* to life - is caught up almost exclusively in thoughts about the past or future, and which we feel and perceive as either positive or negative. Thoughts lead to feelings, and feelings lead to more thoughts. We are either desiring pleasure or fearing pain. The pleasure is in getting our hit, the pain is not getting it, or losing it when we already have it. But if we develop harmful habits and addictions, those pleasures start coming with a price to pay. And the currency is pain…

The trouble is that the material way of life usually means we are thinking negative thoughts and having negative feelings about things, people, situations, and so we are losing out on life, and doubly so: experiencing negative energy and missing out on the now. Preoccupation with our worries and regrets, our fears and desires, our expectations and ambitions, steals life from us. We barely notice today, we are fixated on making a future time better, worrying about it getting worse, or digging up an unhappy past.

Done to the nth degree, as a default approach to life, this brings us unhappiness in mind and sickness in body. Harmony and happiness are nowhere to be found. We are like a dog chasing its tail, always trying to catch it, never getting there.

Materialism and fitting into the system's mould puts our focus and attention *on the future* and *on the external world*, removing us from *today* and *our own inner world*. Such a lifestyle takes us out of the zone where life and the universe are happening, leaving us stuck in our own head with our mind's infernal internal chatter. Life is going on without us, we have pulled out of it!

We lose our connection with the force of life, and instead become disconnected, disoriented and disempowered.

This is not to say we should reject and turn our back on sex, drugs and rock 'n roll, no way! Nor to hate money or deny ourselves other material pleasures of life, nor to cease imagining a better future for ourselves. Materialism is not bad per se, it's our relationship with it we have to be wary of. And we are all pushed on by the system and its consumerist ways of mass advertising and marketing hitting our consciousness daily in all our media. This system devours our money and spirit alike.

What we need to do is find *balance*. We innately know this of course, but we need to step away, find time and space to reflect on our life, regularly. Disconnect from the mad mantra to buy buy buy, rush rush rush, and connect with the rhythms of Mother Earth, and her abundant nature and gifts she offers us. Free of charge!

'Enough is never enough' is the system's mantra, for the grass is always greener over there, look at those wealthy people, those celebrities, they've made it, why not me?

Well, it might seem like they've made it, but I think we all know that a wealthy lifestyle does not often lead to health and happiness, in fact, my experience and observations tell me it often leads to loneliness and unhappiness. Always more is sought, and that suggests emptiness of spirit.

The practical way out is, always, to seek harmony and balance. If seeking out pleasures brings us pains too, then why spend more time going for happiness instead? Happiness comes when we unblock and unburden ourselves from our conditioned ignorance. How to do this?

Easy. Conscious living. A reminder…

Reset your outlook on life using the OOAAI tool (orientation, objectives, approach, attitude, intention, in case you've not memorised it yet!) to give yourself strong foundations for a new approach to life. Just consciously setting a new outlook for yourself will encourage and empower you. You cannot make serious progress until you undo the programming from the system. OOAAI sorts you out in this department.

Then, from this position of inner strength, live out your new outlook by practising conscious living using the OAR tool (observation, awareness, reflection). Now come the riches and rewards from learning how life works and who you really are - an intelligent interconnected gifted unique individual. Never forget it and forever celebrate it.

Work out your guiding intention, orientation and attitude, set ongoing objectives, and develop an approach which will lead you towards health, harmony and happiness. Make a spiritual connection with all that is alive in our world and universe. It can only happen in the now-moment, the only place where life takes place.

So, practise conscious thinking, conscious being, practise bringing your attention and focus back to the now-moment, and focus your energies on making today a good day, not some future today. Get into the journey of life, that's where all the action's at. Make it happen. Your OAR tool is always the go-to means for making any changes to your life because when you observe - others, yourself, situations - you really get to see and discern life at a higher level. Then you can reflect upon things and make informed, intelligent changes.

Self-awareness is your passport to life, today life.

Pay attention to your future, to things you'd like which you don't have right now, yes for sure, but only after you have attended to the journey of your life. Make the journey more important than the destination. Aim somewhere by all means, but if you end up somewhere else, don't let it upset you, enjoy the alternative place. Just reflect upon why it happened this way, and when you wake up the next morning, do things differently. If you keep on observing you can keep on reflecting, and this is real learning.

Making one's key objective in life the Triple-H lifestyle of wellness is perfect because it focuses us on today; this objective is not a destination, it's a way of life. Make choices, develop new habits, interact with people and nature in ways which lead you to wellness and positive vibes. If you live with this as a default in your life, all future objectives or dreams or directions you may desire will be so much easier to achieve, because in your healthy, happy state of mind you can be creative and productive, and inspired to do your best.

You are the navigator and the driver of your own life when you live consciously and spiritually. Not completely, for the system still goes on for now, but more than enough to optimise your time on this beautiful planet of ours. And the more of us who travel this path, the more we begin to help society neutralise and overcome this system, which has dominated our lives for centuries or millennia.

You are the most important person on this planet. Not to others, but to yourself. Be that way, celebrate yourself and share your positive vibes with others. What's not to like about this?

Your challenge is to find the right balance for you in your life between *material pleasures* and *spiritual happiness*, between a *destination-focused* and *journey-oriented* lifestyle. I would hazard a guess that 99% of us need much more of the spiritual zest and quest in our lives, and more today-living than tomorrow-living.

Spiritual revolution is embarking upon changes in our life which lead us towards living in harmony with the world and with other people. The living of life is experienced in the journeying, and so it seems to me that the major focus in life should always be on the journey, but allowing for a judicious amount of planning or dreaming for where we might like to get to. But sacrificing today for tomorrow is a risky choice, for life is only partaken of today, in the now-moment.

A FINAL WORD in relation to the *master journey of Life* itself…

Life represents one long journey while death represents the final destination and the end of life. But life, in reality, consists of many intermediate journeys and destinations. Each of these journeys takes time, and reaching the destination merely marks the end of that journey and the start of a new one. So the journey is a period of time, and relatively speaking the destination is a dot of time; it is a marker of time between the periods. It looks like this:

J o u r n e y endJ o u r n e y endJ o u r n e y end.

We can see from this that most of time and life is being on a journey. The end of one journey merely marks the beginning of a new journey, the end of one today marks the beginning of a new today. It surely makes sense that we spend most of our time and energies focused on the journeys of life rather than desiring and chasing certain destinations.

And so we shall end this chapter's journey as we started it: 'It is good to have an end to journey toward, but it is the journey that matters in the end'. Thank you, Ernest.

A new journey awaits you >>>

11

THE JOURNEY OF LIFE: LIVING CONSCIOUSLY

With a peaceful heart we discover happiness. ~ Buddhist wisdom

Look and contemplate within and see the truth. Looking out at others we are immersed in delusion. ~ Buddhist wisdom

Imagine entering a gigantic maze in the gardens of an ancient castle. The usual objective of being in a maze is to find your way out of it in quick order, often in a race with others, and this intention colours every decision you make. Reaching this destination and succeeding in the challenge, that is to get out of the maze as soon as you can, governs your thought process and focuses your mind on the end point. Where you are is not important, getting out of it is.

Now imagine changing the objective… this time you are to just enjoy being lost in the maze, experiencing all the different pathways with beautiful green hedges, walking barefoot on the grass and feeling connected with Mother Earth's energy forces, listening to all the birdsong, and deeply inhaling the smells of nature. When faced with left or right, you try to choose the one that keeps you in, not to find your way out.

Prolong this experience instead of trying to get out of it. At some point you will come out, it's inevitable, but hey, no rush and just have fun playing the game

while you're in it. And when you do finally emerge, you can explore the rest of the gardens and prolong the experience of your exciting day, connecting with nature and life, and tuning into your own heartbeat and energy force.

As with the ***maze****, think* ***today*** *and think* ***life****. Either do your best to get out of it as quickly as possible without really noticing much, or stay in the game for as long as you can, noticing and enjoying the journey along the way. When one journey naturally ends, enjoy getting on the next one.*

Task

Reread the above, this time substituting the concept of *life* or *today* for the *maze*…

LET'S remind ourselves of my thesis for the spiritual revolution and the vital, unpostponable need for it: thanks to an inadequate, damaging education and thanks to a society that is set up to hinder rather than help us, *we don't know who we are nor do we know how life works.*

We therefore have a problem… individually, collectively. We are conflicted within, and between each other. We don't know how to communicate and collaborate properly, and our damage limitation is by trying to avoid confrontation. But this in itself leads to it.

This is all terribly sad because individuals and the whole human family alike are operating at a fraction of who and what we could be. Our potential as a unique, beautiful human being remains largely untapped. We are struggling.

I loudly declare we want ourselves back, we want connection, we want meaning to our life, we want brotherly and sisterly relations with all. We want to be loving and to be loveable, no more of this negative nonsense we see in our battered human family.

No more suffering I say! We must get rid of it, solve it. This is not idealism or escapism, quite the opposite - it's easy once we know how. Love is how. And love comes from gratitude, and an absence of fear. And that, my friend, comes from busting up ignorance!

Love is the only way for the positive evolution of individual humans and our whole human fraternity alike. And I mean the love that we express outwards from our own heart and soul, not any kind that we may seek for ourselves. But, if you give it out, it will find its way back to you, that is natural law. We only need test it out to find out for ourselves.

And such love will easily arise, flow and flourish, when we practise **conscious living**, which we have mentioned several times so far. *Cultivating conscious living is our central business from here on in until the end of the book, and on into the sunset of our life.*

We now officially shine the light of our attention and intelligence onto it.

WHAT IS **CONSCIOUS LIVING**, what does it do for us, how and why do we do it? Let's investigate.

I said previously that wellness is no accident, that in our toxic world today it must be a proactive and ongoing pursuit by anybody who desires health, harmony and happiness in their life; well, the way to effect the 3Hs is through *conscious living.*

I view conscious living as the engine room for one's revolution. It is the means for teaching yourself how to manage and look after your own health and life.

Through it you become inspired, informed and skilled. It is the catalyst for transforming yourself and your life by your own efforts and deeds, and once you've embraced it, there is no going back to your old de-educated, disconnected, system-conditioned ways. The butterfly cannot go back to being a caterpillar.

Our objectives for choosing conscious living as a way of life are myriad and manyfold. We would like to empower ourselves, transform our way of life, and help heal our planet. We would like to overcome self-limiting beliefs and any detrimental ideologies foisted upon us by society. And we would like to gain control of our own fate and destiny by learning to gain control of our FATE: our **f**eelings, **a**ctions, **t**houghts and **e**motions.

By practising conscious living we empower ourselves by becoming connected, confident and compassionate. We discover our own unique self and, in this way, we feel at one with all other humans and life; we see diversity in unity, unity in diversity.

We shall rise up and roar like a lion, chase that miserable anti-life system right out of town, and create our own loving way of living.

Conscious living reunites us with our nature and human essence - with our own self and with each other. It is the enabling factor that allows us to embrace the 3Ps, aim for the 3Hs, becoming 3I people by focusing on the 3Ls: be proactive, productive and positive… achieve health, harmony and happiness… become an intelligent, interconnected individual… by focusing on learning, living and loving. And you know what that spells… choose PHIL's way!

Now, ignore your neighbours or anybody around you, and give yourself an almighty bloody huge lion-like roar of encouragement!

Be a lionheart from this very moment onwards. Give yourself permission and just do it. It's your life, your world, and you're gonna lead your own way from now on. You are a unique expression of life's creation, a beautiful human being, and miracles and magic will be yours if you drop all fear today. No more bullshit, no more nonsense, no more system suppression, time to flower and flourish.

Conscious living is our way.

There is an initial body of work (I call it 'life inquiry') that needs to be done which, in a nutshell, is to discover who we *think* we are today, how we came to be this way, and how we *think* life works.

To that end, we need to bring light to our existing beliefs, values and habits, to ask ourselves where they came from, and to discover if they support or hinder us in our quest for wellness. We need to shine a light onto our existing attitude, outlook and approach towards life, and to see what, if any, our objectives and purpose for living are.

Conscious living informs us of all of this.

Meanwhile, as we are discovering much more about ourselves, and about the society and culture that we live in, we need to investigate and discover how life *really* works, and who we *really* are.

From this twin approach to information gathering we will learn about the *ideology* of human life, and we will learn about the *truth* of life as it applies to the world and whole universe. I say we are in a collective mess because the ideology from the system runs counter to truth and love, it antagonises our very nature and desire for connection with each other and the natural world.

We learn that there are, in effect, two worlds that we inhabit: the *World of Should Be* and the *World of Is*, or, the *World of Human Ideology* and the *World of Consciousness*. When humankind's ideology does not complement the truth of the universe's consciousness, which is the highest form of life, then we humans will always struggle. And so it is today. With ideology, we humans allow our nurture to antagonise our nature, not to complement it.

Conscious living informs us of all of this.

Brother, sister, no need to take my word for it, discover for yourself. That is the serene beauty of conscious living, it is the individual's means for learning about life first-hand for themselves. It's your life, so you find your own understanding and your own truth. Then you find you. Conscious living connects you back to the life support grid of the universe which the system disconnected us from during our schooling.

So, having discussed what it does for us, and why we might want to become skilled in it, what exactly is it, how do we do it, how do we beneficially use it? We've been on this quest since the book started but now we will give it our full attention.

CONSCIOUS LIVING IS when *you notice and are aware of i) what is happening around you, ii) what you're doing, and iii) what is going on inside you*. We notice and have awareness of life using what we shall call our **'mind's eye'**. It is your mind's eye which is noticing and reading the text on this page right now. Conscious living is connecting your mind's eye to the present moment.

If one is doing something while being preoccupied with thinking about something else, one's mind's eye is on the thinking, not on the doing… wherever your attention, there is your mind's eye. Conscious living is being aware of where your attention is lying.

Look up at the ceiling right this second, and realise you are doing it… there, conscious living. Now look at your right foot and notice it with your mind's eye; now stroke an imaginary cat and watch your hand as you move it… there, conscious living.

It is said, by those who study and research such things, that most people spend over 90% of their lives not living consciously, rather they engage with life through the autopilot of their subconscious mind. Routines, habits, and actions we do all the time are so ingrained in us that we don't have to think what we're doing, we can automatically do them, and often, therefore, we just don't notice that we are doing them. We don't have to think how to open a door, walk, or clean our teeth.

And because of this, or arising out of it, a section of our mind runs riot with what we can call our internal chatter, or inner talk. It is this chatterbox mind which steals our consciousness, diverts our mind's eye from what is going on in the world and from what we are actually doing. It many times directs our behaviour and language. In my massage with the falling water noise, I kept losing awareness of the water because my chatterbox mind was doing its stuff.

This inner talk, while sometimes benign, is our tormentor-in-chief and the instigator of all our destructive words and deeds. Everybody has negative self-talk - you know, doubt, guilt, shame and so on - and this is your internal chatter and part of the system's program we've been talking about.

Conscious living means we can notice this thought production factory within our minds, and that is always the start of solutions to our problems in life.

It's easy to get ourselves into conscious living mode and, until we practise and become skilled in living this way, even easier to become distracted out of it by this inner voice of ours. I'd like to offer you a method for instantly, whenever you think about it, bringing yourself into conscious living. Once we live more consciously we can start availing ourselves of all the aforementioned benefits. My method also carries some associated health tips to help you with your wellness journey, as a free bonus!

The best way to see everything and fully grasp the act of conscious living is to bring your focus onto our four most common daily activities, which ordinarily you are unlikely to be aware of because you don't need to be, you can do them all without thinking about them. I'm talking about *breathing, sitting, walking,* and *eating.*

My suggestion is to practise getting yourself into conscious living mode with these activities first, which means you'll get unlimited opportunities to become skilled at it. Then just apply it to all other areas of your life.

Quite simply, bring your attention - your mind's eye - to the activity you are doing. As soon as you realise or notice that you are eating, breathing, sitting or walking, then you are in conscious living mode. That you were not aware of doing them beforehand is because your mind's eye and attention was preoccupied with doing or thinking about other things. Let's go through them one by one.

WHENEVER YOU ARE next *walking* somewhere, remember reading this chapter and notice your walking, become aware that you are in the process of walking. Keep your attention on your walking, notice how fast you are going, what kind of posture you have, how you hold your head, what your arms are doing, all the while being aware of what is happening around you in case you have to change your direction. You are now consciously walking with full awareness. But your chatterbox mind can hijack your attention very easily (so can your smartphone).

To practise maintaining conscious walking, notice each time your feet make contact with the ground and when they leave the ground. Keep noticing, keep your attention on your feet.

Health tip: instead of rushing to wherever you're going and barely even realising you're walking, set off earlier, slow down from your usual pace, walk upright, chest out and head up, and walk confidently into the space ahead of you. It's you and the world together, enjoy the world's company, embrace her, be that lionheart! Keep doing this for the whole journey, whether it's one minute, ten minutes or more, whether it's at home, in the garden, or out and about. If you become distracted - you will, many times - just return your attention to your posture and feet.

Health activity: find some parkland, lawns, a beach, and enjoy walking barefoot. If you didn't know, this is called 'earthing' or 'grounding'. Earthing is super healthy for us - the earth gives off negative ions which send positive energy through our feet and into our body which we don't get when we've got shoes on. When I walk barefoot I definitely live consciously, I love the sensation of being connected to Mother Earth, for she is the giver of life.

WHENEVER YOU ARE *SITTING down* - and many people nowadays spend a lot of time sitting down - recall this chapter and bring your attention to your body. Become aware that you are sitting down, and notice your posture. Are you sitting with back upright and shoulders open or are they slumped in the shape of a hammock-shaped banana? I used to be a slumper, but I began retraining myself after I started my wellness journey. These days I look around me when I'm out and about and nearly everybody slumps. It's become more of a health disaster since smartphones came onto the scene. Notice what you're doing and if need be straighten your back, open up your shoulders, make your chest point forwards, and relax out of any tension you notice in your neck region. This all becomes super important if you do a lot of computer or desk work.

Health tip: if you slump a lot make it a mission to retrain your sitting posture, and in so doing you will have to become super good at conscious living. It's amazing how quickly we go from a conscious straight back to our default slumping position. I can't recall how long it took me to really retrain myself, perhaps a year or two, not sure. Now I sit upright subconsciously as my default sitting position. This also helps you if you are prone to any back pain.

Health activity: sit down on the floor cross-legged or in the lotus/half lotus position if you can, and practise keeping your back upright for as long as you can. Sit against a wall if it helps you to maintain conscious attention. If you find you have slumped, straighten up. In all these kinds of retraining activities never lose heart, sometimes you have to practise for quite some time to get the real benefits, but when you succeed you really do boost your wellness factor.

WHENEVER YOU ARE *BREATHING*... hah, just joking. Whenever you remember to, bring your conscious attention to your breathing. This of course can be anywhere at any time. Notice your in-breaths and notice your out-breaths, and keep noticing for as long as you can or have time to do so. Just keep following your breathing, feel your chest moving. Do you breathe through your mouth or nose? Do you breathe in a shallow manner?

Health tip: make sure you're always breathing (only quality health info for you in this book).

Health activity: combine with sitting or lying down on a yoga mat or your bed, or anywhere comfortable, and make breathing your only activity. Now focus on slowing down, breathing more deeply in and out, and enjoy the process. As you breathe in and out, you might let your mind's eye do a check up on your body, part by part, perhaps starting with your toes and working your way up to the crown of your head. Or, visualising your heart, say, direct your in-breath there to bring oxygen to it, and then with your out-breath imagine toxins leaving your heart. In this way you can keep conscious of both your breathing and each part of your body, while feeding oxygen to your whole being.

At the start of my spiritual journey, when living in Bangkok, I used to take a long weekend most months at a nice beach town two hours away. I would get up early, go and sit in the shade under some trees on the beach and, as the sun was rising out of the sea and upwards, I would focus on counting 100 deep breaths in and out. My rule was that if I lost count I had to start again. Usually, I ended up becoming so hungry for breakfast that I gave up getting to 100. I challenge you to reach 100! But in any case, the journey is the key, and I was getting lots of good oxygen and circulation while practising holding my conscious attention.

When you are *eating*, notice your eating, notice how fast you eat, how much or how little you chew your food, and what the tastes are like. Now for me, again, I have completely retrained myself in my eating habits. Most people don't just eat, they do other things at the same time, barely even noticing their meal - TV dinners, on-the-go meals, smartphone meals and so on. That is not conscious living!

Most people eat fast, and I mean *fast*. I observe it all the time. Barely any chewing going on, just shovelled down like there's no tomorrow. I recall before I moved to Thailand being a very fast eater myself, usually finishing my meal before everybody else, and in those days I got a lot of stomachaches and indigestion. I knew not why back then. So many pains and bodily malfunctions arise out of our ignorance. Now I'm usually the slowest eater.

Health tip: to practise maintaining your conscious attention when eating, ensure you chew every mouthful plenty of times. You may find that previously bland tastes begin to release pleasures hitherto hidden from you. Your stomach will have less work to do and will be most thankful to you. Ayurveda views the stomach as the seat of health, and is where health first starts to go wrong if we don't take care of it. Try to get into the habit of doing nothing else while eating most of your meals. Especially when you've got good tasty healthy food. If you're busy talking, watching TV, on the phone, you won't notice all that lovely food. Of course, a good meal out with good company is somewhat different. It's the default that counts.

Aside from the four essential habits of life, what else can we apply our mind's eye and conscious living to? The short answer is anything you like, but perhaps a longer answer will be more useful.

Task

Before I give you my thoughts, brainstorm with yourself all the things you can start consciously noticing, observing, paying attention to in your own daily life. Write down your ideas, and then choose some to focus on in the coming weeks.

Practising conscious living, which is the bulwark of your revolution, means wheeling out your new OAR tool. This is your numero uno method for learning about life, yourself, and the strange and often harmful ways of humans, so never let it gather dust!

The idea is to use it as often as you remember, but at some point you will find it second nature to use, and your self-awareness will help you in all matters of healthy and happy living.

Observing others, observing life going on around you, and observing your own self, will allow you to get out of the habit of making assumptions, believing this or that to be true, and being stuck with your societal and cultural conditioning. Instead, you now start verifying everything for yourself, you begin to accumulate a vast storehouse in your long-term memory of real time and first-hand experiences, and you find yourself naturally challenging everything you thought you knew.

Observe others and learn about yourself, observe yourself and learn about others, observe yourself and learn about your body, mind and soul. Observing means learning, big time!

Observe, then reflect upon what it meant and what you can learn. We investigate the cause-and-effect nature of karma in the next chapter, but in essence creating time and space in your life for reflecting upon your experiences and observations is crucial in understanding how everything works, and to see for yourself how all of life is interlinked. Karmic law underscores all of life, and we must live by its teachings if we are to live harmoniously.

What specifically can we observe? I will just list some key things that you may need to address so that you can advance through your spiritual journey into a default state of wellness in your life.

. . .

Task

Read through the following list all in one go, getting a feel for them, and then re-read them and reflect upon experiences you've had in your life pertaining to each one. In this way, you personalise them to your own context in life. Resolve to pay conscious attention to them all in the coming weeks and months. Your learning about yourself, your life, and life in general will go through the roof.

First and foremost, observe what goes on in your body, either inside it and out of sight, or on the surface which you can see. Learn to 'listen' to your body. Tune in consciously to your feelings and sensations, whether good ones or bad ones, and use such feelings to guide you - what caused them do you think? Reflect and always look for causes, and in the same way you can think about future consequences for any action you may take today. Don't run from pain or discomfort, use it to ask yourself why you feel this way. Pain is the consequence of a previous action or the accumulation of past choices and decisions. Change the cause, change the effect.

Observe what goes on in your mind, notice the thoughts produced by your chatterbox mind. Out of such thoughts come feelings, notice these too. Look for negative thought patterns. Notice your full array of FATE: your **f**eelings, **a**ctions, **t**houghts, and **e**motions. Learn about your natural tendencies in this way, negative and positive, and gain control your own fate by taking control of your FATE. Notice what triggers your feelings and thoughts and reactions.

Observe how you react to what people do and say. When you disagree, contemplate why - are they wrong, or are you wrong? Are you both wrong or both right? Does it matter in the grand scheme of things? Reflect upon your views, values, beliefs, 'facts', ask yourself where you got them from. Challenge them, use disagreements to learn from, to trigger discussions to explore their views and your views. Challenge everything you know. Put it to the sword. Research stuff that you find you're unsure about.

Observe your eating habits and how you feel after meals. Observe your energy levels. Observe how well your mind is working, look for connections between positive or negative mindsets and the foods you eat.

Observe nature in action. Observe animals, tune into the sights and sounds offered up by the natural world. It's amazing what we can learn by taking time out to really pay attention on life itself.

Observing means reading and listening with your full attention. Practise listening carefully to others, either as a bystander or when you are involved in the discussion. Notice your inner voice which wants to judge, but override it and keep listening. Observe body language and faces.

Observe your culture and society in action. Observe others communicating, whether in your own life or in media. Are they good listeners? How often do people interrupt each other? Why? Are they respectful? Emotional? Does your society promote uniformity and in-the-box thinking? Does it allow for expression of the self? How do people react to different opinions and viewpoints to their own?

Observe your media input, is it negative energy or positive energy coming to you? How do you react?

Reflect upon things, then observe; observe things, then reflect. Cultivate awareness by observing and reflecting. All three go hand in hand. They promote common sense, your conscience, and consciousness. They lead to increased clarity and compassion. They lead to understanding, learning, wisdom, and they allow you to trust yourself, your intuition and instincts.

We may often reflect that we just don't know, and then we can do research using the *four stages to learning* tool. Get information and input, consider what it means, test it out, and then reflect again. Spiritual living is a lifelong commitment to learning, remember!

Learning enables you to evolve, 'knowing' blocks you. Knowledge is great, of course, but it's only really useful through its application, when we do something with it, and that means understanding is more important. Knowledge by its nature seems fixed, and if we stick with it we may decay. Seeking understanding always keeps our mind open to new ideas, new perspectives, new ways of doing things.

To change anything, we must first become aware of it, see it, hear it, notice it in action. For the spiritual revolutionary making changes is the essential ingredient for their progress and advancement, and therefore conscious living is a must.

But… another memory jogger, your success is dependent on making changes from a strong position. If the foundations are not in place it will be hard to make *and sustain* your changes until such time as they have become new, health-supporting habits. In my experience, creating these good habits tremendously helps us in our battle with our chatterbox mind, which loves to weaken our willpower and resolve, for we are literally rewiring it and taking its power away. Conscious living is empowering us over our conditioned mind, and developing new habits make it all so much easier.

We must therefore re-orient ourselves if we wish to recondition ourselves: if you want polar bears, head north! Our self-education rests upon the motivational forces bubbling away in the background of our mind. Let's revisit our outlook reset tool.

IF YOU DID NOT DO a conscious OOAAI reset to your outlook on life in the *Learning Toolbox* chapter, now is the time to do it. And if you did, revisit your notes to remind yourself of your new outlook on life, and adjust it if you feel it needs fine-tuning. You can of course update it any time you feel it can be improved.

Making clear to yourself what your *orientation* is towards life, what your *objectives* are, what default *attitude* and *approach* to life you'd like to follow, and what your macro *intention* is, is the sure-fire means for hacking into your subconscious mind and recalibrating its set-up.

You will then find this acts as a memory-jogger every time you may need to make a choice or decision, helping you to determine the right action to take. Always the idea is to support your harmony and wellbeing, and to avoid causing harm to yourself or others.

Once your new outlook is an ingrained habit you will be flying.

I mentioned that my own guiding intention is *ahimsa*, the proactive practice of engaging in non-violence. I noted that, in particular, this pertained to verbal violence because spiritual seekers are most unlikely to be involved in any kind of physical violence.

Yet, a caveat is necessary: we must still be rigorous about the physical kind too - many psychological experiments have been conducted that show how ordinary upstanding citizens will commit physical violence against fellow human beings when put into specific roles and are playing out those roles. They, subconsciously, think they are doing the right thing (because that infernal *external authority* is always right!); but harming others can *never* be the right thing. Justifying it to oneself does not make it 'right' behaviour. It is our system programming which tells us that following rules and the law is 'right' behaviour, but what if in so doing we cause harm to other people?? If you live by *ahimsa*, then you may have to not comply to a rule or law. This is the conundrum we often face in human life, thanks to the system which has near strangled us with its millions of laws and regulations and 'taught' us as 'good citizens' to comply without question.

I simply choose the path of never harming others. If I inadvertently do so then I am quick to apologise, and right from the heart too.

A phrase worth repeating is, 'cause no harm, accept no shit'. This latter bit is important too - perhaps somebody, in the role of their job or in the marketplace of gossip, is trying to harm us. What do we do? Well, harm is against the sanctity of life, and we must do our utmost to never let others harm us. Bullying behaviour never goes away until challenged. Now, perhaps we may think that others gossiping about us is their problem, and we really don't care, in which case there's nothing to be done because there is no shit in the first place!

The environment we are in has a *huge* influence on how we act and react in life, and most people spend more time in their working environment than any other environment. *'I was just following orders'* does not cut the mustard for spiritually-minded citizens, we cannot afford to allow the system to 'persuade' us to unnecessarily harm, through words or actions, other living beings. Through the 'excuse' of one's job, in many lines of work, human beings commit and cause much damage, terror, and mental misery or torture upon their fellow brothers and sisters. It is unconscious and unconscionable living, and can only be inflicted by those who feel disconnected and carry no love in their heart. We are literally talking about tyranny here, where people terrorise others, but claim it's their job, or they 'had to'.

Some people may find they have to change their jobs if they wish to become spiritual in their life, and to enjoy good karma. Nobody can hide from karma.

If we live consciously we can escape our conditioning, and will afford ourselves the fullest protection possible against hurting others. And be sure about it, when we hurt others, we are most certainly hurting ourselves. This is a good time to recall my favourite piece of Buddhist wisdom which I shared with you in the *Three Tales* chapter: *To harass others is to harass yourself, to belittle others is to belittle yourself, to destroy others is to destroy yourself... and block your own path to prosperity.*

This is why, for me, consciously formulating one's OOAAI, and living by it, is an essential foundation in any spiritual quest. It means that any time we commit harm, or are about to, we will know about it, and we will be unable to hide from our conscience! Blaming the system or the job or somebody else's actions does not let us off the hook, for this is universal karmic law in action, and we can't corrupt any courts to escape our own natural justice. If, dear reader, you are working in government, or a corporation, take careful note!

Since *intention* is the mother of our whole outlook on life, influencing the success or otherwise of the OOAA components, I'd like to add a few more words about *ahimsa*. The more one explores and experiences its concept in action, and how it beneficially influences our approach and attitude towards life, the more magical it becomes - just a single word, yet with a tremendous power for creating the flow of positive energy in our being, and for neutralising negative energy.

It absolutely relates to being gentle and kind to ourselves, as well as others. If you find yourself with thoughts of guilt, shame, unworthiness and all the rest of it then you are harming yourself. There's no need to act on these thoughts, no need to feel bad. Maybe you can't get rid of memories of things you've done, or had done to you, but you can accept that they've happened and they are now forever part of who you are. No need to feel bad about them though. Apologise to others if need be, forgive others in your mind for acting themselves out of hurt and pain, and job done. Use these negative memories to motivate yourself to enjoy life more, for now and the future.

Thoughts, like actions, are an energy flow, so whether I'm feeling bad about myself, or harbouring negative thoughts about you for perceived slights I feel you have caused me, I am failing in my *ahimsa*. Negative energy is negative energy, and applies to feelings, words and deeds alike. Everything in fact. If I resent you for something, I am harming myself, and in all likelihood I will harm you too. If I blame or complain then I'm creating negative energy and harm to myself at least, and no doubt to the recipient of my grumbles, even if I'm just bending their ear about other 'bad' people.

I'm not talking about what is easy to do, just what is true. Practice is our friend.

What do you think about white lies?! Maybe by telling one you may think you are protecting somebody from being hurt, but will there be negative consequences down the line? I've found an easy relationship with lying: never do it, not even once. It makes life so much easier, and everybody knows when somebody is being honest or telling porkies. Honest people definitively experience fewer problems in life, so be one of them! If in speaking out the truth of things I know I will harm somebody else, then it's best to just bite my tongue and say nothing. It rarely comes to that, but better than telling the truth and causing harm.

I have also found that life is so much easier when you automatically tell the truth; trying to remember the lies, and who you spun them to, is far too stressful!

Sometimes we can't stop negative thoughts from arising, but we never have to act on them or allow them to get us down. This is key, and in following this path I have found that such negative thoughts, in the end, start getting bored with me for not acting on their bidding, and they become fewer and fewer.

To circumvent most negative emotions, reactions, actions, we should live consciously by developing and practising our skills in observation and noticing. OOAAI sets us up for this, as does choosing to live a REAL life: living with respect, empathy, awareness and love. For ourselves, for others, and for all of life.

It means forgiving myself and others for any perceived crimes committed by me or against me in the past; especially, and usually, mental and emotional ones.

This releases us from the bondage of our past, from bitterness and resentment which fester away, acting like a mental cancer, eating us up from within. We don't have to forget, nor will we be able to, but we can use the memories as lessons to help us learn to do things differently, and based out of love from here on in.

And if you go wrong or inadvertently cause harm to others today, out of the heat of your emotions, or from being overly stressed - and often it's to those who we love and cherish - then don't beat yourself up over it otherwise you are failing in your *ahimsa*. I personally find it very easy to apologise for my actions or hasty speech when they escape my guard. I'm sure you will know the absolute power of forgiveness and heartfelt apologies, either receiving or giving them.

Living with HEART - honesty, empathy authenticity, responsibility and trust - is the bedrock of healthy, harmonious and happy people. It is an intention in life, and conscious living is our way of ensuring we are successful. What others do is their lookout: 'I can't control what you do, but I can control my reaction'. If we focus on ourselves then we can generate much positive energy for the whole universe. But always bear in mind, the system wanted to control us, and *control* became the dominant 'glue' in relationships. We use conscious living to spot it in us and in others, and then we practise getting rid of it. Control means force, coercion, imposition or violence, and has no place in harmonious living. It's bullying behaviour.

We will 'fail', and we will feel low and stressed at times, but with a sound OOAAI outlook, and using OAR in our lives, we can create a beautiful default way of life and will spend most of our time living consciously; such downers in life will become less and less frequent, and we will become skilled and noteworthy ambassadors for ourselves, for Mother Earth and for the whole galactic enterprise. Resolve to impress any aliens looking down upon our planet!

Task

I'd like to end the chapter with a task, an ongoing task for the rest of your life, until such time as the janitor from heaven arrives for your collection. Then you can rest in peace, because you will have lived in peace (RIP and LIP)!

One thing we are conditioned to do is to *judge* other people by what they say and do. Many people these days complain that we live in a really divided world, and everybody seems to be right and nobody is wrong! Judging is done by our system-programmed subconscious mind, *not* by our true self, and it decides what or who is right or wrong, good or bad, acceptable or unacceptable. It judges according to its view of the world arising from its beliefs and cultural conditioning. And it is always correct, it is always the good guy. In this way we are actually imposing ourselves on other people, *but only because the system imposed upon us.* At the point we make a judgement our subconscious mind has stopped our conscious observing, listening or reading, and is now preoccupied with its view of that person or what they said.

My task is for you to practise being conscious and aware of this judgemental voice within you, and to observe it whenever it pops up. While you are unlikely to be able to stop this judging, you don't have to act upon it, and as soon as you notice it you can ignore the pesky little thing and get back to your listening, reading or observing. Our world will become peaceful only when we stop disliking others or deciding they are 'bad' people just because we - in reality our conditioned mind - think they are no good. We only hate others based on our own view of them, not based on the actual living flesh, blood and sovereign human being that they are, or that we are. You think the ant hates other ants? That the dolphin hates other dolphins?!

Know the difference between observing and judging, and overcome the negative energy of negative judging. Live consciously, not as a prisoner to your past conditioning by the system.

12

FROM 'GOD' AND GENETICS TO KARMA AND EPIGENETICS

Don't be stuck with your genes, improve them.

You can be emotionally enslaved or spiritually liberated, but not both.

This and the next chapter go hand in hand. Mostly speaking, this one is theory and understanding, and in the next, *Problems and Solutions,* we get practical and look at dozens of small actions we can take as part of a whole package of solutions. We will also look at the master problem in *P&S*. Uncovering this will then prevent so many problems from even arising in the first place. Most of our problems in life are because of our crippling schooling. Real education is always the answer, and that of course is our central business.

Our mission for this chapter is twofold: firstly, to take stock of where we are so far by summarising our running themes, and secondly, to outline two views of our world and our human world so that we can head onwards with focus, confidence and purpose. Each part will blend into the other, for blending is the name of the game.

There is then a third focus in the following chapter, and that is the practical business of becoming problem-solving and solutions-oriented people.

One view reveals to us how we humans, in a less than harmonious manner, live our lives in the modern times; the second view pertains to the universal laws of life and the natural rhythms of Mother Earth. We mainly focus on the latter here, and will then turn to the unbalanced way of living in *P&S*. We would like to know where we are today and how we got here, what is a more intelligent and natural way to live, such that we can bring wellness and harmony into our life, and then we will be informed and inspired to make the changes we need to. Know where you are, know where you want to be, get there.

In this chapter, I use *'God'* and *genetics* to symbolise and illustrate the reasons why the human family as a whole, and many of its members, are living with so much stress and suffering, which manifests itself in us through psychological unhappiness, physical disease, and spiritual emptiness. 'God' and genetics represent an externally-controlled way of life, which 'persuades' us to take little responsibility for ourselves and enslaves us to the system.

It's a perversion and suppression of our innate intelligence, and of our ability and birthright to be free and beautiful beings.

Whether you are the controller, or the controlled, matters not, for either way, your freedom and intelligence are compromised when control is manifest, and in the exercise of control lies no beauty or joy. Zilch. When we seek to control another person against their will, or they do that to us, then in either case both parties are both dehumanised.

It turns out, after considered contemplations, that many people will find themselves in both roles. It's such a key thing to become conscious of, and to do inner work on. Control through force or coercion is anti-freedom and anti-love.

Through **'God'**, the system has told us *how we should live*, and through **genetics** it tells us *how life works*. They symbolise our masters, our directors, the external authority. They come from yesterday's ideas and people, may have been useful in the past or not, but are not serving our purpose at the start of the third millennium one little bit. In fact, hampering and hindering us from living in harmony, by making us ignorant.

The system which we speak of was instigated by men long since dead, yet it and they continue to rule us all. Not good enough, ruled and controlled by dead men, ruled from the grave! We are, by nature, beautiful conscious and cosmic human beings, unique expressions and creations of Mother Earth and the will of the universe. The system suppressed it out of us. No more I say…

We live in an age where we should, no, where we *must*, find out things for ourselves, and in this way we can emancipate ourselves from our enslavements to the past, and to the external authority of a system created by men who walked our planet centuries ago. Luckily, we have a clear path out of our mental prison…

Karma and **epigenetics** reveal to us the **real God**, and show us the way out of our collective mess, but which can only come about through the changes that each individual citizen makes; spiritual revolution is bottom-up, grassroots stuff. It's up to you and me to play our part. Emphatically, my friend, we count as individuals. Using karma and epigenetics to inform ourselves is the path towards personal responsibility, spirituality and wellness. They introduce us to ourselves, and teach us how life works. They are revelations when we 'get' them.

Millions of us are already carrying out our necessary inner work, our life inquiry, our spiritual transformation, and we are part of this huge evolving force for the betterment of ourselves, our humanity and our most amazing Gaia. *Karma is the cast iron, incorruptible law of the universe; epigenetics teaches us, in a practical manner, how karma manifests and works.* Understanding karmic law and the biology of epigenetics acts as a guiding light for each of us, giving us the perfect platform to harmonise and tune ourselves into sweet, soulful, sensational human beings.

At which point we can turn to Ayurveda for heaps of practical guidance relating to diet and lifestyle in pursuing, achieving and sustaining wellness for ourselves.

Why Ayurveda? Because it reflects the principles and

understandings of epigenetics, yet was born and written thousands of years ago!

THESE HAVE BEEN our running themes…

i) We, the modern-day humans, at the individual and collective level, don't really know who we are, nor how life works. Yet, we assume we do know. We can call this 'conditioned ignorance'.

ii) However, the knowledge and understanding we need is out there, and has been for at least 5000 years, as evidenced through the body of wisdom contained within Ayurveda, and as evidenced by the work of many individuals throughout history, including Lao Tze (founder of Taoism), Buddha, Jesus Christ, Socrates, Martin Luther King, David Bohm, Osho, Krishnamurti, just to name a few spanning the last 2500 years. In our time, this century, more and more people are learning for themselves, and are doing so despite mainstream orthodoxy, which is always against change. The system and status quo abhors change, rails against any kind of reform, all it wants to do is control and devour.

iii) Illness and wellness - of body, mind and soul - are no accident. How we feel is always the consequence and outcome of our diet, posture, lifestyle and outlook, notwithstanding the influence of whatever genetic heritage we each received from birth. We work with what we've got. Our beliefs and our diet to a great extent determine our level of wellbeing or not.

iv) Wellness must be a way of life, needing savvy intelligence and a proactive lifelong commitment towards its pursuit and achievement, due to the increasingly toxic environments we live in, which pose multiple threats to our physiological, psychological, social and spiritual wellbeing.

v) Our default education systems systematically discourage and disempower us. They teach us nothing of the essential knowledge and life skills we need to successfully and enjoyably navigate adult life. Not only do they fail to teach us what we need for life, they suppress our curiosity, creativity and ability to learn. We leave school knowing virtually nothing of our body or mind, nor how each work, nor how they work in tandem. Therefore we are impotent to take care of, and manage, our own health and life. Scandalous! Criminal!

Thus, they handicap us right from the off, dividing us from each other and disconnecting us from our roots, our nature and our natural impulses. Our schooling is not empowering and magic, it is disempowering and tragic.

vi) Modern technology, and money-corrupted science and politics, has more easily enabled the anti-life system to infiltrate and infect our food, healthcare, and justice systems. None of them support our wellbeing. Modern day society is crumbling. Out of its ashes the magnificent phoenix shall arise. In fact, it's in the middle of arising. We - all spiritual seekers, soul adventurers, lovers of life - are that great bird. If things look dark now it's because it's 'always darkest in the hour before dawn'. The new dawn for humanity is nearly here, and your personal new dawn *is* here!

vii) Successful people who do things harmoniously, not at the expense or pain of others, all share the two core skills required of a human being: they are excellent communicators and skilled learners.

Learning, like the pursuit of wellness, never stops. We can enjoy and live out our life, we can learn about life, and spiritual people are always doing both: living enhances learning and learning enhances living. Learn to live and live to learn, in a never-ending virtuous circle. In this way we need never fall prey to the forces of ignorance, impotence, illness and fear again. Learning empowers us, and is our liberation.

Communication is the bedrock of relationships, and relationships are the bedrock of a human life. Become a good listener, attentive and empathic, and see how your life improves! Read about life, have things to talk about, express yourself, and be the human you were born to be. Writing is a great tool for reflecting, which itself teaches us so much.

viii) Due to corruption, ego, fundamentally flawed understandings about how life works, and the tentacles of the system which infects all of humanity's advances, we just cannot afford to blindly trust the experts anymore. They put their hand up to lead our world, and we see the mess they got us into. Besides, they all received the same so-called education and psychological upbringing. There are many outstanding professionals, and I mean the likes of doctors, scientists, teachers, journalists, gurus, just that amongst them tread various charlatans, ego-driven characters, and wolves in sheep's clothing. Who is who, and how do we know? Better it is to become our own mini-expert and guru through the practice of conscious living.

The failure of the experts as a whole, in my view, has been part of the evolution's intelligence, pushing all citizens into learning to take responsibility for their own lives, to learn for and trust themselves.

ix) Conscious living is your means for making all the changes you need to upgrade, empower and transform yourself and your life. We can reset our outlook on life using the OOAAI tool, and then we learn from observation, awareness and reflection, and from doing our own research (*OAR* and the *4 stages of learning* tools). We become the intelligent interconnected integrated individual we were born to be.

x) When enough citizens have carried out their revolution, and brought a decent level of wellness into their lives, then they will start occupying positions of influence and leadership in their communities and societies, and the collective human family can rewrite its relationship with itself, and with Mother Earth. Beautiful times will no longer be an ideal, they will be real, and we will forge REAL relationships, based on **r**espect, **e**mpathy, **a**wareness and **l**ove. Spiritual revolutionaries make great leaders, and society always needs good leaders with love in their hearts.

xi) The corporate mindset born of the millennia-old system will continue on its locust-like path of destroying us all, including itself, unless or until we stop it. It is anti-human, anti-life, relentless and unforgiving. Our generations alive today have some essential work to do *now*, for ourselves and for our progeny. That's you and me, dear reader! There is very little time to waste any more.

Bring on millions of spiritual revolutions. Light up the darkness, love out the fear, and resuscitate our intelligence.

. . .

HERE IS a map and outline of our work at hand...

Harmony is balance, and leads to wellness. Wellness is energy, clarity and vitality in your physical, psychological and spiritual domains. All is possible with intelligence and love.

Stress is imbalance, and leads to illness. Illness in one domain will negatively affect the other domains and your ability to operate holistically.

Therefore, spiritual revolutionaries seek to acquire information and develop skills to help them:

- manage their own health and life
- achieve harmony and wellness
- prevent stress and illness
- overcome stress and recover from illness whenever it may strike.

My thesis is that, to be able to do all that, we must:

- know who we are
- know why we are here
- know how life works
- commit to being a lifelong learner
- practise and become skilled in conscious living, conscious thinking and self-awareness.

It means that:

- we must conduct our own life inquiry, through applying the *OOAAI outlook reset* tool and using the two learning tools of *OAR* and *4 stages to learning*
- we should cultivate the 4Ps, namely to be proactive, positive, productive, and peaceful
- we must discover and challenge all our assumptions, beliefs, values and views, thereby exposing our conditioning to our conscious self
- we will need to decondition, re-educate and nurture

ourselves, overcoming thought patterns and habits that do not serve our purposes, replacing them with new thinking and habits which do support our endeavours
- we bring ourselves 'home' to our natural ways as intelligent interconnected integrated individuals living according to natural karmic law.

It turns out that there is one gigantic master problem in life, and once we unmask it and then solve it, we will find that a goodly proportion of problems that previously afflicted us will simply disappear and not come back. For the ones that we will still face from time to time, we will have the skill set and know-how to solve. We will investigate this master problem in detail in the next chapter, but I'll share it with you now so you can contemplate upon it as you read on.

According to all my reflections, while doing my not inconsiderable amount of hammock time, this master problem, from which nearly all other problems arise, *is the sense of separation and division from each other, and from our natural roots, that we feel deep in our psyche, put and installed there by centuries of the brutal anti-life system.* We have been isolated and disconnected from each other, and from Mother Earth, giver of all life. This has perverted our innate intelligence, and confused us into conflict against our nature as social loving animals.

This applies to individuals, groups, and factions, and the whole of humanity

LET's get exploring and see how life is typically lived, and how it might more harmoniously be lived according to our nature. Interestingly, we shall discover that much of our life is spent in the 'World of Should Be', while we should be spending much more time in the 'World of Is'. Hah, work that one out…

Below are eleven theses, understandings and principles of how life works from a common sense viewpoint. I will do my best to let you agree with me! But more important than your agreement is that what I write helps you to visualise and understand things for yourself. However, common sense is the outcome of conscious living, an innate human energy force, and so usually there is little argument against common sense.

We should at the outset make note of two important terms, which we've already mentioned, but which will find increasing usage from here on in. We are talking **external environment** and **internal environment**, or EE and IE for short. Our IE is everything inside of us including our skin, while the EE is everything outside of our skin - other people, the natural world, all situations, information, ideas and so on. Our skin is the demarcating line through which energy between the two environments flows in and out of.

The external environment, *to you*, is the whole world and universe and everything in it, absolutely everything except your internal environment. From your internal environment perspective, I am in the external environment, and from my internal environment perspective, you are in the external environment. Take a third person, call her Emma, from her internal environment perspective, both you and me are in the external environment.

You may like to reflect upon just what this reveals to us.

And on this: that if your perspective of the external environment changes, so does the external environment. Or just read on without pause and see what I say!

Okay, away we go.

i) We humans are born out of our parents, and out of Mother Earth and the universe too. This is natural law, not open to conjecture. We are relational beings, never ever alone or separated. Your life and health (your internal environment) proceed and manifest according to your interrelationship and interconnection with the world and the universe (the external environment). You are inextricably linked with, and interdependent upon, both Mother Earth and the universe for your life, for meaning and purpose, for your sustenance, and for your continued existence.

You, therefore, are *not* your internal environment, you are your

IE *plus the EE*. Think of it like this: **IE+EE = me**. *You are a blend of inner and outer worlds.* You exist in the outer world, the outer world exists in you. Even though not visibly so, you are umbilically connected to the universe, and to Mother Earth. This blend, this connection, is crucial for us to understand and accept as truth of life.

ii) *Your internal environment, itself, is a blend too,* consisting of your body, mind and soul components, which themselves are inextricably interdependent on, and interconnected with, each other within your IE. Your internal environment's interconnection with the external environment is forged through the physical, psychological and spiritual *structures* and *operations* of your body, mind and soul (respectively, the elements of space, water, air, fire and earth; information; and consciousness).

This leads us to understandings that are essential to grasp:

- eat nutritious foods from the external environment for your body, and your mind and soul will benefit too
- consume positive information and ideas for your mind from other humans in the external environment, and your body and soul will benefit too
- imbibe the beauty of Mother Earth and the nectar of cosmic consciousness from the universe for your soul, and your body and mind will benefit too.

By the same token, take in toxic foods, toxic mental impressions, experience no nature or beauty, and your whole internal environment will struggle.

If you combine the two blends in i) and ii), you will find that you are an interconnected blend, an amalgamation, of four components or dimensions of life: your body, mind, soul, and the external environment.

We begin to see that if we poison or damage the ecological systems of our planet, that is, the external environment, then we are doing the very same thing to our own inner ecological systems of our internal environment. And, if we poison or damage our inner world, then we will add poison or damage to the outer world. By the same token, if we cherish life and Mother Earth, then we must cherish ourselves, and if we cherish ourselves we will do our best to never hurt life in the external environment.

(And be sure, if you have that cherishing, then your innate intelligence will flourish; or, if you want to be intelligent, then first cherish yourself, your life, and life out there.)

Can you then see that as individual citizens we have a tremendous influence on both our own inner being and that of the outer world life around us? Can you see the absolute damage and carnage much of our media world pushes out into the external world, and into the minds of our own inner worlds? And, can you see when we see politicians dividing us, trying to control and push us with thousands of new rules and laws, that they do so because they are clearly eating dodgy foods and reading too much negative media and in general consuming negative energy? Each of us is very much only as good as what we consume into our internal environment.

What will happen to you if you go on a news fast and stop listening to divisive negative politicians?? What will happen to you if you seek out positive intelligent media and politicians and listen to them? What will happen to you if you meet intelligent loving people and intelligent loving leaders? Who's in charge of making those choices??!

Optional task: it may be worth a pause in your reading to reflect upon your personal actions out towards the external environment, and your consumptions from the outer world, and to see how they influence each other; and to also reflect upon the same in relation to the wider world of humanity itself.

iii) Thus, as we consume so we produce, and as we produce and give out so we shall attract back in. We can say that our life is the two-way bidirectional flow of energy between the external world and our own inner world. Food and information alike carry energy, everything in life is the movement and flow of energy. Think 'karma'.

If you want a harmonious and healthy life, feed well and

nutritiously! That means the foods you feed your body, and the impressions you feed your mind. But if you eat poor quality foods and take in negative media, you will find harmony and health rather elusive.

Learning to choose wisely is part of the spiritual revolutionary's remit.

iv) Unlike the rest of the animal kingdom (at least, I think so!), who can only react to their external environment, and act accordingly, we humans were blessed with the ability to proactively shape, or rise above, the environment around us. If the human ego-driven world around us is going pear-shaped, we don't have to succumb. We can seek out energy from the life force of the natural world of Mother Earth, and from the cosmic consciousness of the universe, and this energy comes to us free, any time we ask and look for it. Then we can overcome almost any burden by using our spirit, soul, heart, and will to live and love. And, if we contribute positive energy outwards to those around us, then in this way we positively and proactively influence the world. And it will come back to us.

If others are negative towards you, does that mean you have to accept this energy? If the media are fully negative, do you have to consume it? Or, in consuming it, can you detach yourself from it by invoking your soul energy? If the politicians are dividing you, do you have to accept their warped energy? Can you neutralise people's negative energy by responding with your own positive energy of compassion, love and kind words?? Who is in charge of your energy here?

I take my lead from Mother Earth, not from divisive human beings! 'Cry and the world cries with you, laugh and the world laughs with you', that's what my mum taught me and my sister (hi Wend!).

Our soul, once we have activated it, is our guiding light, our personal source of eternal strength, our intuition; it is our micro-portion of the universal intelligence and cosmic consciousness of the divine world. It is limitless and abundant, and when you turn to it, it will never fail you. If it's low in energy, fill up from the station of nature. No cost.

The soul loves beauty, so seek out natural or man-made beauty and let the beauty trigger your soul to light up and inspire your mind, and help you to change your situation and station in life. The spiritual energy force of our soul can always overcome psychological trauma if we let it.

v) In my view and understanding, our mind is the centre of the universe. Without your mind there is no universe for you. Everything you ever say, do, think, and feel is done through the mind. Your mind is your central processor of incoming information and energy flow, and it is your producer of outgoing information and energy flow.

Anything and everything you are aware of out there in the world - in your world or in the media you consume - comes into your mind, and everything you put back into the world is overseen by your mind, and we're talking physically and spiritually as well as mentally and psychologically. This view concords with some of the literature and ancient understandings, and not with other parts of it. This is how things best make sense to me. We can then distinguish between our autopilot mind and our conscious mind, but whichever it is, it's our mind at work.

vi) In this way we can think of ourselves as i*nformation agents*, much like a travel agent or an import-export agent, except we're dealing in the matters of life rather than travel or buying and selling. We are processors and producers of information. In essence this is what our life is, a whole bunch of successive inflows and outflows of information.

Become skilled in the matter of importing and exporting information flow, and you will find the route to wellness and the 3Hs, guaranteed! Interestingly, we live in the era where the Industrial Age is giving way to the Information Age. Information is the hot currency, my friend, so get with it and be on it! We can only act upon the information we have, so if we are struggling, we don't have proper information.

Computers were designed to mimic the human mind: your mind itself is the hardware, how it interprets and responds to incoming information is decided by the software in it. You can service and upgrade both the hardware and software elements of your mind, once you have developed the wherewithal and skill to do so. Life inquiry and using the OAR tool teaches you this.

vii) And we use our mind to adjust, upgrade and recondition both the hardware and software of our mind. This is a truly amazing evolutionary principle, design and creation!! Understanding your mind means you understand who you are and how life works. It's the magic key to all.

viii) Your mind has two influences which fashion and shape it - **nature** and **nurture**. You interpret incoming information and respond to it according to your nature/nurture mix. You are born with the first, and for the initial portion of your life the second one is the product of, and proceeds according to, the society and adult world's input in which you are growing up and being 'educated'.

If your nurture complements your nature you will be in a good space and able to easily find harmony and overcome problems in your life; if your nurture antagonises or runs counter to your nature, you will struggle. Or, to put it the other way round, if you have found that typically you struggle with your physical and psychological health and in your relationships with other people, then your nurture almost certainly did not support your nature. This book is all about re-nurturing oneself to ensure we live in accordance with our nature, and therefore find that elusive harmony and wellbeing. Our nurture has done most of us a terrible disservice. Humanity lost its way accordingly.

ix) Your **nature** is three things combined - your *unique nature* as per your personal propensity, characteristics and preferences; *human nature;* and the *natural/universal law of all life.* I see our nature as the consequence of the position of the stars during our birth (and probably conception too), past karmas which come to us from our genetic heritage and lineage, the natural impulses and urges pertinent to being a member of the human species, which have accumulated throughout the history of humans, and the intrinsic laws of nature and the whole galactic enterprise.

x) Your **nurture** for the first portion of your life is pretty much completely out of your hands. It comes to you from your home upbringing and your schooling which is overseen and shaped by the environmental framework of your society and culture. Ostensibly speaking you are 'free' to become your own person, legally speaking, at 18. But, as an adult your nurture is consolidated and ongoing via the aggregate of human understanding and information (subject to evolutionary forces), as held by and expressed within its cultural traditions and the society's constituent parts. In the main these parts are education and media, religion and science, agriculture and architecture.

In terms of mainstream information flow and understanding, schooling is for kids, media is for adults. Or it was, now we have social media and the internet which kids can access, as well as their schooling. If society is malfunctioning through corruption, inequity and conflict, turn to education and media to find the causes. Education itself is the first and foremost pillar of a society, leading to that society's consequential wellbeing or sickness.

xi) Successful communities and societies, as evidenced by peaceful, creative and productive citizens, can be said to have created and sustained an intelligent nurturing process, for both children and adults, which nicely tunes into and harmonises with human nature and the laws of the natural world, while allowing for the expression of everybody's unique character and self, which is an innate feature of the human being. Such a community or society, as the collective representation of all its individuals, supports the wellbeing of its members with the intelligent recognition that individual and group needs are interdependent.

You might ask yourself where such communities and societies and nations exist. You may need powerful spectacles and super keen vision to find them in our world today.

There are undoubtedly pockets here and there, and at the nation level I think of Finland and Bhutan, although I've not personally been there to see for myself. I suspect some African nations are doing a fine job, but not sure. I have found that island communities seem to have a greater harmony and community spirit and wellbeing, or at least it seems this way to me. I don't mean island nations, just islands within nations. My experience of this has been in Britain, Australia, Thailand, Indonesia, Canada and Spain.

On the whole, though, I think it fair to say that almost the entire world is struggling, societies and individual citizens alike, for all the reasons we've mentioned throughout the book.

There you have it, for me that's how life works, gleaned from my lifetime's worth of experience and reflection, with no small amount of the latter conducted on my trusty, ergonomically superior hammock. We can all go home now!!

WE HAVE JUST HAD a discussion which neatly introduces us to the concepts and natural truths contained within **karma** and **epigenetics**. Karma is sometimes thought to be a complicated concept, but it is not at all. It is the one single law of nature and the universe, and is of the utmost beauty and simplicity (in contrast to manmade law with its billions of rules!), while epigenetics is karma in action. Learn, understand and apply both and you will have your Triple-H lifestyle.

In a nutshell, positive energy or negative energy comes in, same goes out; and, what you give out comes back in. Like attracts like. Karma is simply one action leads to a reaction, and the reaction leads to an action which leads to a reaction, and so it goes on…

What goes up comes down, input leads to output and output leads to input, what you reap you sowed and what you sow you will reap. As with the chicken and egg, it doesn't really matter which one comes first, just that both inter-belong to each other, each feed into the other. Drink apple juice every day for a year, or drink coke every day, and see what happens to you. Actions have consequences, and actions have causes. If you like, think of every happening or action as a bridge between past and future, between cause and consequence.

Of course, there are over seven billion karmas going on in our human world, not to mention all the past karmas of our ancestors; sometimes the karma of somebody else (dead or alive) comes your way, and you don't like it, it feels unjust or unfair or unlucky for you,

you feel you did nothing wrong. But… and this is the key bit… *you can choose your reaction* and *you can initiate new actions*.

If you react negatively, you feed the negative karmic cycle coming your way and you will feel the bad vibes in you; if you react consciously with equanimity, compassion and understanding for somebody's pain and hurt, you block its negative energy from affecting you. And if you pass on that compassion to the other person, they may snap out of their own negative energy and feel your positive vibes. Such is the karmic nature of everything that happens. Everything, remember, is interconnected and karmic law is the glue.

So, you may bemoan your lot in life, you may blame others or bad luck for your woes, you may feel life around you is boring, unfair or negative in some way, but you have the wherewithal to proactively produce positive energy, by practising conscious living. Conscious living allows us to react consciously, and with understanding or compassion, before we are triggered into a negative response by our autopilot mind. This phrase hits home, 'I can't control what you do, but I can control my reaction'. Learn to take time before responding to people, thereby giving you the chance to consciously choose what you say to people. In this way, we can tune into our conscience and remember the fact of karmic life that if we hurt others we hurt ourselves.

This is the beauty of slowing ourselves down, we find it easier to avoid reacting automatically, and instead can use our innate intelligence.

Of course, this iniquitous system we have been talking about, and to which we return shortly, seeks precisely to control you, and if you react negatively it's got you for sure. React through conscious living and you have neutralised or got rid of the pesky blighter. This is our challenge and if you take it on you will assuredly win.

Always we can get out into nature, into the great outdoors. Nature is the petrol station to fill up our mind and soul with the fuel of energy and wellbeing, free of charge - how wonderful and generous she is. When you feel down, you're caught up in negative karma and vibes, just go outside and connect with Mother Earth, she will see you right. And eat the food *she* produces, not all this manmade synthetic and junk food, and other corporate 'food' which has been processed, genetically modified, and had all kinds of toxins added to it under the guise of additives, flavourings and preservatives. They used to be called 'E' numbers, now they go by the code of 'INS' numbers. This cocktail of poisons hammers our organs and immune system. We are poisoning ourselves left right and centre. I read it somewhere, 'You're not sick, you're being poisoned'. Ignorance is dangerous to us, my friend!

Quality information really is the root of it all. We can be ignorant through wrong information or lack of information, and we will stay that way unless we proactively seek out information to release us from our conditioned ignorance. Once this seeking is begun, we realise it never stops, for we discover that learning is the heartbeat of a life well-lived. Mark Twain said it, 'I never let my schooling get in the way of my education'. Indeed!

We have to educate ourselves out of our conditioned ignorance, there's no other way.

The purpose is not to be right or wrong, good or bad, but to just do, be and live the best we can, and to keep on striving to maintain or better our best. Do your best, accept the rest, for nothing more can be done. Afford others the same leeway because it's hard work being human in the societies that this system spawned! Be gentle to all living creatures, it's easy once we reset our outlook on life.

Karma means we reap what we sow, we get what we have seeded, we get our just desserts, and in this way we can look at events, happenings, and the state of our health today, and ask ourselves what we did, or what happened to us, that led to it all. Today is the effect, yesterday was the cause. Observe with full awareness, investigate and reflect, and we can find out the cause. If you like the effect you are experiencing today, seek out and repeat the cause; if you don't like the effect, seek out and change the cause. Live consciously and notice life around you and inside you, and life in this way becomes a constant source of learning, which keeps us in a positive karmic cycle.

However, and check this out, we can use our understanding of karma *to start with the cause* today, now. If you want a certain effect or thing to happen in the future, for example better health or a good relationship with another person, ask yourself what actions you can take today which will lead to the effect you would like to experience tomorrow. Sow the seeds now, today, which most likely will flower and give you the fruits you would like to obtain in the future.

But if, instead, you end up with a sour fruit or no flowers, this is not to feel sorry for yourself, or to say that karma is a load of mumbo-jumbo nonsense, rather you can ask yourself why it didn't go the way you thought. Pain or misery or disappointment are learning opportunities - if we apply the law of karma to our situation. Take time and space out to reflect upon things, and to learn from your contemplations. Don't run from pain or bad feelings, look into them, face up to them, find out what caused them, and then make intelligent changes. This is intelligent living in action!

Karma is simple in its workings, and a magnificent tool for us to improve our lives with. Living by karmic law, and learning from it, is as easy as pie once you have reset your outlook. And then, with your brand new, super duper life-affirming mindset, you use OAR to practise conscious living. Bob's your uncle, job done. You can plant beautiful seeds for future fruits and flowers while enjoying doing the planting today, all the while enjoying any fruits from yesterday's planting. You can react to negative happenings in life with equanimity, realising it is simply the natural flow of energy and you can choose how to react, and you can convert negative energy into not-negative energy or positive energy.

Change your thinking, change your foods, and you change your world. And the world will change too. Go with the flow, let go, live and let live, bend with the wind (Chinese version). Live consciously, choose your actions, choose your reactions. Choose positive energy, choose intelligence, choose the Triple-H lifestyle. Forget about being right or wrong, good or bad, just focus on the energy flow and harming no other person or animal, nor accepting their harm towards you. *Ahimsa!*

What is is, what happens happens.

. . .

In **epigenetics** the 'epi' is a prefix meaning 'beyond' or 'external', and thus we're talking about a biology that understands and explains life beyond the genes in isolation. And that 'beyond' or 'external' refers to the environment in which they live. Life is interconnected, not isolated, and genes are what make up the structure of life. Epigenetics talks of a blend between one's inner world and the outer world - just as we've been talking about.

The understanding given to us from the science of **genetics** tells us we are born with our own set of genes, which remain fixed from birth and carry our fate, level of health, and how long we will live, encoded in them. It effectively says our internal environment is hardwired, and is isolated from and separate to the external environment. It says the state and condition of our mind and body today, and always, is *predetermined* by what we get at birth, and therefore nothing to do with our choices and lifestyle, or the state of the environment we live in. What horse shit and fairy tale nonsense! Just a few seconds of conscious reflection should disavow us of this patently absurd idea, yet it is the bedrock of orthodox biology and medical science. This is incredible, mind-blowing!! What a gigantic misunderstanding, but which, coincidentally or not, has been an equally gigantic financial windfall for the corporations.

Our discussion in this chapter, added to common sense and a deep intuition about life, entirely and quite rightly refutes this reductionist, anti-holistic way of thinking. As does Ayurveda, Traditional Chinese Medicine, the way of Tao, yin and yang, and the very law of nature herself. How could our genes possibly be fixed in a world and universe where nothing at all stands still except that which has no life or which has ceased to have life??

Yet, and it's key my friend, in this way we are, and have been for a very long time, controlled by external forces. If we 'think' we are 'victims' to our genes, then why take responsibility for our own life? We become easy prey to those who deign to control us.

To me, spirituality is bringing the pure, unpoliticised forms of science and religion together into a blend (as with the internal and external environments), rather than any more having to live with them separated from each other, and therefore running counter to the holistic law of karma.

Our genetic heritage - connected to past karmas - of course carries influences on our individually bestowed natural skills, and our propensity towards us liking or disliking this or that; and our genes will be relatively weaker or stronger at birth compared to some kind of theoretical average across a society, but the reality is they are only *predisposed* to act in certain ways.

I am predisposed to being impatient (and when living in England in my younger years I always was) due to my western and Chinese birth signs, but upon moving to Thailand at the start of the 1990s this new environment completely changed me around, and now I find I'm calmer and more patient than many of my compatriots and other westerners. This has undoubtedly conferred health benefits to my whole being.

We are absolutely not fixed, we manifest in the way that we engage and connect with the external world around us, and we always have choices. We are helpless victims *only if we think we are*, whether it's to our genes, other people, or anything else we would like to blame.

What actually *determines* their expression, or not, what decides if our genes turn on or off is the environment *and* our *perception of the environment*, in which they exist. In our discussion that means the EE that we let, and perceive is coming, into our inner body and mind. Primarily that is the environment we live, work and exist in, including our choice and consumption of media. Your inner environment with all your genes and cells reflects what you consume through mouth and mind from the world out there.

We can say, then, that our relative level of health or sickness is directly related to the foods and mental impressions which we consume. We should also note that, it is our perception and perspective of those impressions that influences our body's chemistry and biology, and so our genes are turned on or off by the external environment we are exposed to, *and* by our perspective of it. Change your perspective and to a great extent the world around you changes to match it. I tell you, being human may be hard at times, but the more consciously we live and the more we learn about, and act upon, our capabilities, the more miraculous we realise the human mind is.

So this means what you believe and conceive, receive and perceive, will affect your genes, your body and mind, your health and longevity. Same with what you eat, and everything else you consume. Once we consciously make this known to ourselves, we can only but begin transforming our life immediately. Feed your body and mind well and nutritiously, and you will live well and harmoniously. Karmic by law, epigenetics in action. As your input, so your output.

We - you and me my friend - are in charge, not our genes, nor the system out there with all its invisible tentacles, nor 'God'. Each one of us is an expression of the real God of the universe, of cosmic consciousness and of universal intelligence. The universe is the boss, not other humans! Tune into God, and develop a relationship with the divine cosmic order, and you will be mucho mucho in charge of your genes, their expression, and your own health and life.

Not entirely, no of course not, for we have seven billion plus other people to share the world with, and often we just cannot avoid the consequences of their behaviour, whether individuals, or the actions of corporations which cause so much damage to the rest of us with negative behaviour, toxic chemicals, radiation, heavy metals and the like. Nor must we forget the dastardly system we have to contend with, but we still have many choices that we *can* make. Take responsibility for your reactions and decisions to the fullest extent that you can, and see what happens. Focus on what you *can* change, not on what you *can't* change, cultivate gratitude for what you *do* have, not what you *don't* have.

So a quick summary: in any appreciation for the reality and truth of how life works, not how we assume or believe it works, or how the system tells us it works, we can see clearly that *we are interconnected with, and interdependent upon, the world around us*, which includes the everything of everything. It can impact upon our own internal environment, and our IE can impact upon the external environment. There is no IE or EE, just a blend of the two; remember it this way, IE + EE = me.

The EE is our support network, and represents the grid of life to which we are intimately connected to. You are not alone, you were produced by the universe and you are plugged into it, constantly. Your umbilical cord to your mother was cut, but not to Mother Earth and the universe, you are forever tied to both and they are both rooting for you as any loving compassionate parents would.

Mother Earth and Father Universe are the real God!! How could it be otherwise? They produced *you*, they invited *you* to the party. I think that was the original teaching coming our way thousands of years ago, but as with everything it touches, the system politicised it in order to control us all, including those who think they have power over others. The only power you can use over others that will karmically reward you, with good vibes and positive energy, is when you have love in your heart and intelligence in your mind to exercise that power. Inspire, motivate, facilitate learning, this is intelligent power in action.

Drop the force of control, drop resistance to that which you cannot change peacefully, and you shall empower yourself to be a loving and loveable two-legged creature.

The natural world, cosmic consciousness, the real God, offers choices to you. Which ones you make determine how your life manifests today, and cumulatively so for your future. How you are today is the accumulated and amalgamated consequence of all your previous decisions, choices, and experiences in your life. How you will be tomorrow will take into account the consequences of all your decisions, choices and actions today. So reflect upon your past, and use the lessons of it to help you carve out a beautiful today and many more todays. Use today to enjoy today, and improve the odds of enjoying the next today, and keep on at it. HHH is the way!

Making choices and decisions and taking responsibility for them, based on your interconnection to all living things on Mother Earth, is your path to being the captain of your own ship of destiny. The means for getting on, and staying on, that path is conscious living. So much of it is in your hands if you grab it. The universe wants you to enjoy life, it put you here to enjoy it, not to be miserable or to struggle. Remember this always: your mind only exists in relation to everything it receives or produces. It never stands alone. Life is nothing but relationships. *If you harass others you harass yourself, if you belittle others you belittle yourself, if you destroy others you destroy yourself… and block your own path to prosperity.*

WITH THIS UNDERSTANDING we shall move to the next phase of our inquiry.

We need to clearly uncover and unmask the nature of the beast, aka the system, which moves in us all, so that we can make our changes doable and sustainable. By identifying the master problem, and solving it, we dramatically turn our lives around.

Reveal yourself to us master problem…

13

PROBLEMS AND SOLUTIONS

Change what you can't accept, accept what you can't change. Or suffer.

Go with the flow, bend with the wind, accept and move on.

Picture the water in a stream, flowing along on its journey, onwards and onwards towards its ultimate destination. Then it comes to a big rock. The water simply goes around it, over it, under it, any which way so that it may continue its journey. Whenever it meets such obstacles it takes the path of least resistance to overcome them. Water, and nature, is super intelligent. Now consider that water to be your mind and the rock to be a problem. How do you deal with the rocks that come your way??

While physical pain is indeed a horrible problem to have, in this chapter our focus is on the problems we experience in our mind. We are looking at negative feelings and thoughts. In short, we would like to discover how it is we become unhappy, fearful, lacking confidence, cruel and all the rest of it. Then we will be ready to learn how to bring about solutions. This means a twin approach: solving problems as they crop up, and, crucially, learning how to prevent many of them from even cropping up in the first place.

We have discovered much to this end already, but we will now exclusively focus on problems and solutions. Before I have my say, may I ask you to locate your notebook? I thank you!

Task

Please consider some problems that typically afflict you in your life. Consider things like work, your relationships, home, situations, your own habits and traits. Write them down in your notebook. Then decide how you feel when you are experiencing such problems, what you typically think or do about them, and what you think causes them. If you like, but it's optional, reflect upon some solutions you can apply to them the next time they crop up.

Then read on.

THE OTHER DAY I heard some famous English ex-footballers talking together on a video. They were talking about the addictions and problems they had while at the peak of their skills and fame. They were super famous in their day, winning many trophies between them, and millions of football fans were no doubt envious of their lifestyle and riches and fame, seeing them as having reached the height of success. But these footballers were now revealing a rather different story. Now that they were older, and had recovered from their addictions, they felt able to open up and told of many psychological problems they faced in their heyday, unbeknownst to their fans and the media.

It was interesting because as they compared their experiences, they found much in similarity, yet at the time each thought it was only they themselves who were struggling, while the others looked as if their life was all in order, yet it turned out they were all in a negative mind space.

They said they had nobody to talk to about their problems

because they feared they would be seen to be weak and get ripped apart by the media, their fans and their peers. They felt good if other people were seen to have problems because it wasn't them and the focus wouldn't be on them. They craved approval all the time so they were never happy because they were always seeking this approval.

They succumbed to addictions (alcohol, gambling in the main) because of their unhappiness and negative media reporting about them and their families. It was a way of numbing their pain and escaping from their negative self-talk. But from their addiction they then felt even worse: they thought they were letting everybody down, they were causing grief to friends and family, they felt like they were bad people, felt ashamed, and they didn't think they deserved sympathy or to be helped.

Taking compliments proved impossible because of this lack of self-worth (reflecting on my own life, it took me until well into adulthood before I was able to take compliments and not be embarrassed by them; I think the British are programmed to not take anything which makes us feel good about ourselves, but maybe it's the same everywhere?).

At the point they discovered they were an ill person rather than a bad person, they began their healing process. It seemed this healing was a long difficult journey for them too. It began by being able to talk and open up about their problems to some professionals.

None of this surprised me because I had seen for years how famous people (actors, rock stars, sports stars) often turned to drink, drugs, sex, gambling, or whatever else might help them navigate life with less pain. Clearly fame and riches did not mean happiness. I think all people face the very same problems, it's just that famous and rich people are expected by the rest of us to be happy, so they get even more pressure on their shoulders. They are in the public eye so their fall from grace or humiliation can be much more keenly felt.

The major problems here are trying to live up to an idealised person, to be the person we think society expects us to be. We feel there are expectations on us. We are taught/told when we are young that we have to be good, virtuous, well-behaved and all the rest of it, but we're not taught *how* to be like this, nor are we given the chance to grow into such a person.

This is the problem I've been identifying throughout the book, that in our schooling we are *told* and *taught*, but never shown *how to learn*. Humans have to do things themselves if they are to truly learn how to live life properly. We have to make our own mistakes, but we live in fear of being judged negatively by our peers, by society. We worry about looking vulnerable or stupid. Therefore we don't want to make mistakes, and then we may lie or pretend, or try to cover things up. It's a vicious cycle.

I know the value of being able to make mistakes in a supportive environment. Before I began teaching teachers, I encouraged all my English language students in every class I ever had to make mistakes. But my students weren't kids, they were adolescents and adults. I used to enjoy saying this to them because they would look at me strange, having never heard anybody say such things to them before, especially a teacher. I would then say that we learn best when we make mistakes. Anybody who laughed at a mistake early on in the group's life would get a stare from me! Then I would stop the class and talk them through it, saying that they could even learn from their classmates' mistakes. Once this fear of looking silly was gone, everybody thrived.

If we had been encouraged to be ourselves, to find out who we are and become who we are, then we would not carry into adulthood this worry of being judged by others to be a 'no good' person.

Thus, instead of love, compassion, and encouragement, we are more likely to carry fear and desire in our minds. Fear of being seen to be a loser, of appearing weak; desire for peer approval and status.

We measure life and our own self-worth by what society thinks of us and what we want them to think of us, rather than what we think of ourselves. We are not in control of our own life in this way, and that leads to stress, which leads to sickness. We find psychological happiness elusive because always we crave attention and approval from others. Always we are looking, never content.

This worry about what others think of us is crippling. For a start it makes us wary of expressing ourselves in case we get shot down, which means we cannot explore life or ourselves, nor be ourselves. But it undermines so much of our life in so many other ways too, and does so subconsciously, below the radar of our conscious awareness. I think it lies behind most problems we encounter in life. Reflect upon it and see what you think.

It's come about thanks to a rigid, external authority schooling which never allowed us to make mistakes without being laughed at or punished in some way, whether physically or psychologically. The latter, for wee young kids, can be far worse. My mum often used to say to me and my sister, 'sticks and stones may break my bones but words will never hurt me', no doubt in an effort to prepare us for the inevitable nastiness that comes from other humans when they are in negative judgemental mode. Perhaps it really worked, because I myself worry very little about what others think of me. I am me, and that's it, take it or leave it! I do my best and there's nothing more I can do. I always live with HEART - can you remember this one?! It is living with honesty, empathy, authenticity, responsibility, and trust - and then let life judge me as it sees fit. I don't care! HEART brings you to yourself, it centres you in you, helps you approach life from the inside out, not always trying to conform to the outside society's mould.

The adage which I came across a few years ago fits very well here. We've already mentioned it, and it will help you retrain yourself to worry much less (or not at all) about what others think of you: 'It's none of my business what you say about me'. Use conscious living to remind yourself of it and live by it. It's much more important that you are a good person for yourself, and that you just do your best. If that's not good enough for others, do you really want to spend time with them? If a friend denigrates you, are they a real friend? Find people who appreciate you for who you are. Besides, if they are speaking ill of you, who has the negative energy?

We must be who we are, we must train ourselves to lose our fears and desires. We've talked about a lot of things so far that can help us do this, and it always comes back to living consciously and thinking in the moment, and focusing on making today the best day we can. And if your all-new super-cool outlook in life - your orientation, objectives, approach, attitude and intention - is in place, you're well set up.

And here's the thing: once we drop the fear and begin expressing ourselves and doing things without concern of failure or looking stupid, we become proactive and positive people, and rewards hitherto unknown to us start coming into our life. Including lots of peer approval, the very thing we so wanted in the first place! Moral of the story? Do things for yourself, be yourself, drop the fear and worry, and then good things will happen to you.

Another big source of problems I've observed in human life is when things don't go as we expect or want them to go. People say or do the 'wrong' thing (according to you), they don't say or don't do what you wanted them to, or a situation goes wrong. We get what we didn't want, or we don't get what we wanted. We may get angry, impatient, disappointed, and any number of other negative emotional reactions. I say expectation is the mother of disappointment.

It comes about because we've been instilled with values, and told what is good or bad, right or wrong, normal or abnormal, and we judge according to this conditioning inside our autopilot mind.

We can so easily impose ourselves on family members, or our partner in particular. The people we love. We want them to be a certain way, and when they are not, we may feel disappointed, let down, angry and so on. We blame them, complain to them. Parents will blame the kids, a partner blames their other half, but why blame? How does that help?? And in the karmic chain of how things work in life, perhaps the parent somehow pushed their kid into some kind of action? If we push, others may resent this and push back. We will see what they do, but can we see what we did ourselves to provoke them into their action?

I want you to do this or that, but am I not imposing my way onto you?? Why can't I just let you find your own way in life?

Then there is the problem of inequity. People look upwards with envy, or downwards with disdain. Some may feel unworthy by comparing themselves to others, while other people may feel entitled to greater things than others because they see themselves as somehow more important, more worthy. In Asia in particular, the concept of VIPs is strong, people literally consider themselves as very important people - clearly more important than everybody else. What arrogance! Fela Kuti, one of my very favourite musicians, used to fight his whole life against corruption in Nigeria where he was from. He had one song called VIP which, he sang, stood for 'vagabonds in power'…

There are many kinds of problems we can have in life, with hundreds of emotions and thoughts, actions and reactions that our mind experiences and produces. I would like to offer you an analysis of 'the problem', and we'll look at all aspects of it. At the end of my analysis, I offer you a very simple approach for how you can solve every single problem you face, aside from the problem of one's very survival. Poverty is not in our remit here, I start from the basis that we have our food, clothing and shelter needs met. We are talking about striving and thriving, and how to do so.

WE ARE *RELATIONAL BEINGS*, we have relationships with everything we perceive, remember, or imagine. We relate to the world as it happens to us now, to our memories of the world, and to our anticipations of the world. You and your inner world relate to everyone and everything in the outer world. You eat, drink and breathe it; you absorb and mentally grasp it. You blend with whatever your attention is on, whether it's out there now, in your memory bank or in the future. This blend is your relationship with the universe and all in it. You are this blend and the feelings it generates in you at any one time.

By 'outer world', we take this to mean everything beyond our skin: encompassing all other people, places, and things, as well as everything in outer space. Everything except our own inner world. We see and perceive this distinction of two worlds, but the physiological, psychological and spiritual reality is that we are a blend of the shared outer and our personal inner. The world is out there, but it's also in here, inside our own minds and bodies. And we are in it. There are no vacuums or black holes.

What we want to be able to do, through skilled practice and management of our inner and outer environments, is minimise problems and suffering in our life while maximising our positive relationships with everything out there. First, we learn about the life and make-up of a problem, and then from this informed basis we can work out any changes we need to make. Always: step one is understand and learn, step two is using this understanding to take intelligent action.

The principle and base instinct of life *is to feel good and avoid feeling bad, to seek out pleasure and avoid pain, and to feel secure.* This is our innate/subconscious motivation and driving force in life. We just wanna feel good baby! We want the good vibes and the good times, and if it's uncomfortable, disagreeable or painful, our innate impulse is to flee or neutralise these *perceived* (key word) bad vibes in any way we can.

The gigantic master problem, the mother of all problems, *is holding a wrong, or flawed, relationship with our external environment, with the world out there.* This is the consequence of our conditioned ignorance handed on through multiple generations via our education. The unstated hidden assumption and understanding, upon which we approach life, is that we are living separate to each other and the world about us in which we live. We feel disconnected, and being social animals this is a terrible thought. Fear enters our psyche. Psychologically and physically, we think we stand alone in our body.

We do not, though, it's a grand mistake, a terrible misunderstanding!

We do not see the relational nature of who we are ourself, which blends with everything else we perceive through our senses, and which we remember from the past or imagine will arrive in the future. We do not understand that we are a blend of the outside world and our own inner world of body mind and soul. Our approach to life is thus based on a misunderstanding and misperception. Sad to say, we cannot 'see' properly. And for this reason, until or unless we consciously attend to such matters, we don't really know who we are, nor how life works. Once we can see with clarity and understanding, most problems won't even come into existence. Hence the power that observation brings us, because then we teach ourselves to see.

The source of all problems is that we seek to feel good *exclusively from the external world out there,* we have become *externalised* in our approach to life, as if life is a one-way flow from out there to inside of us. We seek our pleasures from out there, we seek meaning for our lives from out there. We want sensory stimulations such as drugs, alcohol, comfort foods; we seek to be admired and thought important; we seek validation and love from others; and we seek status symbols and loads of money.

We depend upon the world out there to supply what we seek. But even when we get what we sought, off we go again seeking more, looking for a new hit, a new destination.

Because we are seekers. And enough is never enough to a seeker because by definition a seeker is always looking for something he or she does not have right now. We get what we want, but the pleasure is fleeting, ephemeral, so we seek more. Desires become our chains.

We are addicts. All of us. And the stuff we're addicted to is out there. We were conditioned this way. Nobody is to blame, but this is the way we are. The now-moment is apparently not good enough. We are always headed somewhere, rarely if ever happy where we are now. I suggest because we're not rooted in ourselves, we're chasing life from out there.

We are forever looking, meaning we are focused on destinations and not our journeys. We are driven by our desires to get stuff which we think will make us feel good. We fear pain, and when it comes we try to get rid of it, flee from it, or kid ourselves it will go away.

Seeking enslaves us to desires and fears, enslaves us to our society, to the outside world. We are not content, we do not experience inner peace, life is not good enough now, and it is so because seeking is always thinking the grass is greener yonder, greener in a future time, and so we completely fail to see the grass we already have. If we could only see the grass we have, if we could only notice the current moment of time, if we could only be focused on today, we could then water this existing grass of ours, take care of it, enjoy it.

All because we are seeking, instead of accepting. Once we learn to accept the grass we are on right now, have gratitude and reverence for it, we can focus on tending to it here and now. If it's not green enough, water it!

We have failed to look inwards, failed to look within ourselves and discover all the beauties that already exist within us. We are so busy looking out there, thanks to the way we were conditioned by our society, that we forgot to look in here. It's the same in the dimension of time, we are oriented towards tomorrow and the future, not with today, yet today is the only place and time that life can be experienced. There is no life yesterday, it's just a memory; there is no life tomorrow, it's just a thought, a worry, a dream. You better live today or not at all.

It's the same for rich and poor alike, and even the powerful become powerless in their constant chase for more and more, controlled by their desires and greed. In fact, they have more desires, more needs, and so are even unhappier. In orienting our lives in this way, we have ceded control of our own life to others and to the out-there. When the pleasures come, fine, but as we all know many pains come along as well. We love our thrills, but they come with ills and spills and then we, erm, seek pills to fix us.

The trigger of our problems, the thing that gets us into a stressed, upset, disturbed state of mind, is always *something in the outside world* which hits our consciousness, grabbing our attention and focus. That something can be other people, situations, happenings, anything at all that takes place outside of our internal environment. The trigger may come from our own personal world where we live and work, or it may come to us from the media we consume.

We must note that the trigger, while always relating to something or someone in the outside world, may arise within our own minds by remembering a previous happening, or by imagining a possible future one. We may regret something we did or remember a past grievance, or we may fear or worry about a possible future problem happening. These internal thoughts are always in relation to something or somebody out there.

Our impulse, due to the *source of all problems*, is to then blame this trigger for our negative feelings and thinking. We find ourselves blaming other people, the weather, bad luck, anything at all. It's their fault, they caused us a problem.

Blame, though, regardless of the righteousness of our position, and however justified we believe we are in blaming another person, will not get rid of the problem. In fact, it acts as fuel for keeping the problem alive. Blame is negative energy. Nobody likes being blamed, but if we are the blamer, then it is we with the negative energy.

We may even blame ourselves from time to time, for being stupid, spiteful, causing harm, and so now we feel shame or guilt or unworthy… more negative energy.

Blame and solution cannot coexist, it can only be one or the other. Take your pick. I will say that the blame game is a shame and makes us all lame.

The reason being is that the trigger of a problem is *not* the cause of the problem. *Trigger* and *cause* are equated as the same thing in our subconscious conditioned minds, but this is a mistake which exposes us to repeated suffering of problems.

We can only solve a problem by addressing the *root causes* of the problem.

The cause of our problems is *our reaction to the trigger*. I would like to repeat that: the cause of our problems is *our reaction* to the trigger, *not* the trigger itself. Please realise this crucial understanding, for it's the beginning of the end of so many problems in your life.

In some manner or other, we resist or reject the trigger. And we can view life as a constant series of triggers day in day out until our final day, so we're never going to get away from triggers, triggers are here to stay for the duration of our life's journey. And remember, our own mind may be the trigger as much as somebody, or something, else may be.

So, the reality of **the cause of a problem** is this: *it is our non-*

acceptance of life as it presents itself to us. We resist or reject the out-there. The trigger from out there may happen in our own life, or it may be something we hear about in the media we are consuming. It may be a memory of a past trigger or an anticipation of a future trigger. Whether present, past, or future, for some reason we don't want the trigger - we don't like it, we think it's unfair, it's stressing us. It may well be unfair or distasteful, but *it* is not causing us our problem, *our reaction to it* is causing us our problem.

How so?

The trigger, the 'it', is out there - somebody says or does something, a bad situation arises, events go against us, the trigger comes from out there. The reaction is in our mind. Thus, the bare reality of it is this: the trigger of the problem is out there, and the cause of the problem is in our own mind. Trigger external, problem internal, the problem is *not* out there.

You may begin to see the beauty of this understanding, because suddenly we realise that we can be in control of this process...

I'm not saying the trigger has nothing to do with our problem because clearly if the trigger hadn't happened or wasn't there, we'd not have a problem. But how do we get rid of the world?!?

The trigger and *our reaction to it* combine to create our problem. Remember, we are relational beings, we are blends of outer and inner worlds. We absolutely cannot say that the trigger is our problem, no, the reality is that *our reaction to the trigger* is our problem. It is our reaction which creates the blend of our inner world and the outer world, and our reaction is *determined by our perspective.*

Now, the whole purpose of a spiritual revolution is to gain self-control over our perspective. In this way we can control our reactions to triggers, and therefore we can choose whether the trigger is to be a problem for us, or not.

One example to illustrate this from the football world, and we'll make it Arsenal at home to Spurs, fierce local rivals from North London. After ten minutes Arsenal score a goal. The reality is that a player in a red shirt puts the ball into the back of the Spurs goalkeeper's net. 1-0. This is the external reality, but nothing happens in isolation, it needs a witness. This goal, experienced and seen by all members of the crowd and both teams, is the trigger for wild elation in some people and morbid despondency in other people. The goal is just a goal, the trigger is just the trigger, but it's how it is perceived that gives the trigger any kind of meaning or energy force. The same trigger provoked a problem for some, and magical feelings for others. The trigger, clearly, is not the problem.

Our reactions to the event or situation define what kind of energy we receive from the outside world. Me and a good mate of mine have travelled from our home town to a favourite island of ours a couple of times. On the plane journey I'm comfortable and relaxed, he's a bag of nerves, and then when we get on the boat I'm now in stomach-churning fear while he's fine. It's not the boat or the plane, it's how we relate and react to the outside world, how we perceive things, that leads to our problems. Now, where do these reactions come from?

Our mind.

We can easily say then that the cause of our problems is our mind when it reacts negatively to something that happens out there. And if it is our mind that creates problems, then it's our mind which can solve them… just bear that in mind (!) for a short while.

The cause of our mind's reaction is *the contents of its memory*, and we're calling it our *long-term memory (LTM)*. In this memory bank is contained a lifetime's accumulation of everything we have learned, experienced, been taught. Whenever we react to triggers out there, our reaction is automatically provoked by the mind consulting this gigantic memory bank to make sense of this trigger, be it good or bad. Our mind, via our LTM, is therefore reacting to life now, by consulting our past. This is how our conditioned self works, we judge the present by what we learned in the past and by what happened to us in the past.

It comes back to us as being agents of information, and when our autopilot mind reacts to incoming information according to past experience and past information, held in our long-term memory, we have little control over ourselves and our life. Our past governs our present. We are controlled by our past. We may think others control us, it's why we blame them when things are not to our liking, but the reality says it's our perspective borne out of our own past which controls us and causes us our problems… or makes us feel good.

It is said that if we don't know our history we are doomed to repeat it. I think this applies to us as individual citizens too - if we don't know our past we are doomed to repeat it.

Now, once we start to look within this long-term memory of ours, to see what it is that triggers us into negative energy, we may well start to wonder where its contents came from, and how they got to be in there. And as a spiritual revolutionary we will certainly be inquiring into our LTM's contents, for it's central to finding out who we are and how life works.

We have been saying that we were rather deeply conditioned as kids in our schooling and upbringing, but especially via our education because all members of society went through pretty much the same education process.

I teach my teacher students that our LTM = KLUSE+2V. The long-term memory's contents are contained in the compartments of **k**nowledge, **l**anguage, **u**nderstandings, **s**kills, **e**xperiences, **v**alues and **v**iews. I set them tasks in the classroom to help them discover what their own (hitherto subconsciously held) KLUSE+2V contains. For your own life, conscious living is your means for discovering your own.

Knowledge can be any kind of information that we take to be true. *Understandings* include all assumptions, beliefs, and conditioned 'facts' that came from society, which usually we simply took to be our own. Some of it is misunderstanding masquerading as truths and knowledge.

I encourage you to go inside yourself and find out your own LTM's contents, and begin the process of challenging it all to see if it serves your life or holds you back. One good way to learn is when you find yourself disagreeing with something or somebody. In this way you can then ask yourself if your own understanding is correct, and you can question where your values and views came from. Discomfort or pain are great teachers if we look for their causes. Learn the art of questioning your own answers.

The effect of our problems is negative energy in the form of negative *feelings* and negative *thoughts* in our mind, and any negative *actions* we take in response to the trigger. We may feel anger, resentment, unhappy; we may think of life as being unfair, depressing, worrying; and we may blame, pretend, or bottle up. Our triggered conditioned mind has taken over the controls of our entity and whole being, directing our mind into various feelings, thoughts and actions.

You, the conscious living you, have to restore order within your mind to get out of this negative energy created by your long-term memory's contents automatically reacting to the out-there. Living consciously and practising awareness is your way out of this enslavement to your emotions and thoughts. We can observe our feelings and thoughts and learn from them, and if we do this, we can become conscious of our knowledge, language, understandings, skills, experiences, and our views and values. Then we can make informed changes that will improve our life. We can't stop our feelings and thoughts, but we don't have to do what they tell us to do. Observing them neutralises their power over us.

To finish this analysis of the mighty problem we shall sum up its process. **The manifestation of a problem** is this: *conditioned approach to life >> KLUSE+2V >> trigger from out there >> non-acceptance of trigger >> negative feelings and thoughts >> negative energy >> suffering >> action or suppressed non-action.*

Where do you suppose the solution lies with the life of a problem?? Have a ponder yourself, and then read on to find my simple approach to all problems and how to solve them...

A REMINDER: the gigantic master problem, as we traverse the landscape of time until we reach our final destination, the one constant of all problems we ever have, *is our non-acceptance of life as it presents itself to us*. We resist what is, or what happens, and we resist past and future situations and happenings that we may recall or think about.

We are resisting a trigger from out there with our autopilot thinking, and out of this comes our problem. There can only be two solutions to a problem: change the trigger, accept the trigger.

But you do have a third option, and so let me introduce you to my **'1-2-3 approach to solving problems'**: *one problem, two solutions, three options.*

You have a problem of some kind triggered by something or somebody out there in the outer world, and we can think of this problem as *a disturbance of your mind.* Take a look in your notebook at the triggers you wrote down earlier. Pick out one problem, or go through them one by one…

You have two possible solutions only: either *change* the thing, situation, person out there or *accept* it. There are no other solutions.

And the process of changing it must be done non-harmfully to you and to others, through practising *ahimsa,* otherwise the harm you cause others will come back to you as a karmic payback.

Of course, if it's happened already, you can't change it now, but you may be thinking about what you can change to· avoid it happening again in the future, because many problems we experience come from triggers which keep on repeating themselves. For example, a nasty or overbearing boss, in which case if you are to change him or her you will need to communicate in a non-threatening way to ask them to desist next time. I'm not talking about what's easy or difficult here, just only about our choices. Maybe you'll have to change your job. Many people in Thailand do this as their way of solving this particular problem.

If you can't change it, and often we can't, then you must accept it. If you can't accept it then you must change it, peacefully, creatively, intelligently. If you want a solution, it must be to accept or change the trigger. By accepting it you are changing your reaction to it.

In golf I joke that the game is great for helping us learn to accept the unacceptable because we hit so many bad shots which we just wish we hadn't hit. Yet, if you dwell upon the bad shot, complaining and feeling bad about it, you will almost certainly ruin your next shot, and so you spiral into even more negative energy, and a nice healthy walk turns into hell. That is the lot of many of your amateur golfers. I use golf in this way to train myself to accept pain. Then, often, the pain goes away!

Now, here's the beauty of this 1-2-3 approach. What if you feel you can't accept it, and you can't change it? Well, you have a third option, and that is to do neither, just to continue suffering with the problem. Sometimes this might offer you less pain than accepting or changing, so it's always an option. But if you don't want to suffer from the problem anymore, or you're bored with it happening so often in your life, then you know what you've got to do. Unresolved problems that we bury in our minds have a habit of resurfacing.

At least you know your options.

However, bearing in mind it is our negative reaction to, and our negative perspective of, the happenings in the world out there that leads to our problems, what do you suppose happens if you have somehow changed your whole perspective of things in life? Maybe many of the problems which previously afflicted you will no longer even materialise as problems because you no longer see happenings out there as unacceptable.

This change in perspective comes to you by resetting your outlook and mindset with the OOAAI tool, consciously choosing your orientation, objectives, approach, attitude and intentions in and for life. Prevention of many problems is the best action.

My mindset in my OOAAI is that I would like as much positive energy and as little negative energy in my life as possible. This is more important to me than deciding if others are right or wrong, good or bad people. If I see bad people doing wrong things everywhere, then I simply have negative energy in my being all the time, and I am hurting my own experience of life in this way.

My own struggles have always been with impatience, seeing injustice and suffering, and seeing bullying behaviour. I do not 'accept' cruel behaviour, but I have trained myself to not get enraged or angry about it anymore. I neutralise the negative energy coming my way into not-negative energy, through my understanding of karma. I understand that people act like this out of their own hurt. I may try to change them peacefully, and always by first trying to get them into conscious living mode, because only then can they see what they are doing that hurts others. However, usually people resist ‘help’. So, I practise not reacting, and although difficult, practice does make it easier.

So, that is your problems and solutions for you. Nearly all problems are in our head, in our mind, produced by our perspectives of the world around us. If it’s happened, you can’t unhappen it, but you *can* make changes to avoid it happening again. Or, you can move and get away from the triggers that you can’t change. Change your job, change your home, emigrate, drop toxic friends. You only get one life, there are no dummy runs, no dress rehearsals, no second goes, you know the score by now!

Prevention is perhaps the easiest approach, and it comes back to OOAAI and OAR and doing your own research and learning. Conscious living. Observe with awareness, read and listen to others, reflect upon all this input; seek out understanding of what is and what happens, rather than judging everything to be bad or wrong. Use your spiritual power to liberate you from being tied to your emotions, which themselves are automatically triggered by the conditioning we all received while kids. Inquire, decondition, self-educate, and Bob’s your uncle.

14

3DH5DL: A FORMULA AND FRAMEWORK FOR UNDERSTANDING LIFE

Understand your mind, understand yourself, and you will understand others and understand life. Understanding your mind is the central key to a life of much reduced suffering and emotional pain.

'You just don't know, really, what your mind is going to do to you sometimes. You can control it to an extent but certain situations are going to bring more tension and you have to kind of channel that the right way, play the right shots.' ~ Jordon Spieth, brilliant golfer

'You can't afford to let your mind wander… you've got to stay in the moment.' ~ Mike Atherton, cricket commentator talking about being a batsman

Only we can liberate our minds, nobody else can do it for us. We do it by understanding the mind.

I'm in two minds about it. I was torn between two minds. I can't make my mind up. I was out of my mind with worry.

The core questions in the human life are: Who am I? What am I? Why am I here? How does life work?

More questions, pertinent to the above idiomatic phrases, are begged: Who, precisely, is it that is torn between two minds? Who is in two minds? Who is the **'I'** that is torn? And, you're in **two** minds? Which minds would they be? And when we say I can't make **my** mind up, who or what is the possessor of 'my' mind? To whom does the 'my' refer? We see the two sportsmen referring to themselves as the possessor of their mind. Lastly, **who** was out of their mind with worry, and where were they if not in their mind?

When we can answer these questions, we are in a beautiful position to live the most beautiful life we can live. This chapter brings us to the answers, building on everything we've learned so far.

We have now reached the denouement and culmination of everything we have been talking about. We have reached the heart of everything: now I officially introduce you to yourself! Simultaneously I officially conclude how life works, and then it's all down to you. We've covered both in bits and pieces during the whole journey so far, but here we bring it all together and explicitly define and discuss it. 'It' being my formula and framework, 3DH5DL, for who you are and how life works.

If I was to distill the essence of our journey together into a brief snippet, take everything else away, and leave you with just one thing, it is this: carry your OAR tool with you today and every day for the rest of your life's journey: *observe* life with full *awareness*, then *reflect* upon what it might mean. Using the OAR process puts you in conscious living mode and that's where life, and life's answers, are at.

OAR is your personal teacher and the only one you ever need. It doesn't mean you do everything yourself, it means that you know when and how to get help from others, and when and how to help yourself. It enables you to become your own skilled learner and autonomous citizen by your own questions, actions and efforts, and that is all a human being ever needs. Using it, you can self-educate to any degree you wish to. It is the means to uncovering and becoming the innate intelligent interconnected individual that you were born to be. It brings you to self sovereignty.

Truly, the ability to observe rather than judge is such magic. Observing keeps the mind open, judging shuts it down and traps you in the past. Observe others and the happenings of life, observe yourself and the goings-on in your inner being, and in so doing you cultivate your awareness of the world out there, and you cultivate self-awareness of your own inner world of mind, body and soul.

When we feel connected to each other and to Mother Earth, and to the whole cosmos up there in the night sky, then we feel free and full of love and joy. Our soul is dancing. Conscious living connects us; observing and being aware is conscious living, and reflecting is the learning part of the process. OAR is your spiritual revolution's heartbeat!

Observe, be aware, reflect, learn, observe. Reflect, be aware, observe, learn, reflect. Be aware, observe, reflect, learn, be aware… do you see what I'm saying?

You will no longer be enslaved by the system's conditioning, instead you will find your own understandings and truths, which will lead to your self-empowerment. Confidence and trust in yourself feel super good inside you.

Observation and awareness unlock all the keys to the magic of being human.

Most importantly of all, OAR will help you evaluate for yourself the efficacy of everything I've written so far, as it applies to you and your own life, and the same for the rest of this chapter and book, and the same for anything else you ever read or listen to, and then on into your evolutionary journey, until such time as the janitor from heaven arrives for your collection.

What a blinding tool!

But, we have a little more work to be done with this tool, and then we'll get to 3DH5DL.

. . .

Task

I want to be absolutely sure we are both on the same page when it comes to the cognitive processes of observing, being aware, and reflecting, and what they each mean in the reality of practical living. You've done plenty of observing and reflecting already with previous tasks, to raise your awareness of, and gain key insights into, life; and you may recall my story about my massage with the falling water noise. You can also find your notes relating to the tasks you did in the *A Dozen Tasks* chapter.

This is a task for raising your awareness of *self-observation* and *self-awareness*. This specifically applies to noticing what is going on *within* your skin-covered organism!

You can do this task right now where you are, just make sure nobody will come and talk to you, in person or on the phone or on social media. Turn off any TV, radio or other distractions. I think 15 minutes will be long enough, but go for as long as you wish. I think it best to sit down, and to do so in any way that you feel comfortable. If you want to get out into nature, then that's great too, just make sure you can sit down okay. Probably best to shut your eyes.

(I was doing this very activity a few years ago in one of my very favourite resorts out in the country. I sat down on a log on the ground, near a beautiful stream. The nature all around was just resplendent. But I shut my eyes and tuned into the birdsong and other noises, and noticed my mind doing its inner chatter. Then, at some point for some reason, I opened my eyes. And there, right in front of me a few feet away, was a quite a thick and long snake moving along on its way. What a freak-out. I quit my communion with nature there and then!)

Your task is to observe everything going on *within you* as you sit there for 15 minutes. Not literally with your eyes, but with your *mind's eye* which is in charge of focus and attention. Don't try to do anything or not do anything, just focus on observing within you. What do I mean by 'within you'? It means observe and notice anything happening in your body and anything happening in your mind. You can notice and feel your sitting posture, your breathing, and any other bodily sensations that may be happening. You can visualise different parts of your body, doing a sort of mental scan of them by noticing how each part feels, tense or relaxed. Notice if you start thinking any thoughts, or are already thinking about something. Focus on the noticing, so if you do find you are thinking, observe and listen to your thoughts as if you were listening to a movie or somebody else. If you stop your thoughts, notice the silence in your mind, and then notice if you are suddenly preoccupied with thoughts again.

In summary, focus on the goings-on inside your body and mind, be alert and focus on observing, watching, noticing it all, including noticing that you stopped noticing! Do at least 15 minutes, and if you are enjoying it all, go on for as long as you wish. I'm not suggesting you lie down in case you fall asleep.

I would like to offer you two optional extra tasks to do if they take your fancy. Both you've done already, but you might like to do them again to remind you of what you discovered the first time. In both of them, ensure you can be sitting comfortably and go for a minimum of 15 minutes too.

i) Listen to some music, focusing carefully on all the instruments. Notice if thoughts pop up in your mind to interrupt your focus on the actual music. Notice what happens inside your mind during the whole time.

ii) Sit in some nature where you can hear the constant noise of water, birdsong or other noises. Do the same again, focusing on listening only to the water or birdsong and other sounds which come to your ears. Notice if any thoughts come along, notice everything.

Please don't read on until you've done the task/s.

You will now know precisely what observing, being aware, noticing and reflecting mean in practise. We are on the same page! If we focus our mind's eye on the goings-on within ourselves, we call it *self*-observation and *self*-awareness. Recalling and replaying what we observed - out there, or in here - is the reflecting process, and it gives us the chance to discern and learn from the experience.

So far, we have emphasised the interconnected and interdependent nature of life and of human life, but that modern society around the world has this erroneous idea that the opposite is true, that we are separate and disconnected from each other, and from Mother Earth herself. I have said in this way we are conditioned into ignorance, from which arises most, if not all, of our suffering. We have a flawed perspective going against the alignment of nature.

In short, the degree to which the *nurture* we received as kids failed to complement our *nature*, rather it antagonised it, is the degree to which we will find problems and negative energy dogging our life.

When we re-educate and re-nurture ourselves, through the process of our spiritual revolution, to work *with* nature, then we move into a life characterised by wellness and the 3Hs. We use the OOAAI tool to create for ourselves a new conscious outlook, giving us a firm foundation for success, and then it's all about practising, and becoming skilled in, conscious living.

We are almost ready to discuss my unique formula of 3DH5DL, but in keeping with the theme of our journey together so far, and to enhance your learning experience, I'd like to get you thinking about it first, so that when I offer my input it will be more meaningful for you.

Task

Please turn to the first two paragraphs of this chapter and consider the core questions I posed, along with my pertinent questions relating to the idiomatic phrases and quotes. My suggestion is to spend some good time reflecting upon your ideas and answers, and to make notes in your notebook. Then, as you read my own input you can compare it to your own thoughts.

Read on when you're ready.

. . .

3DH5DL CAME to me on my hammock somewhere after the turn of the century, and when it did, I knew I was ready to write this book. I think it also marked the start of my wellness journey back in 2008 when I first began proactively changing my diet and lifestyle to support and enjoy good health. Perhaps it was my new orientation towards health that provided me the missing piece to the puzzle of life…

For donkeys' years I had practised going deep into my mind and reflecting upon the ways of life and how it works, and the ways of human life and how it works, with all its violence and wars, terror and horrors, yet with all its art, beauty and music, love and kindness. Were we all schizophrenics I kept wondering. How can we be capable of such brutalities and yet such beauties?? Hitler, Stalin, Pol Pot, Mao and many other brutal dictators who killed huge numbers of their own people, yet Martin Luther King, Buddha, Socrates, Jesus, Mohammed, Osho, Krishnamurti, Rudolf Steiner… how can it be?

And what of ourselves, ordinary citizens who seem to find so much unhappiness, conflict and confusion, and who struggle with our health and in our relationships? We all want to be happy and healthy, to love and be loved, but it seems to be so elusive most of the time. How can this be? Those who are happy and healthy, how do they do it?

I was onto it for myself in my new life in Thailand, but I needed to be able to articulate things to other people. Since 2000, life gradually brought me more tests and challenges and problems which I had to deal with, after my previous decade of the utmost beauty and freedom, and there's nothing like stress and problems to learn from and focus the mind.

And then it came to me, my formula. On my hammock in my beachside bungalow, yards from the water's edge. Palm trees everywhere, with the dragonflies, butterflies and huge bumble bees going about their business of living, and with no human noise save the odd chug chug chug of a longtail boat that would arrive in the bay, and traverse it until it was out of sight and out of sound again…

'3DH5DL!' popped into my head suddenly. It's who we really are, and it informs us how life works. I got excited, gently swinging in the hammock, and started challenging it, looking to see if I could find any holes in it. I couldn't.

For me it encapsulates everything. I'm not offering it to you as a 100% guaranteed answer as to who you are and how life works, but I am offering it to you as the basis for you to easily gain your own personal understanding of who you are and how life works. It certainly continues to work for me. I think you'll find it works for you too, for I've had years to challenge my formula and be sure about it - I challenge all my understandings in life all the time. But it has always stood up to the tests I've put it under.

So, back to our core questions: who are you and how does life work? What do you think? What did you notice doing the task above? Can you recall what we've said about us as individual human beings being a blend? About energy flow? About how many identifiable components there are to us? About the relationship between your internal environment and the external environment?

We bring it all together now.

3DH5DL stands for **three dimensions of health** and **five dimensions to life**.

While we are identifying these different dimensions for our purposes of understanding, the working reality of life is that they don't exist separately, they integrate and operate as holistic wholes. But, just as we can break down a machine into all its separate parts to understand what each part does, so that we may better understand how the whole machine works, so we will do the same with our own self and life itself.

The three interconnecting dimensions of health operating within your body are **physical health, psychological health** and **spiritual health**, which relate to your body, mind and soul respectively.

Your overall level of health, and sense of wellness or illness that you feel within your body and mind, is indicative of how well your body, mind and soul are functioning as a whole. We've said that our own internal environment 'feeds' off the external environment, and in turn our IE produces back out into the EE; that is, input and output of energy flowing back and forth between us and the external environment we live in.

If positive input comes into the body then this boosts not only your physical health but also your psychological and spiritual health, on account of all three working synchronistically and interdependently. Similarly, positive mental input will boost your physical and spiritual health as well as your psychological health, and nutritious soul food from nature will boost your physical and psychological health, as well as feed your spiritual wellbeing. On the flip side, negative energy of any kind coming in will affect all three dimensions in a negative manner.

Clearly, then, we see that our sense of wellbeing is dependent upon all types of incoming energy whether of a physical, mental or spiritual nature. *To the extent we can actively choose our energy sources is the level of freedom we have to promote, or attack, our overall health.*

Presumably, nobody would willingly choose to attack their own health, but everybody can see the health woes facing so many of humanity's members, and therefore there must be other forces which influence our choices.

One major influence is ignorance - we cause ourselves harm without realising or understanding what we are doing. Another is addictions, which can be very hard to give up despite us knowing that they cause us harm. My view is that if our schooling did a proper job we'd not enter the world ignorant of health matters, we'd have a much more positive and supportive society and community to live in, and addictions may well never get off the ground in the first place. And, dear reader, prevention is so much easier than cure!

The five interconnecting dimensions of human life are **body, emind, imind, soul** and **external environment**. (I'll get to the distinction between the two minds in a mo.) Therefore, what I'm saying is that you are 5DL, I am 5DL, each individual human being on the planet is 5DL. This is who we are, *an amalgamation of five dimensions* which operate holistically and interdependently within the physical boundary of our body.

Previously we've talked about the nature of life being that

everything in our world and universe is interconnected and interdependent. We said that within the boundary of our skin were the body, mind and soul which were interlinked and which constituted our internal environment, yet with the external environment coming into us in the form of energy input we said we were in fact an interdependent and interconnected blend of IE + EE. We are physically made of stuff from the outer world, mentally made of information and ideas from the world out there, and spiritually made of the cosmic consciousness of the universe. That means four dimensions within us, and I mean mind, body, soul, and EE, since the structure of our entity and being is made of the EE, and it comes into us as a source of energy and sustenance to keep our life going. Remember, IE + EE = me!

But to really understand how life works, to fully understand who we are, and to really understand the root source of all our conflicts and inner unhappiness, *we must take it to be that we have two minds.*

Now, I must issue a quick rider and caveat to precede our discussion of these two minds and how they influence our life, and then no more reference to it to avoid constantly repeating myself. So listen up!

It's this: unlike the brain and heart which are of physical matter like all other body parts, the mind and the soul have no physical make-up and have never been seen by any human beings ever. They cannot be seen any more than the space between you and the stars up yonder, yet we know it is there. We all came to understand that the mind is housed in our brain and the soul is of the heart. Many in the western world and in the orthodox sciences will even reject the soul because they can't see it or prove it exists. Well, that's for them to square with themselves.

Now, you've got me telling you you have *two* minds that can't be seen! Well, maybe we have one mind, two minds, or several minds, I simply cannot guarantee what we've got or show you any evidence, I don't think anybody can. This, in my view, is why we have the notion of God - whether it's the 'God' we've been taught about, or what many understand to be the divine presence and cosmic order of the God of universal intelligence and energetics - because humans over the millennia have realised that much is knowable about our world, yet much is also mystery, belonging to the unknowable.

This unknowable is unbearable for many human beings, and, might I suggest, leads to insanity.

Yet…

Accepting the mystery and unknowable is accepting God, the divine presence of the cosmos into our lives. Seeking certainty about everything leaves no room for our soul or for God, or for the magic and joy of cosmic consciousness and ineffable love. And then happiness and ineffable love are unavailable. But happiness and love is what we all want!!

What I'm sharing with you now is that, when I conceive of these two minds, which I'm calling the **emind** and the **imind**, then everything in life makes so much sense to me. It doesn't mean I suddenly have uncovered the mystery bits; just that by accepting them as mystery and as unknowable, I am liberated from that part of me as a human which so desires to know, to be certain, to prove something to be so. There is the knowable, which we come to learn about and understand by our own endeavours, and then there is the mystery, which remains that way. My friend, I so love the mystery! I only have to look at a starlit night to connect with it. How far away is the next galaxy? How old is our planet? No idea! But I love these questions and not having the answers. Oh, the books might say this or that, but what does such a number actually mean?

So, from now on I shall be talking as if we do indeed have two minds. The English language seems to support this when we say 'we are torn between two minds', or 'I'm in two minds'. (As I discuss these minds, you might like to reflect upon everything we've discussed so far on our journey together. I think it might blow your mind!)

THE PURPOSE in viewing ourselves as having two minds is for me to express and share my understandings with you, so that you can have a thoroughly successful spiritual revolution which will empower you and transform your life and relationships with everything here on Mother Earth. I think you will find that the idea of two minds really helps you in all your work. Once we accept this, we can see precisely why we get so much inner conflict, because it's the two minds in conflict. Remember, we say that understanding something is liberation from it, so with two minds we can liberate ourselves from inner conflict, and then we can revolutionise our relationships with others and with Mother Earth herself.

The **emind** stands for **ego-mind** and the **imind** stands for **intelligence-mind**. Each has very different functions and ways of working, and that is what we need to get to grips with. If you would like to dwell upon them and how they differ from each other before reading my descriptions, then do take a pause and see what you think…

No doubt you will have heard of the ego, left and right brain, conscious and subconscious, and other terms which apply to the mind, but our work together is now based on us all having an **ego-mind** and an **intelligence-mind**, and exploring what each does.

This is where all your awareness-raising tasks throughout the book, and in this chapter, come in. I would like you to specifically think about the observation tasks you did at the outset of this chapter, because they are current and vivid in your memory.

I asked you to notice and observe the goings-on in your body and mind itself. I will proceed with one assumption: that you noticed thoughts in your own mind, *as if they had a mind of their own*. You will have noticed that such thoughts came to you from somewhere (in fact, from your long-term memory), but that you did not choose to produce them.

Just as we can notice pain in our body, a stomachache, gas, throbbing and a multitude of other physical sensations, so we can notice thoughts and emotions in our mind - if we're looking and being aware of them. To feel the pain or discomfort of your headache means you are in the now-moment, in the present, and if you notice your own thoughts and feelings then so too you are in the present.

Here is the simple, core, revelatory difference between the two minds: *when you notice and observe thoughts and emotions in your mind, this is your* ***imind*** *doing the noticing, observing, and being aware of such thoughts; and it is your* ***emind*** *producing the actual thoughts and feelings.*

The **ego-mind** is the actor or player if you like, while the **intelligence-mind** is the moviegoer or audience. The **imind** can watch, observe, notice, and is aware of, the **emind** in action. The **emind** acts according to its conditioning. Please reflect upon this deeply. These are your two minds.

Everything else I relate to you in this chapter is designed to help you become well acquainted with the differences between your **ego-mind** and **intelligence-mind**, but in essence, the core understanding of your whole life in action, in the past, now and forevermore, is that when you can see your own thoughts in your mind which you did not proactively consciously choose to initiate, then you are seeing them with your **intelligence-mind** and it is your **ego-mind** coming up with these thoughts.

Your **imind** is the eye of your mind, allowing you to observe everything in life, including your own conditioned mind (**emind**) at work. Your mind's eye, your **imind**, puts you in conscious living mode. If you consciously choose to think about things in a discerning or inquiring manner, then you are using your **imind**.

Whatever I say next will be useful, but there's no substitute for your own practice. Just use the OAR tool to observe with awareness. Every time you observe yourself and others you do so using your **intelligence-mind**, and you will learn more about your **ego-mind** and their **ego-minds**. And the more we learn the more we realise how conditioned these **ego-minds** are. We are, in fact, enslaved by them until we do our own inner spiritual work on ourselves.

It's almost as if we have another voice, another person inside our mind.

All you ever need to do from now on, then, is become more and more aware of, to notice more and more, the thoughts which whir away in your **emind**, your internal chatterbox. It is your **imind** which has the awareness and noticing capacity, and which observes everything. When your **imind** is noticing and observing your

emind activity - thoughts, feelings, reactions to triggers - then this is self-awareness, and it is the basis for you being able to absolutely empower yourself and transform your life. **Imind** gives you control over your emotions and feelings, your actions and reactions, and your language and behaviour. Emind is the boss in life, until such time as we become aware of our imind, and whenever we use our intelligence-mind it overrules ego-mind.

Watch yourself, watch your thoughts, and watch your emotional reactions to the things happening out there, the things people say and do. It is conscious living in action with your attention and mind's eye turned in on mind itself: it is your mind in action watching your mind. It sounds strange that our mind watches our mind, hence my separation of our mind into the ego-mind and intelligence-mind, each with their own functions and behaviours.

As you notice and observe how your emind reacts to life's happenings you will become more and more amazed at this incredible entity of creation and evolution. It's not all bad, but all the bad things humans ever do come from this emind of ours. Spiritual revolution, we can now say, is all about taming the destructive tendencies of our emind, and we use our imind to do this.

As well as observing inside our own being, we can of course observe others, watch them, listen to them, notice them, and we can do the same in nature and with the situations and happenings in our daily life. When we observe, and are conscious we are observing, we are in intelligence-mind mode with full awareness of life going on around us. In this observation and aware mode of the imind we get to learn so much about ourselves and our world.

Observing always means learning.

Now - and this is a crucial part of our revolution, and subsequent ongoing evolution - in our relationships in life with other people we talk and listen a lot. We are social animals and we communicate all the time - either with each other in person or online, or we are in the mode of reader, listener, or viewer of other people in the media as 'bystanders'. When we hear or read someone say something and judge what they say, or who they are, to be good or bad, right or wrong, acceptable or unacceptable, and all those kinds of automatic values-based reactions, we do so with our ego-mind. When you judge, it is your emind doing this, and your emind is judging other eminds, not the people themselves.

So if I say you are an arrogant person, a bad person, then the reality of this is that my emind is judging your emind. But you are not your emind, I am not mine, you are five dimensions, so am I, and our emind is but only one of those five dimensions. I am projecting my emind onto yours, and saying you're no good. Unfair of me! But no, wait, not unfair of *me*, unfair of *my ego-mind*. But, here's the thing, it's our eminds which do all the damage in life, and yet, beyond conscious thought we assume this emind of ours is who we are. Once we can see it in action, we can clearly realise no, this pesky inner chatterbox, the emind, is not who we are. From this realisation awaits your liberation from having to do what it tells you to do or say. Conscious living is imind in action, and it shows us the actions of our emind.

Our ego-mind is conditioned while we are young, by what I've been calling 'the system', to judge everything in this manner. The system 'taught' us what is right, what is wrong, what is knowledge, what we should believe and what we should think. If you want to unveil that system, if you want to see it up close and personal, practise using your imind to observe your emind in action, and to observe others acting out of their own eminds, and you will expose the system and all its negativity. We are not bad people! The system just made us think like this. The nasty system tried to infect us with its own badness, and did a very good job considering all the damage and destruction humans do to each other, and their planet, out of their ego-minds.

Spiritual revolution is to reverse, once and for all, this nasty nonsense perpetrated upon us by the system for centuries. Citizen by citizen, until it's spread around the world.

THERE ARE CULTURAL, societal, national differences in ego-minds. Emind reflects your environment and culture, most especially during your childhood, but it is ongoing through media, a gigantic emind if you like, which has an insidious influence over people's eminds.

Being British, my emind is highly sensitive to people jumping queues, which is anathema in Britain, and for several years living in Thailand I had a serious problem in shops because back in those days queuing to Thai people was a much looser arrangement. I - my emind - used to get so frustrated as I queued up like a proper Englishman and Thais would come and unashamedly barge right in at the front. I bristled inside and could not stop myself reacting negatively, but always kept it inside me.

I now look back and clearly see that this situation would trigger my ego-mind into anger and a sense of injustice, and it would provoke my innate impatience, filling me with negative energy. My emind was in control of me.

But what I really want to say is that it is in this impulse by all of us to judge each other's actions that we develop most of our problems. We blame them if they do something 'wrong' or 'bad' or 'unacceptable', and then dislike them if they're a stranger, or perhaps start building up resentments, bitterness, envy and the like if they are friends or colleagues. We may complain to them, and this causes negative energy flow between us, but the reality is that if I complain to you about something you have said or done, then it's my emind complaining and in all reality you will react negatively with your own emind, and there you have it, conflict has arisen. All blaming, complaining, moaning is the emind in action.

So, the emind judges, based on installed values and ideology, whereas imind observes, listens or reads carefully. As and when the emind pushes a judgement into our mind's eye, we stay with our imind to ignore the judgement and continue listening or watching until the end. In this way we can learn, and avoid creating a negative energy flow. Double win. Emind is only in control when we are not in the imind's conscious living mode. With imind in action, emind loses its power over us.

Also, we find it super easy to judge others negatively because we can clearly see their actions or hear what they say, but, until we know about our imind, nowhere near so easily do we see our own actions and words, and how they may be triggering problems in others. Herein lies everybody's propensity for hypocrisy and the pot calling the kettle black.

Only when we conceptually separate our mind into two minds, learn about our emind and its programmed ways, and that we can watch it with our imind, can we start to retrain ourselves into a more harmonious, happier person. The very act of spotting, with our imind, a negative feeling or thought arising in our emind is enough to take the heat out of the negative emotion. This is the beginning of the end of being controlled in our life by our emind's reactions to everything. The nasty system, and its ways of conflict, be damned! Spiritual liberation conquers emotional enslavement.

People may have done a 'bad' thing, but nevertheless we ourselves only have a problem if, through our emind, we react negatively. If we observe instead of judge, then by engaging our imind we firstly avoid complaining to the person, and secondly we may reflect that they are stressed and don't actually mean to cause any harm. We accept, the emind's negative energy is neutralised, and the other person's emind is not further antagonised.

I have seen it thousands of times in myself and others: if I react negatively with my emind to somebody else, then their emind will respond to my response with yet more negative energy, and so will my emind, and bang, we're both caught up in a ping pong battle until one of us backs down. One will back down and then feel a sense of injustice or unfairness. Perhaps the emind will remember that, and then emotions like resentment and bitterness start building up inside our emind, and this is like a mental cancer, eating away at us over time.

But, if somebody says something bad to me that my emind doesn't like, and I instead notice it with my imind, I can now feel empathy for their negative energy and space, not react with my emind which I've now neutralised with my imind noticing it, and now their emind has nobody to argue with! Eminds are looking for trouble when they're in negative mode, but if none comes back they run out of steam.

Eminds in positive, beautiful or fun environments are fine, but any time they think something is wrong, they engage in negative thoughts and feelings and then their owner feels negative energy.

Since the emind contains the system's programming/nurturing in it, from our schooldays and upbringing at home, in effect the system is controlling our life through our emind. Any time we get ourselves into the now-moment, into the present, we are in conscious living and in our imind, and we can prevent, neutralise or override our emind's automatic reaction. Conscious living nullifies the system. Just try it and keep on trying it. If you easily get angry or frustrated or impatient in life, just learn to notice it as it arises or as you are in the middle of the negative emotion, and as soon as you notice it you have disidentified and disengaged with it.

In quiet moments where you have created time and space to reflect, think of typical triggers in your life which make you react negatively. Write them down. Maybe do it now. Then, when they next occur you can intercept your emind's negative reaction with your imind, and in so doing you gain control of yourself. This is a revelation of the highest order!

Reflect upon things away from the heat of the battle of daily living, regularly creating time and space for you to do so, and then resolve to live consciously through noticing and observing things, or reading or listening to somebody without allowing your emind's judgements to stop your imind's focus. If your emind got the better of you today, got you emotionally uptight and perhaps you lashed out at a friend or a loved one, in your time to reflect you will be using your imind, and can feel that you'd like to apologise for your actions or words. The positive power we get from genuinely apologising, or receiving an apology, is powerful.

These ego-mind thoughts and feelings are *part* of who we are, but they are not *who* we are. We are 5DL, body, two minds, soul and the external environment, which means we have five influences upon our overall single entity. How many people carry self-doubt, insecurity, unworthiness in their mind? All of us! Well, dear reader, it's not you. It's just your emind reflecting whatever conditioning it received, and continues to receive.

When you use the outlook OOAAI tool to reset your

orientation, objectives, approach, attitude and intentions, what you're doing here is creating new foundations for your life, and this will be the start of overcoming the system's programming into you during your childhood. You use your imind to do the resetting and deprogramming.

We talked about reconditioning and re-educating ourselves, what we are doing is consciously hacking into our ego-mind to change its habits and reactions. We are overcoming the system's program and installing our own. After a while you will find that you no longer react automatically to negative triggers because you've practised accepting them with your imind, rather than resisting with your emind. At some point there won't even be anything left to accept. What you've done is retrained your autopilot into being a more positive supportive emind!

I COULD WRITE MORE and more and more on this, but I think and hope I've clearly distinguished between what your emind is and what your imind is. Now all you need to do is use OAR to guide you into your own full discoveries and understandings - observe with awareness and then reflect upon what you noticed. OAR is your door to enlightened living.

I shall shortly end the chapter with a sort of list of typical activities from both minds, and that will give you a nice working list to absolutely raise your awareness. Then it's a matter of practising using your imind to neutralise negative emind reactions until such time as you actually have retrained your emind to not even react negatively to this or that trigger.

Before that, a word on your **body, soul,** and **the external environment**, the other three dimensions of your 5DL, and how they link to the two minds.

Ostensibly speaking, the emind links to the **body** as being the unique entity and existence of who you are as an individual human being, the obvious bit of you which is you and not anybody else, while the imind links to the **soul** as being the universal expression of cosmic consciousness, awareness, and universal intelligence. Soul and imind are the same in all of us.

Yet interestingly your emind, while being unique to you, will share much in common with other members of your community or society or nation if you all received a similar schooling, upbringing and cultural input. However, your astrological charts and karmic and genetic heritage bless you with certain traits, preferences and skills. These will play out through your emind. I think therefore that our emind has elements of both nurture and nature in it. Let's remind ourselves, emind is not all bad, just that all bad comes from it.

Through the **soul** we are all one and the same, existing in an infinite timeless field and ocean of oneness, awareness, and universal intelligence. When we are in the moment, living and thinking consciously, we are operating through our soul and our awareness of this is through our intelligence-mind. Through imind and soul we are fully connected with everything, as is our nature to be so. Out of this connection we experience feelings of joy, unconditional love, empathy and so on.

For me, and many others I've communicated with, our soul is the micro version of the universe and the universe is the macro version of our soul. With our soul we are whole. We are intelligent individuals connected with everything else. To be connected like this should be our aim and our game.

If you were brought up in a happy family and home, eating a healthy diet, somehow received a proper education which sought to enable you to flower and flourish, as an individual human being, according to your natural impulses from your karmic, genetic and astrological influences, then your emind will reflect your positive start to life and you will have a healthy body. However, if you had tough or traumatic times at home as a kid, got the usual woeful and fear-based schooling that exists nearly everywhere, and imbibe the typically toxic media, then your emind will be filled with negative programming, impulses and instincts.

To the degree that you had a bad start in life, and thus an emind full of darkness, and are therefore likely to commit dark thoughts and deeds as an adult if in a non-supportive environment, then this is the degree of work you have to do to spiritually evolve and escape your emind's programming. But everybody can escape, just that some may have more work to do than others.

If you eat lots of sugar, eat junk foods and processed foods, drink lots of fizzy drinks, smoke, drink too much alcohol, take pills and drugs, then this is your emind looking for sensory pleasures to numb its pains, memories, traumas. You may know at an intuitive or even intelligent level that what you are doing is harming you, but your emind which is demanding such stuff will convince you that you can handle it or that you are not addicted and so on. Also, drugged or boozed up we appear to gain temporary refuge from our chatterbox emind that does all the negative self-talk.

It is clear that if the ego-mind gets a certain conditioning (past and/or present), it has no qualms in damaging the body to which it belongs. I've seen people in Asia literally almost kill themselves in the process of trying save their face, which is their emind completely out of control.

Turning to the **external environment**... this world of ours is a huge smorgasbord of offerings! There are those aspects of it from the Human-made World, which include culture, society, ideologies, concepts, education, media, science, religion, medicine, money, law, architecture. There are aspects of it from the Natural World, such as climate, geography, food, water, and all the various ecological systems. And then we have all the more galactic aspects to the EE such as the sun and moon, the planets, the stars and the whole universe itself. What minute little particles we are by comparison.

With the emind, we react to the external environment according to its conditioning, pretty much as with the rest of the animal kingdom; while with the imind, we either observe the happenings of the EE without reacting emotionally or behaviourally, or we use it to proactively direct positive energy flow into our external environment around us to make it better for all.

This positive energy comes from, for example, natural whole foods for the body, constructive and inspiring media and books, being with positive people, enjoying the arts and beauty, imbibing the delights of nature. I invite you to add to the list.

We use our imind to educate ourselves on important matters relating to health and wellness, and in so doing we help reorient our eminds towards healthier pursuits. More use of imind equals more positivity and more reconditioning of our emind.

On the other hand, if our environment brings us toxic foods, negative media, negative people, then we're feeding the dark bits of the emind and suppressing the imind and soul, and we're in deep trouble. Our only way out is to change our environment as much as we can, and to practise conscious living to neutralise that which we can't escape from.

Too much materialism means an out of control, overfed emind and little room for spiritual counterbalancing, and this is when our psychological and physical health suffers, as do our relationships with other people, and then addictions and harmful habits kick in.

Emind is the great disruptor and controller, carrying the system's anti-life, anti-love forces within it from what seems to me a few thousand years of human subconscious psyche in the making. Just take a look at its CV, and see which apply to your own emind:

- it's political and ideological, inflexible
- it puts us down and puts others down, things and people are not good enough
- it gets greedy, entitled, envious, selfish, always wanting and wanting more
- it follows orders if there is a threat of pain, yet will easily be addicted to substances that cause pain
- it creates fear, anxiety and worry
- it is always trying to take us out of the current moment because its life force is in the past and future
- it can be vindictive, brutal, cruel
- it can be hateful, intolerant
- it deceives, lies, cheats

- it can make us feel unworthy, stupid, powerless
- it brings shame and guilt to us
- it can make us feel small, or it can humiliate others
- and the list can go on and on and on.

Emind has various recognisable voices in the head - see which of them apply to you sometimes or frequently: *the worrier, the controller, the judge, the self-doubter, the rager, the idler, the uptight, the perfectionist, the moaner, the blamer, the entitled, the deceiver, the liar.*

It is also against change, and will resist being taken from its perceived comfort zone even if being in that zone is harmful to your health.

But always remember: the emind is not you, it's a program from your society, and from the whole past of human existence. And always remember too: it's not fixed - you have the imind and soul available to help you turn your life around, to reprogram it, or to fine-tune a few things if you've already done a lot of inner work.

If you are a person with power, who has hurt and bullied others by force or coercion, then you can fix this. If you have been a victim, taken advantage of, easily led, reluctant to express yourself, well... you don't have to be any longer, you can fix it. Starting right now.

Resuscitate your hibernating intelligence-mind, tap into your soul. Redo the tasks throughout the book and in this chapter, create your own tasks and challenges, and in this way you get real practice in conscious living. And, whenever you're in a rut, ask yourself what your current diet looks like. Seek out fresh produce and whole foods to eat, minimise animal foods and drink lots of juices, herbal teas and water. A nutritious diet can very quickly bring positive feelings into the body and from there you can build momentum. See the *Desserts* section of the book.

Oh, and remember you can always invoke your imind into action by remembering to focus on your breathing, sitting posture, walking posture, and eating. You can always sit in nature, or an urban setting, and listen to the sounds and view the sights, and then notice as your emind does its best to hijack your mind's eye with its thoughts and judgements. Get good music into your imind and soul, get nature in there, find inspiring voices on the internet if none exist around you.

Let's end on a positive note with a list of imind actions and ways of being. Learning and intelligent living are at the heart of its remit. One, traditional, method of learning is memorising and I have just the task for you…

Task

i) Look at the list of the following cognitive actions and ways of being that your intelligence-mind can carry out, and memorise as many as you can. Give yourself, I suggest, four or five minutes. After your time is up, write down in your notebook as many as you can remember.

The imind observes, notices, realises, is aware, reflects; it is timeless and spaceless, is conscious and consciousness; it discerns, intuits, understands, concentrates, pays attention; it learns, reads, listens; it loves unconditionally, respects, trusts, empathises; it collaborates, empowers, transcends, transforms, cultivates, creates, produces, motivates, inspires, enables, encourages, enlightens, emboldens, harmonises, helps, gives, shares, cares, builds.

And you used your imind to do that task!

ii) Choose some of them, say half a dozen or so, and resolve to really put them into your daily life, to make a habit out of them in the coming days and weeks. If you like, memorise your choices and go through them each time you go to bed, and let them swim around in your mind as you sleep.

YOU, **the real you**, are the holistic sum of the ever-changing influences of five dimensions. Your body is your house or temple, your emind is the program of your subconsciously-lived life which reflects your education and environment, your imind is your link to your soul which is supreme intelligence, joy and ineffable love, and your soul is your micro portion of the universe inside your being. All four dimensions are inextricably linked to the external environment, in terms of their structure and their continued need for sustenance and 'food' from the EE.

Your personal evolution is enabled and harmonised by creating a balance between your earthly body and universal soul, between your material and spiritual needs, and between your needs and other people's needs. You will also be looking to find a beautiful balance between your autopilot, instantly-reacting emind being in charge, and using your conscious living imind to guide you in your life.

Emind, or your ego as it is usually called, is not to be got rid of, you can't, its voices will never leave your mind until you die. But by using your imind and soul, practising conscious living, and committing to being a lifelong learner, you can reeducate and recondition your ego-mind so that it serves you so much better in life.

In essence, by your proactive efforts you create for yourself a less destructive and more agreeable ego-mind, but on the occasions it brings you trouble you simply turn to your imind for solutions, to help you mitigate any damage, and for apologising or forgiving if need be. And that might be saying sorry to yourself - your 5DL - for the actions of your emind dimension.

Thus, spiritual revolution is not about getting rid of anything, it's all about living in balance and harmony, and that requires us to get good information and cultivate our natural inborn intelligence that we were all born with.

Then we can naturally evolve as we navigate along the highways of life.

15

YOUR BODY IS YOUR TEMPLE, YOUR SOUL MAKES YOU WHOLE

What is your relationship with your body? Do you take care of it, or take it for granted? What do you feed it? What do you put on it?

How do you feed your soul? How often do you feel connected with your soul? What is your soul?

I would like to open by saying that just deciding to treat your body like a beautiful temple will, in itself, help you transform your life and turn your health around. Your body is literally your home, your constant forever home, you will never leave it until you are done with this life. If you can't love your body, you can't love your home and you can't love your life. Everything starts and ends with your body.

Revere it, take great care of it, make it a beautiful home to be in and make this your very starting point for your spiritual revolution. Anything which encourages vitality, vim and vigour in your body will do the same for your mind and soul, your whole being. Taking care of your body is taking full care of your physical, mental and spiritual health. It's hard to live spiritually and harmoniously if our body is sick or lacking in energy.

And I specifically mean the contents rather than the surface! Image is great, of course, we all like to look good and so we should, but not at the expense of substance. Take care of your inner body and you can be sure the outer will reflect your inner wellbeing. You will shine and exude wellbeing. Focusing on substance makes image great too, focusing on image is often liable to neglecting and messing up the substance. Many products on the market selling to image are full of toxic chemicals, and what goes on your body goes inside your body.

Be good inside and you are made. Feel good by your own feelings, feel good within by connecting with nature and the universe, don't depend on, or pander to, peer approval. They don't have to live inside your body and mind, you do. Make them hospitable places to be.

Despite what I've just said, and looking around society, especially in the last couple of generations, one would think much of humanity doesn't care two hoots about its body. In fact, it seems to treat it more like a garbage dump for all the things which will make it not function properly. All things which will look after it and promote its wellbeing have been eschewed in favour of all things which will attack it. If we poison our body like this, remain ignorant of it and what we are doing to it, then we will never ever have psychological and spiritual wellbeing. We will forever be pretending we are mentally and emotionally well, often deceiving ourselves as well as others while inside we are unhappy and unfulfilled. This is the astonishing emind at work, being ignorant and/or practising deception to hide its crimes from your imind. Imind, if engaged, will not allow toxic stuff to come into the body.

If we eat a diet of corporate-made convenience foods which are processed, full of chemicals, or genetically modified, then we cannot live with a sound mind, nor will we experience much of our soul, if anything at all. Impossible my friend. At very young ages we may appear to get away with it, but it doesn't take long before the body goes way out of shape, and various ailments and diseases begin to appear on the horizon, afflicting the body, and therefore the mind and spirit. Past actions are now karmically catching up with us. And without making changes we will not escape this karmic path we have induced upon ourselves. Karma takes ignorance and inattention fully into account!

In the past, many religions and religious sects somehow made it seem like the body should be neglected, and any love of it would mean we were going against God and against the sanctity of the soul. We should focus, they said, on getting rid of our ego, getting rid of our emind, by getting rid of all attachment to our body.

Pure nonsense I say! Emind and body are an integral part of who we are, neglecting them is neglecting our self, our essence, our inner wellbeing, our 5DL. Look at all the stunning temples, mosques, churches and other religious buildings, beautiful works of art, yet we neglect our body?! No more of this absurdity I say, make your body your shrine.

Our modern-day material world says consume, consume, consume, like there's no tomorrow. Eat this drink that, anything you want, do this do that, booze, drugs, smokes, pills, anything you want, that's individual freedom and that's the way to go, yeah baby! (And we make our profits selling it all to you, but we're not talking about that.)

No madam, no sir, that is not the way to go. All the pleasures experienced by your tongue and emind may feel good today, but we all know there'll be a price to pay, even if we have not yet received the bill. Our emind will convince us of anything if there's pleasure and sensory stimulation to be had. Take sex, one of the biggest stimulatory pleasures we can feel in our body, how glorious and wonderful it feels! But, overdo it and you will suffer and pay the price with your health. And for sex, read alcohol, drugs, pills, comfort foods and anything else which stimulates our tongue and body, thereby stimulating and feeding our ego-mind. Pleasure today, yes, but most certainly one day this will become pain. That's karma and it's non-negotiable.

I read once that when we get stressed we drink more, and when we drink more we get stressed more. It becomes a vicious cycle.

Same for any other addictive substance. One must cut the cycle if caught up in it. Good foods are always a good place to start, the body wants good foods with nutrients in them, not toxic chemicals that the food corporations think we should be ingesting all the time. Feed your body, not your tongue.

I'D LIKE to share an observation with you to sum up our era which is marked by heavy consumerism, consumption, and so-called individual freedom. I will relate things in the order that I thought about them, which is not chronological. I am going to tell you my tale straight to help make my point relating to the matter of health and us seeking a life of wellness. 'Fat' in many contexts has become a rather derogatory term, and of course I mean no harm to anybody here, but we must face up to health problems rather than hide from them, and that means collectively as well as individually, and it means not shying away from language. Being overweight, fat, obese will definitively impact negatively upon one's health and longevity.

As you know, I arrived in Thailand in 1991 and ended up living here. I quickly noticed barely anybody was overweight, all had a 'normal' body size. I met so many people on my travels and so many more in my classrooms and teaching work, and Bangkok itself which is a teeming metropolis. An overweight person was very rare, an outright fat person was even rarer, and obesity was nowhere to be seen. This was the case for some or all of the 90s, can't remember. I just clearly recall seeing things when I got here, for it contrasted with my native nation England which at that time was now fighting a real obesity problem.

Fast forward to about four years ago, so nearing 2020, and I went to Burma for the first time with some colleagues to team-teach many Burmese teachers at Moulmein University how to deliver student-centred lessons. Burma by now was just opening up to the world after years of being closed by its military rulers, and these teachers after their training were going back to their towns and villages, and in this way education was going to be the way for lifting people out of boredom and poverty. When I travel I'm super alert and feel super alive, and I realised I was noticing the same things in Burma that I had noticed in Thailand a generation previously. No overweight or fat or obese people, none. I was there for a week, in the third biggest town of the country.

I then started thinking about it and realised that by now Thailand had many more overweight people, and quite a few fat and obese people. This rise in body weight in Thailand came about at the same time as a massive rise in the availability of western-style fast food, junk food outlets, and an increased consumption of factory-farmed meat and refined sugars. The natural Thai diet, as in Burma, is full of whole foods, herbs and spices. But convenience foods were now everywhere.

Round about the same time, now back home after my exciting trip to Burma, I watched a documentary film of the Rolling Stones giving a free concert in Hyde Park in London in 1969. That is, a generation before I went to Thailand. Now, there were half a million people in the crowd that day, and you know what? Nobody was overweight, nobody! I then started looking more closely when watching old TV footage of sports events or TV series, both in the UK and US, and it was clear that in the 70s very few western people were overweight, even fewer were fat, and obesity seemed pretty much absent.

Here's the thing. In Burma today it is like Thailand one generation before, which itself was like the UK and US one generation before that. Developed nations started getting fatter, then developing nations followed suit a generation later, and one imagines that third world nations may some time soon face the same problem. Shitty 'foods' are spreading around the world, brought to us all by the whole corporate juggernaut, and are ruining people's health and wellbeing.

They then need the corporations' medicines and pills…

This change in the typical body shape of citizens, in my view, is the mark of material 'progress', and the advent and spread of junk foods, processed foods, GM foods, and so-called 'modern' factory farm approaches to food production. In Moulmein there were no fast-food restaurants at all, not even any factory-farmed meat that I could see. We had chicken which was sinewy and more chewy, and reminded me of how chicken tasted when I was a boy back in England. In Thailand in the early 1990s there very few fast-food shops, and I recall as a kid in England in the late 1970s the first KFC shops arriving on the scene. I can also say that about the time I went to Burma, I also went for a holiday to Hanoi in Vietnam, and I saw only one KFC outlet, no other fast-food outlets. I saw no weight problem with the Hanoians.

I share with you my anecdote to illustrate how humanity's health is rapidly going down the toilet as it eats more and more unnatural foods. Hospitals are super busy, pharmacies are doing a roaring trade, and demand for pills has gone through the roof. Nations everywhere spend huge amounts of their money and resources on sickness and disease. It's because we eat convenience, toxic, chemical-ridden foods which exert a tremendous burden on our body and its ability to process all this incoming poisonous junk.

To be frank, much of humanity is now addicted to eating shit. It's by design because it's addictive to the tongue and thus super profitable. I saw a BBC documentary a few years back during my main research into diet and nutrition, in which they talked about jobs within the food corporations going by the title of 'craveability expert'. They were tasked with making foods so that our tongues would trip the taste fantastic, triggering our eminds into demanding more and more of them. These corporations are deliberately stoking addictions, but which do no favours to our wellbeing whatsoever, and which will only send us to the hospitals and pharmacies down the line when the karmic price is due.

And as I did all my research back in 2008 and over the next few years, I alarmingly discovered, just as I was embarking upon eating a much healthier diet and feeling really good about it, that even all the good foods such as vegetables, fruits, nuts, seeds and grains were being grown with tonnes of chemicals sprayed onto them, in soils being depleted of their natural levels of minerals and other nutrients by these massive monoculture farms. And then I found out about the meats and dairy foods coming from animals living in factory farms which are akin to concentration camps. Zero compassion for fellow living beings.

What are we humans doing to ourselves, the animals, and our planet?

I have said that we live in a disconnected manner from each other and from our planet, thinking we are separate to everything, and this agricultural system of ours is the consequence, a simply dreadful relationship with our foods, our food production, and the rampant poisoning of our soils, rivers, waterways and underground water reservoirs, while treating our livestock in the most brutal way imaginable.

It is from such animals (I call them MPOs - meat-producing organisms) that most of today's meats, cheeses and other dairy foods are produced and made. And how could an animal living in a concentration camp, where it can barely move during its life, not be completely sick? Yet this produces human food. In recent times the mass media like to warn us gravely of climate change, but nary a word is mentioned about our farming practices and corporate-made 'foods' which surely must be ravaging all the ecosystems, not just of Mother Earth, but all the humans who eat such 'foods'.

As we are an amalgamation of five dimensions of life, it is indeed abundantly clear, when we look into such things, that by poisoning our foods, air, drinking water, and general environment, we similarly are poisoning our own inner ecosystems. For the rivers think of your blood, for the soils and earth think of your flesh and bones, for the air think of your lungs.

Regardless of the merits of the climate change argument, in my view focusing on this is a terrible diversion from the real damage being done in our name, and it is the usual suspect thinking that comes from the absurd idea we humans are separate from Mother Earth and her ecosystems. Modern humankind has still not learned about the natural law of karma. Stop trying to change the climate and start treating the earth, air and water with respect! Stop decimating forests and treating trees with zero respect, stop depleting the soils, stop your factory farms, stop this monocultural approach to food production. Stop treating the symptoms and get down to the root causes. Then we can be sure the climate will do what it does.

Stop poisoning everything that lives. Including us.

Anyway, if we want to treat our body like a temple, and every single spiritually-minded person will do, and every single human being who would like to live with wellbeing and inner peace of mind will do, then we must find good foods to consume. We must learn about the nutrients and the toxins.

We do indeed do that in the diet chapter in the *Desserts* section. If we have a struggling body, full of tension, pains and ailments then there's no way we can be happy and feel an inner peace and joy about being alive. Body comes first in the spiritual seeker's journey, no doubts in my mind. I mean no doubts in my imind.

It's mind-blowing to me we were never taught about our body at school. In biology I was taught about the amoeba and the sheep. Not my own body!! Now is the time to correct this incredible ignorance they pushed onto us. And I can tell you, from all my research (don't take my word for it, research it for yourself, it's contentious!), that the way our mainstream doctors are trained in medical college, they themselves don't know the full proper way our body works. If they did know, why are billions of people sick and dependent on pills to keep them going??? And, did you know, they get virtually zero training about food and nutrition?

One example which I've experienced, to illustrate. Knee problems. My massage lady (hi Hong!) has studied traditional Thai medicine, herbs, natural childbirth, massage for several years and is a super source of intelligence for me relating to how the body works. I've known her and regularly availed myself of her professionalism for over five years, and we talk a lot about the inner workings of both body and mind. She is clear that most of the time a knee problem indicates hip problems as the root cause. The knee itself is fine, but the struggling hips are creating blockages of energy which affect the knees. She works on the hip and then the knee problem goes away! She tells me the problem is that with so many people living too sedentary a lifestyle, doing too much sitting down, the hips are relatively unused and this creates tensions and energy blockages, which often are felt in the knee. Yet, in western nations many people not even 50 or so are having knee replacement surgery when in all likelihood there's nothing wrong with the knee! Just learn to give your hips movement. Use it or lose it. Your hips are the central hinge in your body, linking the two halves.

Trouble is that our modern-day medical system only focuses on the symptoms, does not seek to address root causes. Too many healthy people is a drain on profits. Remember, everything in life is interconnected, and so is everything within your body. Just because you have a headache doesn't mean the problem is in your head! Many of our problems are caused by overburdened organs. But again, we're not taught or informed of this.

I would like to present to you my basic understanding of the body which comes from all my varied research. I'm not going to dive into books to remind me of things, I want to show you what I, an ordinary citizen, can learn and remember for myself, and therefore so can you too. I absolutely encourage you to do research and get to know the contents, systems and processes of your body intimately. Ayurveda and Traditional Chinese Medicine (TCM) will be great sources, especially the former which has so many more books in the English language to help us learn. There are any number of natural health websites which you can read and learn from too. Whatever unique bodily ailments you suffer from can be your starting point for your research.

However, as you may already have found out: there is so much conflicting information out there about everything to do with health. One day we may have a mainstream healthcare system set up for wellness rather than illness.

One thing you will find, I'm sure, is that the more you learn and understand about the inner workings of your body, the more you will want to treat it well and the less you will succumb to previously harmful habits and addictions. Shattering our ignorance of our own body helps to shatter the hold that addictions have on our eminds. Just by treating our body better and making it feel healthier and more vibrant helps us to recondition our emind into less damaging impulses.

I think some key parts to know about are your immune system, tongue, liver, kidneys, stomach, intestines, blood, lymph, hormones, muscles and bones.

YOUR TONGUE IS PRETTY small but it can do tremendous amounts of damage to you and to others! It can speak with acid, bile and cruelty. It can be cutting and truly awful towards other people and often the very ones we love the most, and it moves in these ways, saying these words, according to your ego-mind's workings when there is no imind to restrain it.

But the real damage it can do to you is when it loves those tastes which come from the junk, processed, and sugary foods. It craves such tastes and easily becomes addicted to them. Eating such foods all the time is like pouring acid into yourself in slow motion. They are eating up your insides, and overheating your organs, the engine of your body. You are asking for many future health ailments and diseases, misery and pain, and to die before your time. You will simply have to break any control your tongue has over you to achieve wellness in your life. One of America's finest herbalists in the 20th century, Dr Christopher Ray, who travelled all over the nation in his mission to try and get a herbal dispensary in every county, said his biggest challenge in helping people heal themselves was their tongues! People just do not want to change their diet, but if you want wellness there's no choice.

Consider your teeth, eyes, ears, nose, all in the vicinity of your brain and all of which need looking after. If we are good, we clean our teeth twice a day (but check out the ingredients and ask yourself if you'd like to find a different kind of toothpaste), but who actively takes care of their eyes and ears and nose? Ayurveda promotes proactive care and maintenance of these crucial sensory organs. I've paid the price somewhat with my eyes because when I was young nobody ever said anything about the need to proactively look after them. Same with the ears. However, clean up your body, detox, change your diet to whole foods, read and listen to positive and informative things, ensure your body gets lots of movement, and slowly but surely all parts of your body start improving. You can do eye exercises, and you can use a neti pot with your nose. I frequently pull my ears this way and that way in my morning routine, which is said to increase energy flow everywhere.

Let's go inside, where we can't see, and, as they say, out of sight out of mind. But no no no, don't ignore this part of your body anymore! Nearly all of your body is out of sight. First and foremost, you will want to know about your organs, namely the liver, kidneys, heart, lungs, spleen, pancreas, stomach, gallbladder and the intestines. I think that's the lot. Learn what they do and what their role is. The key ones I always think about are the liver, kidneys and heart.

In traditional Chinese medicine they are intimately interlinked whereby the kidneys are the mother of the liver and the liver is the father of the heart. TCM talks about the five elements of life - wood, fire, earth, metal and water - which relate to the five major organs of our liver, heart-mind, spleen-pancreas, lungs, and kidneys respectively. Each organ has its specific duties, and each interlink with the others, as per the interconnected nature of everything on our planet and in our own bodies.

Your organs are your engine. When the engine functions well, so does the rest of the 'machine'. Overwork your engine, or feed it poor quality fuels, and you can imagine what will happen...

Your liver has many functions, including the processing of all toxins and pollutants. If you take care of your liver, you will live well. Healthy livers lead to healthy livers of life, get it?! Poor quality foods, alcohol, pills, chemicals, heavy metals are all poisons which have to be processed by your liver. When you get any kind of ailment, chances are your liver is struggling.

Your kidneys are a major elimination organ, along with your intestines and skin. Kidneys that have lots of toxic stuff to eliminate begin to struggle, and two symptoms I know very well are lower back pain and a sort of ringing sound in the ears. It's simple, if I drink too much beer, eat too many animal foods and sugary foods then my back starts playing up. Weakened kidney function. Taking in the wrong foods and alcohol and so on taxes the liver, which has to process it all first, and I've read in TCM literature that the overburdened liver turns to the kidneys to get some essence from them to help the liver do its hard work, and this in turn weakens the kidneys. Whenever I return to my wellness wagon, all symptoms disappear in short order!

They don't tell you this anywhere in mainstream, and certainly not in the hospitals.

Each organ is also linked to certain emotions, and when the liver struggles, we become more susceptible to anger and impatience and frustration. Excessive worry leads to kidney struggles, and kidney struggles lead to excess worry. When the heart struggles there is little happiness or love available for you. Certainly, when my diet is good my natural impatience disappears, and I feel great joys in my heart. Clearly a happy liver means a happy me.

The stomach is these days said to have its own mind. Gut instinct, yeah! In Ayurveda they consider the stomach the seat of your health. I notice so many people almost gulping down their food, ignoring the role that chewing one's food thoroughly has in beginning the digestive process, and so their stomach has so much more work to do, and this will lead to problems and symptoms. One of my students once told me to drink only a little water with meals, and certainly not any ice-cold water, because it hinders our digestive work.

Which leads us to the processes in our body, which include digestion, assimilation, excretion, blood flow, and lymph movement. You may eat healthy foods, but if you can't digest them properly and therefore utilise and assimilate the nutrients, you may not benefit much. That you can't do this will be from years of eating the wrong, toxic foods, which start piling up inside your intestines, unable to be fully digested, and slowly blocking your body's absorption of nutrients. When the organs cannot process the waste, they send the 'sludge' to other parts of the body to be stored away from your viscera (where all the organs are housed) which is too important to be blocked. And so our body gets blocked up over time, and therefore even nutritious foods may not do us much good until we have detoxed all the crap out of our system. Joint pain, arthritis, kidney stones, gout, all such ailments are down to a poor diet.

Symptoms of any kind in your body will inevitably mean blockages, and that your organs are overworked and your blood flow is impaired. Solution? Take care of your organs and blood!

When we do detox, if we do, then this induces the stored toxic sludge to move back towards the organs for processing and excreting. Also, it leaves your body through your skin, your biggest organ of elimination. This is when we feel pains and problems in our body, but this is a healing reaction rather than illness. You will need guidance on detoxing from those who have done it themselves, or just do lots of research. More on this in the upcoming food and diet chapter. I've only done one detox program, about a decade ago, and it was for two months, but I still had three meals a day. There's a whole industry on detox, but be careful as always with conflicting information. A good diet and plenty of movement for your body means automatic detoxing, not so fast, but steadily, and you notice improvements pretty quickly.

My wife and I did a three-day apple juice fast once, but aside from that I've not really done any fasting. I often plan to, but never get round to it. I've met a few people who do a one day fast each week. Pick a day, and drink a juice, or just drink water and/or herbal teas. In this way your body gets about 36 hours of no food to digest, and can instead then use its energy and resources to direct towards regeneration work.

Our body is constantly reacting to the external environment, whether to the foods coming into our mouth, or the impressions, information and ideas coming into our minds. Such reactions involve the release of hormones and chemical exchanges, and this will give us good feelings or bad feelings depending on what is coming in. Stressful situations trigger adrenaline for example, to give us extra muscle strength to deal with the perceived danger. Too much of this overworks the body and its organs, leading to ailments and diseases over time.

Hormones and their release are governed by various glands,

such as the adrenals, thyroid, pineal, pituitary and so on. I've read, for example, that a lack of iodine leads to thyroid issues which in turn leads to various symptoms. I've also read that fluoride in tap water leads to a struggling pineal gland, which in turn is responsible for much of our spiritual connections in our life. Everything in your body is interlinked! Be savvy about chemicals and toxins and limit your intake as far as you can.

With muscles, it's very much a case of use them or lose them. Essential to give them workouts, and we look at that in the next section of the book. But briefly for now, muscles need both contraction and expansion, and often in our modern lifestyle people's muscles get little expansion, just contraction. Make sure your muscles get both. I do morning stretches, and take breaks from computer work to expand my hands and fingers and other muscles.

Bones lose their strength when we eat too many animal foods, refined sugars and flours, processed foods and fizzy drinks. Such foods lead to too much acidity in our body, and so it turns to the bones to get some calcium out of them to neutralise your pH and bring your body back into balance. Eat plenty of alkalising veggies and fruits! Drink green juices, take superfoods, make sure you get those alkalisers into you, and then you will have strong bones and a strong body.

There is so much more to the body! This is just a brief tour off the top of my head. As you know well by now, one of my key messages is that information and understanding is the responsibility of each of us, and it's far better that you do your own research than me do it for you and post it here. Why should I be trusted on such important matters?! Not only that, we each of us have a unique constitution and unique challenges, albeit within the framework of core understandings and knowledge of how the generic human body works. That said, there is more on the body in the *Desserts* section.

The best research you can do is on yourself, meaning to change your diet to a healthy one that will help your body detox itself from years of too much damaging stuff coming in, and being stored in the gut or elsewhere in the body. Then, keep a written or typed 'food and feelings' diary which will help focus your observation and awareness on your inner feelings in your body as it changes and begins to rejuvenate itself. You will quickly notice that a new improved diet will transform your mental and emotional mood and feelings.

I must finish this visit into the body with mention of our immune system, blood and lymph. Your immune system is responsible for dealing with things like viruses, unfriendly bacteria, parasites, germs, and all kinds of manmade environmental poisons and pollution. When you have a healthy diet and healthy body, whose organs are not overtaxed and are able to deal with incoming toxins and chemicals, your immune system can easily manage incoming invaders, meaning that you rarely get colds or the flu. When you regularly get colds or the flu this is your body's innate intelligence doing the work it needs to in order to detox the build-up of mucous and other baddies in your body. It will give you a fever to sweat some of them out, and it will make you feel low in energy to try and force you to take rest and stop eating, so that it can rid itself of the baddies you have put into it. Loads of excess mucous will come out through your runny nose.

I regularly got colds and flu living in England when I was younger, and I put it down to the diet there which includes so much dairy and meat, and so many refined sugar and flour foods, all of which produce mucous in our body. Nowadays, hardly ever do I get a cold. Sometimes I feel a cold trying to get into me, but I just take vitamin C, echinacea, and other herbs or superfoods and chase it away most of the time. The immune system is your castle, your army of soldiers, your best friend. Look after it: don't feed your tongue, feed your immune system. The next section covers this.

I can't really articulate too well how the immune system works, but it's really just important to be aware of it and that you can either attack it or boost it by your dietary and lifestyle choices. Take care of it, your liver, your kidneys and your heart, and I think your body will be most thankful to you and reward you with wellness. I can easily recommend you research all this stuff by turning to books or websites on Ayurveda and TCM. I've learned a lot of my stuff on health from these sources. They carry thousand of years of tried and tested understandings, treatments, prevention protocols and so on.

Your blood carries nutrients and toxins (up to you which) to your whole body, while your lymphatic system carries waste in its lymph to be excreted when doing your number two. Blood is naturally pumped by the heart, but lymph has no such pump, and only flows properly when your body moves a lot. So, lack of exercise, a job sitting down all the time, and you are asking for constipation issues, skin eruptions, varicose veins and the like. And when the lymph gets backed up, this is like the pipes of a sewage system getting blocked up…

The body is a simply miraculous creation, with everything it needs to protect you. Creation, God, Mother Nature know best. Our only trouble is that humanity, thinking it knows best, has decided to poison just about everything it touches, including our very bodies, and this means our immune system and organs have so much work to do, hence we get sickness and disease, and hence hospitals and pharmacies are so busy. As the body struggles, so too does the mind, and we feel unhappy, angry, worried and all the rest of it.

It truly is staggering how ignorant and arrogant our species has become over however many years. In our ignorance and arrogance we think we are intelligent and all-powerful, yet look at how little we know about our body, mind and soul, and look at the state of our health.

They want to give us pills, vaccinations, surgeries, but the universe and universal intelligence knows best, not humankind. A judicious use of those medical interventions may be useful on occasion, but many people take pills as if they are food. These in turn begin to tax our liver and other organs thanks to their chemical and synthetic ingredients, adding to the already existing burden from our foods, polluted air and drinking water. All their medical interventions carry warnings of such side effects, so this is not conjecture.

I have read it, 'You are not sick, you are being poisoned'. I said this right at the outset of our journey together, that humanity is poisoning itself and our planet.

As I write this chapter we're in 2020, the year of the 'covid' virus. Regardless of the debates about it all, one thing is absolutely certain to me from my investigations into the media and governments of the major 'developed', 'civilised' and 'free' nations of the world: there is almost no information on how to boost our immune system, how to prevent ourselves falling ill, how to take care of our liver and kidneys, nothing told to us about diet, sunlight, fresh air, walks in nature… an abomination of ignorance, or worse. In fact, just about all government advice in western nations has been to do the very things which attack our health. Not a word about the immune system, and requesting the public to do things all of which subject it to much stress and a bigger workload. And I include fear, psychological separation and suchlike, which attacks our mental health, which of course leads to a decrease in physical health. Poor old soul is well trodden on.

If we want to be healthy, it's simple: develop healthy relationships with the external environment. Eat good foods, breathe fresh air, drink clean water, get your sunlight and imbibe nature. And I certainly recommend you partake of herbs and superfoods to add extra nutrients to your body, in healthy times as well as to treat specific problems, and take pills only when absolutely necessary. I've hardly taken any pills in my life, my mum always said when me and my sister got colds that the so-called remedies didn't work, and that they blocked our body from doing its innate healing. If you cut yourself your body fixes the cut naturally. That's your immune system for you doing its work. Same for inside your body. Treat it like a temple, and your immune system and organs will reward you.

However, as an individual we may not be able to choose the air we breathe, our drinking water and so on. All I can say is that when you sit down and think about it, reflect on the ways you can help boost rather than bust your body - you will find much you can do within the limitations imposed on you by your external environment and/or the government.

Meanwhile, put pressure upwards on the movers, shakers and leaders of your community and nation to ensure you get clean air, good drinking water, and whole foods.

If you don't love your body now, make good changes so that it will change and then you can love it. Make it look good! Make it feel good! Love it, adorn it, revere it, keep it clean and in tiptop shape, and just see how you feel in your mind and spirit. See how your soul leaps into your consciousness, triggering your imind into action and allowing it to monitor and neutralise any negative emind activity. Sincerely, a spiritual person will be most wise to take great care of their body. It is your home, and nobody in their right mind will knowingly continue dumping rubbish into their home. Only an emind programmed into ignorance will do that.

THE SOUL. Your soul makes you whole. If you are unhappy, unfulfilled, wanting, empty, depressed, stressed, or if life simply seems rather meaningless and boring, this is a strong sign your soul is hidden from you. If you are wealthy and/or powerful, yet wonder why you're not happy, then you need to find your soul and overcome attachments and cravings for evermore money and power. Such desires from your emind control you, stopping you from being free despite the 'luxury' of money and power. You can buy goods, but you can't buy happiness and health.

Increasingly so, through my two generation's worth of life, this is the situation. The system, which promotes this consumptive acquisitive approach to life, is eating us all and itself. In the process, it displays total disregard for the ecology of the planet that gives us all life. Consuming, eating, devouring, like rampaging locusts without thought of giving back to the world from which it takes takes takes, is insane destructive behaviour.

The love, joy and harmony that an active soul can bring to people has all but been removed from those living in mainstream 'developed' societies. I see the same in developing nations where economic progress brings the same overly material problems to the people, encouraging the pursuit of money, possessions and sensory stimulation over health and harmony.

We need soul, we need spirit, we need essence, we need love, and we need courage to unleash it all. We need spunk and funk, and no more junk! Until then humanity will continue with its struggles and problems and conflicts. You not have soul, you not whole!

When we work on improving our diet, and filtering out toxic and negative mental information and ideas, we start creating fertile internal conditions for activating our previously suppressed soul. Happiness, inner peace of mind, joy cannot be found 'out there', rather, such inner states of being arise only with an active soul. Boosting physical and mental health naturally boosts our spiritual health, and once our soul becomes active it in turn repays the favours to our body and mind.

Soul is connection. Materialism is disconnection.

Task

I have a Nina Simone song I'd like to task you with listening to, and you can look up the lyrics online if you like too, however, she sings super clearly. I'm not allowed for copyright reasons to put the lyrics here. In my view this song illustrates perfectly the soul in action, better than any effort by me to describe it in words. You will know your own soul too, better than I can tell you, and often you'll feel it when you are in nature. All humans, especially urban-dwelling ones, are instinctively drawn to nature when possible, and it's simple, it feeds our body and soul with negative ions, infusing us with joy and good vibes. Have you ever noticed food tasting better by the sea or by a lake or river? And how good picnics are?

Nina Simone's song 'Feeling Good' expresses this innate joy just beautifully. Give it a listen now and put some smiles into your heart and soul! Only read on once you've listened. And listen several times if you like!

. . .

I THINK she's captured in language the essence of our soul, and how we know what it feels like. In my view of things Nina is completely connected to her soul when she writes and sings this song, and it's all about nature knowing how 'she' feels. Soul is hard to define in language, but when we *feel* 'it' and when we *experience* 'it', we know it.

When we feel at one with the world, at ease, we offer no resistance, when we feel like everything is as it should be, there is nothing vexing us, nothing is out of place, when we are tuned into nature, tuned into the rhythms and natural pace of life, and tuned into all the happenings of the natural world, as Nina is in this song of hers, then inner peace and harmony is ours, and an indescribable joy fills our heart and being and we are at one with our soul.

In this moment, in this feeling, I am my soul, my soul is me, there is a sense of oneness. I am the universe and nature and the universe and nature are me, we are but one with no separation. This, for me, is how love and joy come into being, when I feel completely connected with all of life.

Nina sings about the nature as if she and the nature are one and the same, hence nature knows exactly how she feels because she is that nature, that nature is her. She is one and the same as the fish, the dragonflies, the birds and the butterflies; she is one and the same as the sun, the river and the stars. She sings of a new dawn because, I think, when we're in soul mode there is no old, no known, everything is continuously new in the timelessness of cosmic consciousness. It's like everything is upside down from what the time- and space-based emind knows and experiences about life.

The blend that we have talked of, the blend of the outer world and our inner world, of what we perceive outside of us as received by our mind's eye, is in perfect harmony.

And in this harmony the emind is silent. Only when the emind is silent does the soul arise.

Also, in Nina's song she uses present tenses, singing about now and the current moment she is in and feels she is in. When we feel our soul, we feel good *now*, and we don't need to acquire or buy anything, we already have our spiritual connection to the world and the universe. Soul is experienced only in the now. Soul arises out of conscious living.

Being part of something bigger than ourselves, and feeling connected to our brethren and sistren, to Mother Earth and the universe, happens through our soul. Our soul is our protector, it can give us everything we ever really wanted, and I don't mean material acquisitions and short-lived pleasures. I mean a feeling of compassion and love outwards, for other people, animals, nature and our whole world. Through this compassion we feel at one with life, and deny emotional pain and trauma breathing space.

In the soul we are whole. Life feels good. We are connected.

Yet, the human experience is not always like this, and that's fine, aspects of enjoying being human come from going with the ego-mind. We are that glorious mix of body and soul, emind and imind. Our challenge is to enjoy the emind without letting it ruin our own self or others. Regular experiences of life through our soul will solve this. Proactively speaking, giving to, caring for, and sharing with others feeds our soul. All such connection does. Natural whole foods feed your soul. You know all this, you just have to act on it!

We are five dimensions, and we are the blend of them all. Feed your soul, and feed your body well, and you will find your imind. Harmony and contentment arrive.

DESSERTS

Welcome to the sweet stuff! In this section of the book I share with you a buffet of ideas, strategies, plans and tasks for putting into practice all you have learned thus far, and for cementing your commitment to pursuing and enjoying wellness as your default way of life. Most of it is from my own experiences on my own path of spiritual revolution and evolution.

It's an ongoing journey until our final days, so I continue to struggle to keep my ego-mind in check. By and large I do very well, but I've had years of practice. This is the key. You can always recognise the emind, that pesky dogged operator, it's the inner voice telling you to resist change, that you're not good enough, that you won't be able to succeed.

Ignore the blighter. It's not you, it's your system-installed program!

Oh, and be aware, it's highly adept at coming in through the back door while you're not looking… I know this well, it happens a lot. Alertness and awareness are our friend, imind to the rescue. And remember the wellness wagon for the testing times.

So, please bear in mind that many physical and mental

challenges will come your way as you seek to transform your life. Practice and persistence are key, and in goodly time you'll become a skilled navigator and driver of your wellness wagon, falling off it fewer times, and finding you can more easily get back on it, and with the minimum of delay.

16

MOTIVATION: TAKING THE RIVER TO MARS!

Motivation relates to an instinctive impulse or deliberate intention to either gain a reward or avoid a pain.

I think a more than satisfactory place to start the sweet section of your meal is with the small matter of *motivation.* Without motivation it's very hard to do anything, yet, having motivation to do something, to change something, does not necessarily mean you will do it. You will certainly need it to help you initiate an action, and you will need it to continue with your action until such time as it's a new habit. This is what it's all about really, identifying our harmful habits and thought patterns, and then taking action to swap them for good habits and more positive thinking. Also, we can reflect upon what might be missing from our life, that which doesn't sparkle and reward us enough, and similarly take action to change things.

Without sufficient motivation it will be hard to initiate action and change, but also without sufficient reward from embarking upon this new action, it will be hard to sustain your new ways. To act, and to continue acting, you need *ongoing motivation* to carry you through until it's second nature.

My whole teaching career has been based on motivating my students, but as I became more experienced and skilled in my work, I realised the best thing I could do for them was to motivate them to motivate themselves. Motivated people in life are much better able to make changes, learn new stuff, take on challenges. They can also more easily overcome laziness, or the emind's reluctance to give up its habits.

Understanding motivation is key to helping you make it work in your favour. When I studied for my master's, I did my thesis on learner motivation and learner beliefs, a subject matter that interested me right from the first class I taught back in late 1991. There are only really two forces lying behind motivation: to obtain a reward or to avoid pain. In education they are often likened to the carrot and stick. In our schooling, it was nearly all stick, mostly the threat of failure or looking stupid drove us on. Certainly, we were not motivated by fun or enjoyment. Nor from the joy of learning, because they never taught us to learn.

I wanted my students to have their cake, and to eat it. I wanted them, metaphorically speaking, to get some fish to eat, a fishing rod to catch their own, and to become skilled in using the rod. In this way they could enjoy their lessons, and become a skilled operator by their own efforts once the studies were over.

However, without any rewarding learning experience in our education, we are much more likely to carry fear with us as a motivator. This is not conducive to living autonomously or enjoyably. The spiritual revolutionary must replace the stick with their own carrots. Enjoy the journey of change, enjoy the fruits of your efforts.

Having goals to aim for will motivate us, but I think it's super important to enjoy the journey, hence the aim to be healthy and happy today. If what we do each day is intrinsically rewarding, makes us feel good about life, then we remain motivated and life is easier and more fulfilling.

So, to that end, I would like to introduce you to the chapter title,

Taking the RIVER to MARS! Are you ready for a trip to the red planet?

This is a motivational tool for yourself to initiate and then sustain your motivation to make positive changes to your life. (If you are a parent, teacher, leader, you can help others do the same.) As you begin adopting healthier approaches to daily life this will help you counter any emind resistance.

Firstly, **MARS!** stands for **motivation, action, reward, 'sweet!'**. Be **motivated** to improve something in your life, to change something, to give up something harmful (an action, habit, thought pattern), or which no longer serves you, use this as a driving force to take necessary **action**, and then when you experience some kind of **reward** you will exclaim **'sweet!'** and will want more of the reward, and so you can sustain your motivation to continue your action, get more rewards, and so on. Job done, you're in a virtuous circle! Mars is the red planet of fire, and fire in the belly is a motivation in itself. Use your desire for health, harmony and happiness to feed the fire in your belly.

Once you have sustained your new action for a while, it's no longer a new action and will be your new habit, new thought pattern, new way, which will serve you well in your life, and now that your emind is retrained and reconditioned, you can do it instinctively and without any need for willpower anymore. Just make sure at the start of a new journey, when you take new action, that you observe and notice any improvements to your life and use this to consciously counteract any efforts by the emind to pull you off your wellness wagon.

But what action to take? You will be travelling to the planet of reward, fun and sweet delights via a **RIVER** which you can think of as the *River of Motivation*. This will guide you into making choices and decisions as to what changes you would like to make. **RIVER** stands for **relevant, interesting, variety, engaging, reflective**. It's very hard in life to sustain motivation for doing something which is not useful or enjoyable, so choose accordingly. Choose things which **interest** you and which you feel are **relevant** to boosting your life.

Go inside your inner being with your intelligence-mind to find out your natural skills, what *you* like doing, what is beneficial for *you* in your own context of life, and what your positive traits are. Do things which suit you, your own temperament, and likes - art, music, sport, media, travelling, cooking, the list can go on and on, so many things for us humans to do. Even branch out and choose to succeed in something your emind has previously told you you don't like, or that you can't do. You never know, there may be hundreds of things that will inspire you and reward you. Seek out things which reward you and don't let that emind resistance block you. So-called 'failure' is just a learning episode for spiritual revolutionaries!

By the way, because the emind is programmed to avoid looking stupid or being seen to fail, and worries about what others will think of it, it will often try to block us from doing anything it thinks we can't do. In this way, it reasons, we can't look stupid and we can't be seen to fail because we didn't even do it. You will have to tell it you're no longer listening. Who cares what other people's eminds think, and ignore your own. Their iminds will be impressed anyway, so just do what you want to do and forget about peer approval. Let them approve or disapprove by their own choice.

'Variety is the spice of life', they say. Well, it certainly is for me. I like routine too. For me, it's about balancing routine with spontaneity, and ensuring different things are going on in my life. **Variety** is really important and does indeed spice up one's life. Don't be a one-trick pony, you may get bored with it and then what of life? Put some pep and verve into your life and enjoy it. Take up new activities. I have loads of different things I like doing, so if one gets boring sometimes, many other things to choose from.

Engaging means that whatever it is you do, you want it to put your imind, heart and soul into gear, you want your inner being to feel *connected* to it. To do something well means we need attention and concentration, and in this way we connect to it and we will do it to our best ability. Remember, connection is harmonising our inner being with the outer world. Engage and connect with people, with animals, with nature, or with whatever it is you are doing. Engaging brings us into the now-moment, it has us living consciously. When I do my hammock time I connect with all the flora and fauna about me. I'm not 'doing' anything per se, but my mind is doing lots.

Reflection. Just do lots of it. Incorporate it into your daily life, make it as common as eating meals or walking. Reflecting is done by your intelligence-mind, and the more you use your imind the more you encourage your innate intelligence into action, then the more you will learn and heal, and the less control your emind will have over you. Then you feel at one with the world.

Reflecting on what has gone wrong, on what caused us discomfort or harm, on any problems or challenges that we are experiencing, helps us overcome the situation for the next time, and to learn about ourselves and about how life works. If you're in the process of giving something up, or starting something new, regularly reflecting upon your progress will help you sustain your motivation, and it will remind you to continue. Sometimes I simply forget to do something because it's not yet a new habit. Reflecting is a great tool for your memory, and it's a great tool for making you observe things and being more aware.

When things go well, reflect upon them, seek out the causes so you can make it all happen again. Reflecting upon action - either during it or after it - is an essential life skill in my view, and is your best teacher in life. Many people keep diaries for this reason. Writing is a top reflection tool. Consider doing this yourself, but if you do, you will need to pick a regular slot of time in order to make it a habit, otherwise your emind will make you lazy to do it. I have kept my food and feelings diaries for months at a time, and would fill in the day's foods and how I felt during the day after dinner each evening. In this way, I began to learn about how different foods affected my moods, emotions, feelings. I seriously regret not keeping a diary in the 1990s when I was first living in Thailand, I've only got my memories now, and many of them have disappeared!

One thing all alcohol imbibers need to know, if they don't already, is that alcohol increases negative energy, thoughts and feelings in our inner being and this often translates into negative actions and reactions in our daily life. I know very well that if I drink too much or too often that I more easily become frustrated or impatient and a less nice person (I am an Aries, a fire sign, and in the Chinese zodiac I'm a dragon, yet more fire!). Others will become super lazy, and others may find they worry more or become depressed about life. It can easily demotivate or downpress us.

I have noticed sugar has the same effect, and all chemicals that are in any foods you consume will definitely lead to more negative emotions and feelings inside you. Reflecting upon such things by observing your body and emind, by being aware of your inner being, is the way out of this predicament. Until one even realises the chemical connection, we may just take for granted how we feel as being 'normal'.

So there you have it, my RIVER to a motivating life, using MARS! to check up on your progress and to remind you to sustain new actions, attitudes, approaches until such time as they become new habits, meaning you will then be doing them instinctively as second nature. It's all about swapping stuff that does not support your wellness journey for stuff that does. Don't starve the emind though! It will rebel badly and burn you. You cannot suppress it, you can only retrain it, or neutralise it by spotting it in action before you react to its emotional imperatives and instructions.

Being spiritual does not mean quitting on all the pleasures of life. Alcohol, gambling, blueberry cheesecake, coffee, chocolate are great so long as we don't do too much of them. How much is 'too much'? That of course is the million dollar question. However, as we all know, they are addictive and so can easily burn us. By observing and listening to one's body and emind at work, we can, with practice, learn what our limit is. For some, certain things must be completely given up. It's up to each individual, but with reflective thinking as part of your life you can find out anything.

This is why resetting your outlook in life is so crucial, to give you a strong foundation of conscious direction and attention. And it's why observing your body and emind, being aware, practising conscious living, and reflecting upon things is crucial to your wellbeing and progress. It's why you cannot live according to the experts or spiritual gurus or healers or whoever. Only you can know what's best for you, but that is only true in your conscious living mode when using your imind.

All over the world people are driven and controlled by their emind and they assume they know what's best for themselves and that they know who they are and that how can anybody else know better. If they are speaking with their imind, great, but mostly I easily see they are talking through their emind, or rather their emind is talking for them. It is their emind in charge, not themselves. Eminds are certain they know, certain they know what is best, what is right and wrong, good and bad, and they are dogmatic about it all. No flexibility, never wrong, always right. This certainty comes from the system which installs it into our eminds.

Be motivated to achieve wellness, which means taking actions to change things about your life, which means imind over emind. Do things which make you feel good, don't cause you harm, and practise overcoming any emind resistance.

17

LIVING THE REAL DEAL

A reminder of a caveat, which I think is necessary for this and the next chapter. It is this: everything I say is my personal understanding, albeit all of it from my own research and much of it from my actual experiences in life. I do not say to you it is definitively true for all, just that I've found it to be true for me.

The caveat is necessary for two reasons. Firstly, when one starts researching food and the whole topic of healthcare, it quickly becomes apparent that nowhere else in all of humanity's endeavours and evolutionary progress does so much conflicting information batter your brain. It's like a cognitive minefield out there. A 'mind-field' minefield!

Secondly, and crucially, yet still largely unrecognised in the mainstream, there is no one-size-fits all when it comes to what will make us ill or well. We all know how huge the diet industry is, but in my view, nearly all of them are playing with people because the best diet for you does not mean it's the best diet for me, yet always they propose their diet for everybody. Paleo, vegan, low-carb, high-carb, raw and many others. Good for some perhaps, but not good for all, good for some of the time perhaps, but not all the time. Some of them are likely to be health-depleting for people of differing constitutions.

Therefore, on account of these two really important considerations, I shall do my best to focus on dietary (and exercise) information that is likely true for all, and in the main, that means what not to eat rather than what to eat. We're on much firmer ground in this way. When I think things are debatable, I'll say that.

Actually, there's a third reason. When I read this or that book, website or source of information on food and health matters, so often people write with full certainty, implicitly implying they carry full authority for what they 'know' to be 'true'. For example, 'Eggs are good for you', 'Cooked food kills the nutrients'.

This will encourage a false sense of security ('confirmation bias') in the reader who wants something that they read or hear to be true. For example: 'Chocolate is good for you'. Well, many people would love to read that!! Maybe it is, maybe not, maybe some kinds are, others not, just a little bit is, too much is not... lots of riders and provisos to consider. Another one people love to read is 'red wine promotes good health'. And suddenly people are chucking down one or two bottles a night! Yet, elsewhere I will read that both chocolate and wine are detrimental to health. It's a minefield of information.

Caveats aside, however, the one guide which will likely lead you to a diet which is specifically good for you and your own personal constitution, and which I place great store in is not a diet per se, rather a whole diet and lifestyle guide to living with health, preventing ill-health, and treating and healing oneself should ailments strike: we're talking Ayurveda. That chapter closes out this section of the book.

There *is* one diet, though, which takes personal constitution into account; it's based on our blood type. There's not a lot of corroborating information on it, it's mainly from one person, Dr D'Adamo. Last I checked it still had no real studies which could prove its worth, but neither to disprove his views. It was a big bestselling book back in the 90s, and I just alert you to it because unlike the other diets it does make distinctions between different people. I have some experience of it which I shall relate to you in the next chapter.

Caveat over, buyer beware, your responsibility, it's your spiritual revolution, so you have to verify things for yourself! But also, when we give ourselves time to think about such things in our upcoming discussion, it's mostly or all common sense. Yet, the system did its best to suppress even this out of us.

It's not really possible to become spiritual, to have good relationships with others, and to enjoy a default of wellness and happiness in life, if one is still prey to emind forces such as blame, intolerance, worry and all those negative emotions which our ego-mind foists upon us in reaction to things going on around us.

We simply must learn how to overcome such impulses and instincts which kick in when things or people in the external environment trigger them. Blaming others and complaining about things ensures we remain victims to circumstance and other people in life, and under the control of the miserable, anti-life system implanted in our eminds. Remember the adage, 'I can't control what you do or say, but I can control my reaction'. Well, yes you can, but only if you are in imind mode. In emind mode, until you have restrained and retrained it, you will be controlled by (the eminds of) other people and external forces.

Thus, our inner work is all about promoting use of our imind, and using it to retrain and recondition our emind to become a more acceptable, and less destructive, part of our overall 5DL (body, emind, imind, soul, external environment). Conscious living, instigated with your OOAAI outlook reset and then practised using OAR, is your best friend.

An essential part of your outlook reset towards life is to live in a REAL manner. Being **REAL** means elevating the energy forces of **respect, empathy, awareness** and **love** into your consciousness and five dimensions of life, and making them a benchmark for your life. **Respect** yourself; have **empathy** for yourself when you say or do things you then wish you hadn't, for this is an entirely human thing; **be aware of** yourself and **aware of** your thoughts, deeds and words; and **love** yourself, cherish yourself, love your life.

Incorporate REAL living into your intention or orientation of the OOAAI tool, and then set about making it an inner habit and way of being. You will find it easily enables you to live with authenticity and integrity, and with courage and confidence to be your own self, a unique beautiful expression of creation and Mother Earth - be your own REAL beauty. For me this is human nature, just that our nurture took us away from it. Let's get back to our roots.

When faced with awkward decisions or choices, use it as your basis for action, ignoring any worries about what others may think about you, and ignoring emind calls for you to choose for its own gains, if it will be at the expense of the wellbeing of others. With it installed in your consciousness, you will easily notice if your emind wants to deceive others or gain unfairly for itself, and you can then avoid taking such action.

It opens up your conscience which, when you allow it, becomes your guide for living as harmoniously as you can. Hurt no-one, but accept no hurt either!

However, the real beauty of REAL living is that once you **r**espect, **l**ove, and have **e**mpathy for yourself, once you are **a**ware of your own inner being and the whole range of activities of your emind, you will automatically understand and have empathy for the problems all other human beings face. And you will want, with your heart, soul and imind, to be loving towards them too.

We see our own struggles clearly, and so we have empathy for the difficulties that face all human beings, and our relationship with ourselves and all others radically changes for the better.

We come to see that the root cause of all problems humanity faces - whether we inadvertently or deliberately create them for others, whether we feel others are pushing them onto us - is all the conditioned eminds at work. We can dislike, disagree, disapprove of what others do, or even what we do ourselves, but let's just remember that it's not you or me causing harm or strife, it's our emind. Go easy on yourself and everybody else. Life is for living and enjoying, not succumbing to the emind's blame and complain game.

I have always viewed seriousness as a disease. Smiling and laughing is the way, it comes from the heart.

By living in a respectful, empathic, aware and loving manner you can easily get back on your wellness wagon whenever you fall off it, and you needn't be hard on yourself, nor think you look weak by apologising to others if you've hurt them. But, also, when you are journeying along just beautifully, give thanks to creation and the universe for your wellbeing and notice your good vibes, never take life for granted. Spread your love and cheer around, share and care, give and live - your soul will reward you deeply for your actions.

The system trains us to live according to its fixed dogma and ideology about what is right and wrong, good and bad in this world, but this simply does not support our nature, nor the karmic laws of the universe. It drains our energy. No more of its nonsense, it's just a choice to say 'no'.

It is also a most beautiful basis upon which to DEAL yourself a cracking hand of cards to play a top game of life…

DEAL RELATES TO **DIET**, **exercise, attitude** and **lifestyle**. I think everything and anything you can change and improve upon in your life comes into one of those quadrants. Use these four major areas of life to help you decide what changes you're going to bring into your life. Remember the single word that counters and prevents stress: *harmony*. It's all about doing things to create balance within our 5DL, and harmony with others and with Mother Earth.

We'll take them in order, but my section on **diet** will be a brief one because the next chapter deals with this quadrant at length. This reflects my view changes in diet can lead to the quickest and most noticeable improvements in one's overall health. My back problems and various niggles and tensions departed in just three or four days when I changed my diet back in 2008. It was dramatic and a complete revelation to me. Rainbow magic. I know that others report the same experiences, and I know from meeting people and from my research, that changed diets lead to reversing long-standing illnesses and diseases. I sincerely recommend diet to be your first port of call.

The first thing to say about **diet** is that it's futile going *on* a diet, because if you go on something you will come *off* it, such is the law of gravity and of karma. It's no wonder that most if not all diets fail. Furthermore, don't think diet in terms of losing or gaining weight, think diet in terms of achieving a healthy body and mind. Then you make natural, not forced, changes.

So, what we do, then, is *change* our diet. Forever. You choose a diet which overall supports the proper functioning of all your bodily systems and which boosts your immune system so that it can deal with potential invaders in style.

By the word 'diet' we are thinking simply in terms of 'the foods that we eat', not about calories or half starving ourselves.

Feed your immune system and health, not your tongue. But that absolutely does not mean all health-boosting foods are tasteless or yuck. Just as we retrain our emind so we can retrain our tongue, and once retrained we get fully rewarded and we stop, or dramatically reduce, our consumption of those health-attacking foods. Once I was on my new healthier, diet my eating pleasures went up, not down.

And recalling that life works through the holistic operations of your physical, psychological, and spiritual health, boosting your body's wellbeing with nutritious foods will also bring peace and clarity to your mind, and release your soul to bring you feelings of joy and love.

What you eat, for better or worse, has a dramatic impact upon your health, and not just today, but cumulatively so. Cancer, for example, the scourge of our times, doesn't suddenly appear in our body overnight, it is the consequence of long-term and ongoing exposure to stress in our body and mind, and diet is a big factor in that.

Your diet will definitively influence how long you live, and whether your life is cut short. It will also determine to a very great degree how often or not you get sick and experience bodily ailments.

This is epigenetics and common sense. I'm planning on dying while drinking juices and herbal teas, not pumping my body full of painkillers!

Bearing in mind my opening caveat, what can we know as sure as sure can be? Let me offer you some key understandings, which we shall investigate further in the next chapter. If you just do these, you will make huge gains in your overall health in body and mind, and in that way you are nourishing the soul, allowing it to flower and flourish within you to then repay the favour to your body and mind. You become a holistic bouncing ball of health!

i) Eat whole foods, avoid eating corporation-made foods. This alone would probably outdo every single diet out there. It's a very sad (some say criminal), but excellent rule of thumb that nearly all foods made by food corporations deplete our health. There is also nothing you can do more, as an individual citizen, to help protect and heal Mother Earth. Huge food corporations employ practices that are doing unimaginable damage to our planet. Did you know, for example, that many processed foods use palm oil, the production of which has meant devastating habitat and rainforest loss in places like Borneo? And if you don't know about high-fructose corn syrup, then find out! Probably all of it is made from genetically modified corn. I literally almost never eat or drink anything made by a corporation, right down to our choice of cooking oils, sauces and so on. This is a seriously green footprint you can give yourself. Buy local, heal global!

Whole foods means vegetables, fruits, mushrooms, nuts, seeds, unrefined grains and things like brown pastas and bread made from them, herbs, superfoods, naturally produced eggs, naturally made yoghurt and cheese, unhomogenised milk, meat from animals that did not live in human-made factory farms or concentration camps, and fermented foods. No added chemicals or toxic ingredients.

ii) This means avoiding - to the very best extent that you can - junk foods (why put rubbish into your body?), genetically modified foods, processed foods, refined foods (sugar, flour, salt and oils), meats and dairy foods from factory-farmed animals, eggs from caged or factory chickens, and packaged foods with labels and lists of ingredients that include long strange-sounding words and INS numbers.

iii) Locally-grown foods did their growing in a similar environment, climate, and topography to the one you yourself live in, so they have energetics more attuned to your own living organism.

iv) Avoid, to the largest extent possible, chemicals, pesticides, herbicides, fungicides, additives, preservatives, flavourings, and all those other toxic additions to our food chain which our livers and kidneys have to work so hard at in processing and eliminating. A happy liver is a happy heart is a happy mind. I have read that giving up meat gets rid of most of your chemical intake.

v) Reduce your consumption of animal foods, especially dairy which easily clogs up the system and produces much mucous in the body. Some do well to eliminate meat and dairy entirely, or just dairy, and some feel they need to have meat in their diet - but just avoid eating too much of such foods at a minimum. I eat very little dairy, and perhaps 5-10% of my diet is meat, but I personally never cook it. One day soon I may give up meat entirely.

vi) Limit coffee and alcohol consumption and eliminate fizzy drink consumption. Just get rid of the latter, it acts like acid to your teeth and body. Take tea or herbal teas or just get used to drinking water, perhaps with a splash of lime or lemon in it. You can always make your own fresh lemonade, ginger beer, and any number of soft drinks using fresh whole food ingredients. And of course, smoothies and fruit or veggie juices. Carrot, apple and ginger is a favourite of mine when I can overcome my laziness to clean my machine.

By focusing on just these things you will give your body a beautiful makeover, it will in time find its natural weight for your unique constitution, your skin will glow, you will feel higher levels and reserves of energy, you'll sleep better, you will gain clarity of mind, and vitality will be your middle name.

You don't have to reduce the amount of food you eat, skip meals, or count calories or anything like that. In fact, once you eat whole foods, your body will be getting the nutrients it needs and the satiety gene will kick in at mealtimes, and tell you when you've had enough. I can tell you from my own experience that once I got started on my new approach to diet and life, I got a serious kick out of eating healthy foods and just *knowing* that I was helping my body be healthy. I began to enjoy and appreciate eating my foods so much more, and in no time at all I made my mealtimes of central importance to my life, around which I created the rest of my routine. I didn't fit eating into my life, I was now fitting my life into my eating! Health and mental wellbeing comes first, everything else second.

Wherever you are on your own journey towards wellness, might I suggest you change your diet to a new improved one, and then give yourself two weeks to see what happens to your body and mind. Eat your usual three meals or so, if you snack make it a healthy one. Monitor your progress and apply the MARS! principle to it, let the rewards you feel sustain your new diet until it becomes habit and a default in your life. In this way we change our diet rather than going on one, only to come off it.

E STANDS FOR **EXERCISE**, and again I have found quite a lot of conflicting and potentially harmful information out there as to what exercise we should do and how much of it. I can only give my thoughts on the matter, based on my research, understanding and experiences.

We can think of three clear-cut types of exercise to help us get a picture of things.

The typical western idea of exercise is to go in hard, and at its extreme we can picture the street jogger, flushed face contorted in agony, pounding the polluted urban tarmac for several kilometres every day in the belief that the harder we push ourselves the more we will benefit, and the more the weight will drop off. Perhaps the thought of almost being on the point of collapse, struggling to gulp in the air as one's heart is racing faster than Lewis Hamilton's car, means good health for the body. Unlikely, and according to Ayurveda, not good for people with a certain constitution type. Anything which gets the heart working harder and the breathing deeper is aerobic exercise, but moderation is the key. Many people working in the health industry have told me it's a fallacy to overwork the body, and a fit person doesn't mean necessarily a healthy person. Consider that burnout is not good. Some sportsmen, fit as a fiddle, die young before they've even retired from their sport, and I always assume they've overdone things.

The typical eastern or Indian idea of exercise is yoga, and this is not necessarily nice, easy and gentle! Yet, undeniably, you don't really have to go anywhere, which especially makes it useful if you live in an urban environment.

At the start of my mission to pursue wellness, I signed up for two weeks of yoga lessons. I was astounded at how much my body was stretched, pulled, tested and given such a huge workout in just four square metres of space - it was seriously hard work! I also recall after five days of this seriously strenuous exercise going to my local pub for the Friday pool league night and not drinking any beer. The thought of it felt like an insult to my body, which by now was flying with energy and vitality. I recall smiling inwardly to myself about being in a pub on a Friday night and not drinking beer, a previously unheard-of phenomenon... how my life was transforming itself!

So, while yoga is not so much an aerobic exercise (or maybe it is?), it is nevertheless a quite brilliant workout for the body. As somebody who hates running this is much more my cup of tea. And it really gets to all the muscles, which is in my view the primary purpose of exercise. A big thing in yoga too is breath work and cultivating good breathing practices.

The third clear-cut type of exercise, the preferred version for perhaps the bulk of the human population, east or west, is none of it. That was me for most of my life until I hit 44 and changed my whole lifestyle around. I had a year of playing weekly tennis with a mate in the late 90s, and took up golf in my 30s, and before all that, at the outset of my new life teaching and living in Bangkok in my late 20s, I did a year or so of weekly taekwondo which I loved, but then we lost our premises and it fizzled out. But other than that, I never really did any exercise except for lots of walking which I now realise is a superb activity for keeping fit. Some cutting edge doctors who do health, say walking is the best exercise we can do. I think it is, it moves our muscles, our lymph, and oxygenates our blood and improves our circulation without over-stressing our body.

Doing no exercise clearly appeals to our lazy gene, but anybody pursuing wellness will of course need to overcome this. Consider this, 'use it or lose it, abuse it and lose it'. Don't do none, don't do too much, find your balance. That applies to our body and our muscles. Now, should we pound the streets jogging while going through such pain, and is yoga, being a non-aerobic exercise, enough for us? Do we need aerobic exercise? What constitutes a useful level of exercise to support our endeavours to promote a healthy body for ourselves? As with diet, the answers are personal, hence you'll need to become your own expert on this.

Remember this, though: life is energy and energy is movement, and therefore to me, the key factor when considering any exercise program for ourselves is simply to make sure we move our body. But what exactly is 'movement'? Well, we can move our body, move our muscles, and we can move oxygen, blood and lymph. For example, and as I do every morning, if we sit down and do deep breathing activities, we are doing exercise by ensuring a good flow of oxygen and blood which moves around our body more effectively than most people's default of rather shallow breathing.

Thus, think of movement and you are thinking exercise. Doesn't have to be the painful jogging variety. If you're thinking of losing weight, I'm pretty sure you don't have to engage in aerobic activity per se; I think that's just down to ensuring you eat only whole foods in your diet, minimising animal food consumption, and avoiding all the refined and processed 'foods' which are what cause so much weight gain.

Another key factor is the ability of the emind to choose the third type of exercise, that is, not doing any. For many people, their emind will come up with any number of excuses to avoid doing exercise. This is why I always say that developing good habits is so useful, because then we have the habit and the momentum to tell the lazy emind to take a hike, or a running jump.

Now, factors like time and space come into consideration, for many will say they are too busy. What, too busy for health?! So let me say that if you do just 15 minutes of whatever you choose to do each day, you are providing your body with so much more than if you do nothing. And even a lazy emind will struggle to convince you that 15 minutes is too long. Half an hour even better. Of course, if you can do an hour or more then that's fine, but so long as you don't overdo it. You need to find the right balance for you. Again, use the OAR tool of observation, awareness and reflective thinking to monitor things as you take up new fitness programs, and then adjust them as you see fit.

My personal approach is this. I like to walk as much as I can, which unfortunately in Thailand is not so easy considering the challenges of street dogs and pollution in urban settings, and snakes in the forests. I usually play golf each week which does give me several kilometres of walking. But my mainstay is about twenty minutes each morning of various stretches that I do to work out all the different muscles in my body, like a sort of bespoke version of yoga. I recall some official yoga asanas, but forget so many others, so I just focus on my muscles, contracting and expanding them. Being a teacher, researcher and writer, I do lots of work sitting down, which only contracts muscles, so expanding them is really important. I do lots of bending, stretching up and sideways, twisting and the like. I can also do more aerobic kind of stuff with rapid movement of the arms and by doing lots of sitting squats. My body is so much more flexible, and this keeps me committed to my morning program. I may miss the odd day here and there, no harm done.

After my stretches, which I do in our garden, I come back in and sit down in the half lotus position (which I'm proud that I can do, when I first tried it my knees and thighs were nowhere near the floor, now they sit flush to it), for maybe another 20 minutes or half an hour. I do a mix of meditation and deep breathing exercises to really get the oxygen and blood flowing all around my body.

I also do more stretching here, swivelling my head to the left and right ever so slowly, and then as I look ahead, I lift it up towards the ceiling and then down towards the floor, as far as I can and as slowly as I can. I learned this from qigong I think. I do several rounds of this. I also bend my upper half of the body forwards so that my head can just about touch the floor. I pull my earlobes around this way and that, tap the top of my head and all around my face and neck and shoulders region with my fingertips for a few minutes, and then massage the top of my head vigorously. I do various other kinds of things whenever I think of them.

My point here in describing my own routine, my friend, is that all this exercise I do, roughly 40 minutes or so each morning is all done in a tiny bit of space, so anybody can do this, indoors or outdoors, and if you do nothing else I think this is an excellent support for your health and wellbeing. It's an anti-lazy emind fitness regimen!

In addition to this regular stuff, whenever I have the time and money I sign up to a gym for a month and go there every day, but I barely use it. Instead, I use their swimming pool and get daily swimming in which deals with most muscles, and after that I use the sauna for about 20 minutes or so. Sitting down in the sauna constitutes exercise? Yes, assuredly so! Just think movement, and I can tell you there's plenty of movement going on with all your sweating, which is also getting toxins in your body hastened out of it. If I do the sauna first, I notice that I can easily do so much more swimming without getting tired, the heat no doubt has really helped my muscles be flexible and loose.

I also have some one-kilogram weights at home which I can use to give my arms a workout. No need for heavy weights, although if that's your preference, fine. 15 minutes of one-kilogram weights is quite a burden to handle!

And the other semi-regular exercise I do is cycling, but only around the local roads so as to keep away from the street pollution.

We also have a rebounder to jump up and down on which is a tremendous form of exercise, and again takes up no space. 15 minutes at a time is fine. This is perfect for moving your lymph around your body, thereby helping your body's elimination systems and stopping the lymph backing up. Static lymph means your bodily wastes don't get eliminated and are instead stored up in parts of your body which, in time, will lead to ailments, not to mention weight gain. If you have constipation issues I'm sure you could buy a rebounder and this will really help you.

Now, to finish up on this quadrant, aside from all the usual games and sports and gym stuff, what else can we do to maintain the shape and wellbeing of our body? I'm just going to list a few ideas and leave it with you as to what you choose to do. But build in exercise regularly, whatever you do, and you can see that time and space are no excuses!

Walking is excellent, walking meditation even better, so be aware of your posture and walk upright. I spent the first half of my life with a sort of slumping posture, head down, but no more, now I'm upright and psychologically facing up to the world of challenges. Ensure your sitting posture has a straight back too, and retrain yourself if you need to like I did. Other ideas for you to consider for your own life, to add to the already discussed ones, include tai chi, gardening, trekking, running, earthing, massage, self-massage, dancing, aerobics, gymnastics, on-the-spot walking or jogging, acupressure, and simply go online for more options.

Your joints, muscles, lymph, and lungs all need regular movement to keep them in good shape.

Do think about your hips which are the central pivot to your body; your lymph, which needs body movement to carry wastes out of your body because it has no pump of its own; your blood, which wants plenty of oxygen coming into it; a straight back which links your cranium with your sacrum, and carries your nervous system's ability to work without blockages; and ensure that your major muscles get plenty of expansion as well as the more usual contraction.

A STANDS for **attitude** and is super important in my view. We've talked a lot about this already in the *Main Courses*, so a few reminders will suffice here. But at that time, we had not yet discussed the distinction between our emind and imind

When our emind controls most of our life, as it does until we find out about it and its nefarious controlling ways, it is always prone to negativity thanks to its programming when we were kids and had no choice over our start in life. I come from England and complaining and blaming is a way of life! It's like a national obsession, and at some level perhaps it lets off steam, but not when it's all the time. I found a much lower level of moaning and blaming when I came to Thailand, and a higher level of tolerance for the things people don't want to happen, but which happen. Since then, having met people from all around the world and done plenty of travelling, I have noted a correlation between the more one has materially, the more one is likely to complain and have a negative outlook towards life. Unhappiness is very much linked to material desire.

Undoubtedly for me, having seen it happen time and time again, there is a self-fulfilling nature to life based on our attitude and outlook on life. As my mum taught me and my sister, *'laugh and the world laughs with you, cry and it cries with you'*. For example, people who worry a lot send out a certain energy into the world, and this can increase the chances of what they are worrying about actually happening, especially if it relates to the actions of other people. And when it does happen, this confirms to the worrier that they were right to be worried! And thus a cycle, attitude and outlook becomes set.

An emind can easily push another emind into the direction it doesn't want the other emind to go.

Epigenetics is emphatically clear with its message that how we perceive the world out there has a direct influence on the biology and chemistry of our body, and my own 3DH5DL formula and its interconnections between mind and body say the same thing, so clearly attitude of mind, outlook, mindset have a real bearing on the outcome and quality of our life.

If you have low tolerance for the 'wrong' things happening, then you will be an angry, impatient, frustrated person, and in the process allow your life to proceed in a tense and rather inflexible manner, which does nothing for your physical or mental wellbeing. If you think you're no good at something then you won't do it and you surely will be no good at it! If you think you don't deserve happiness then how will you get it? Hope? Luck? Accident? And if you think you're not good enough, then you're not good enough! Not good enough, my friend, make it happen! Assert your imind authority over that emind of yours.

Expect bad things to happen and they invariably will because that's how your perception filters are set up, choose to make good things happen and they are more likely to. Ensure you have a sound intention. We humans can do incredible things if we use our imind properly.

So, for me, if we train ourselves to have an *attitude of gratitude,* to be thankful for being alive, and if we hold a certain kind of humility that little old wee me exists in this gigantic world and universe of ours, then we will have positive energy inside us with which to face the world and all the daily challenges that come our way. Such energy forces within our being are much better able to handle any negative energy coming our way, and fully accept and love the good stuff that comes along. Gratitude sets us up for imind conscious living.

I am a mere dot passing by on the landscape of time. This idea keeps me humble and my emind in check, but at the same time I feel I fully deserve my dot's worth of life and my happiness because the universe expressly invited me to its party. Why would it want me to be unhappy, fearful or undone by self-doubt?? Be a partygoer in life!

Be that dot my friend! In this way you can always counteract whatever negative nonsense your emind may be trying to get you up to - just remind the blighter that it's only a dot, that will annoy it. When you do do negative things, you know what's going on and you know how to overcome it, just give yourself a bit of time to heal, don't berate yourself, and then get back on your wellness wagon. Can't be perfect, it's the default that counts. Strive to be perfect in the full knowledge you can't be! The striving ensures you're on the journey, living consciously. Job done.

Attitude is not just positive thinking, it's a connection with life and with Mother Earth and the universe. They invited you here.

Out of this connection much positive thinking arises, and you don't have to try and force it.

L STANDS FOR **LIFESTYLE**, and this is a buzz word for a decade or two now, probably coinciding with the advent of the word 'wellness'. Whole books are written on this, so our mission is to simplify everything, and then you can use the 4Ps to be proactive, productive, positive and peaceful, to do the 4Ls of learning, living, loving and leading, and aim for the 3Hs of health, harmony and happiness to guide you in your decision-making and choices for what you do in your life.

I say the latter because I'm adamant that to counteract emind apathy and its capacity to derail us we need to develop good habits and supportive thought patterns. A default life of wellness has room for spontaneity or laziness built into it, always allowing you to not do things, to do things that are not healthy but which you simply want to do today. Your rules, break them when your emind really wants you to. Never starve the emind, it will come back and bite you. Just give in to it from time to time.

The Hs are your aim, the Ps remind you of the need to pay attention to your lifestyle which is often all you really need to do to ensure it's a good one. Conscious living always solves everything, and it happens to you when you are living, loving, listening and leading.

Stress, emotional pain, physical ailments are all signs that your lifestyle is out of balance, so don't run from such feelings, use them as a trigger to investigate where you've gone awry, and then get yourself back on your wellness wagon. Nearly always if we reflect on causes we'll find them, and never doubt your common sense or intuition.

Lifestyle really is just about ensuring you get the right amount of *work, rest, exercise* and *play* to suit your own nature. It's about creating balance, which allows health and happiness to arise out of your inner harmony. And out of your inner harmony your emind has little room to create inner conflict for you and life will proceed in a rewarding manner.

While I enjoyed nearly all my jobs prior to going travelling to Thailand, when I found teaching by accident, I found my total vocation in life, and my ability to enjoy life went through the roof. After all, we spend about half our waking life working. If at all possible, find yourself *work* that suits your knowledge and understanding, your likes and skills, and that helps you put back into the community in some way, or at the very least does not cause harm to others or to our planet.

Be aware that work is one of the major potential causes of stress, and this usually arises because of taking on too much work, taking on too much responsibility for others, or having an overbearing boss or stressful co-workers. Or, your job may 'require' you to be harmful to the harmony and wellbeing of others.

Without *play* because he was too busy working, Jack was a dull boy and the family never got to see him. *Play* is being proactive with your spare time, doing things for yourself or with your family - hobbies, games, being in the great outdoors, travel, socialising, there's a million things we humans can do. By *doing* stuff like this we feel contented, fulfilled, and the joys of being human come to us from our brush with conscious living, which uplifts our spirit and soul.

Play is super important to me for sure. My list of fun time pursuits includes photography, travel, getting out into nature's playground, playing snooker and golf, playing games, reading, and listening to reggae and African music.

Perhaps the music belongs to the *rest* portion of life. Rest is recuperation time, not just for your body but, equally essentially, your mind too. If we overuse our body and mind we abuse them. They need downtime for regeneration. There is the sleeping kind of rest, and then various ways to rest without sleep. I also think just being easy and hanging out with friends is relax time.

The main thing that marks out rest is when the body and mind barely need to work much. Much more passive and receptive than proactive and productive.

Doing what I call 'alone-time' is an essential part of my life, and it has nothing to do with being lonely or alone. It allows me to pull back and detach from our modern-day pace of life, to relax by myself, enjoy my own being and company, and to reflect upon life. It's imind and soul time. I first came to really experience its joys and rewards back in the 90s, in my hammock on the impossibly beautiful white sand beaches of Thailand's southern islands. I didn't realise back then that I was actually practising a form of meditation. I just loved the silence and stillness that I could experience around me and within me, without interruption by other humans or media or any such distraction, while soaking in the soothing energy and vibes offered me by nature doing its business of living.

In today's world with the internet and social media, I find alone-time even more important, and for me it certainly does not include going online.

It's like doing meditation or a more mindful kind of living, where you are in observation mode, just relaxing on your own somewhere nice and being aware of yourself, your body and mind and their inner movements, and life going on around you. In *A Dozen Tasks* you did some of this. Alone-time gives us the chance to reflect upon life too, and this may include keeping some kind of diary. I said earlier in the book that to maximise our time alive we should give ourselves time to learn about life, as well as being busy living it, and alone-time gives us that opportunity always.

I do my alone-time, meditation, mindfulness in nature, at home if there's no distractions, or in funky creatively-designed teashops, cafes and eateries which have chilled music and soulful decor. My soul feels connected when beauty, nature and inner stillness are in my consciousness.

Alone-time, I have found, is quite rare for most people, and perhaps many actively shun it, or their emind does, not wanting to come face to face with themselves. Many people do anything to ensure they are busy all the time, but the body and mind just cannot cope with this and burnout will be inevitable, or some kind of physical ailment or illness will manifest to force the person to slow down. Innate intelligence has its ways of telling you you are out of whack.

A specific word on meditation and mindfulness is in order. I believe, especially in western countries, there's a bit of confusion about meditation and what it constitutes. Firstly, for me it's a way of slowing ourselves down in a busy world where the information highway is overloaded and the material world runs on steroids. It's not about not thinking and stopping thinking, because until one is super-practised that is almost impossible, and then people think they've failed at meditation and give it up.

It's much more about tuning into, and being able to see, our emind at work. Meditation is really more about observing with full awareness, while sitting comfortably or lying down, all the goings-on in our mind, in our emind. It means seeing our emind's inner thought production factory at work. The idea, I believe, is to watch those thoughts as they arise, or to drop them. But when I drop thoughts, other ones come along presently to take their place!

In my own practice I do make efforts to stop thinking, and after many years of on and off meditation practice, I can sometimes go half a minute or perhaps a minute, not really sure, without any kind of thinking, and I do this in nature, tuning into birdsong to help me. What I've started doing is lying down for a while, and I have found that strange zone between being awake and asleep. I think it goes on for a good half an hour or up to an hour, and my thoughts are more dreamy and dreamlike, and I observe they're not particularly connected to reality. It's deeply restful for sure. There are different frequencies the brain can be at, and I know my lying down meditation takes me out of ordinary thinking.

Meditation offers people the chance to see that their tendency to anger or worry or envy, whatever one's emind does a lot of, is in fact not themselves, rather just a reactionary force to external triggers. We learn that we can use our imind to counter this negative energy. Life gets better. Don't give up if you can't stop thinking, just watch those thoughts like they're a soundtrack to a movie. I have observed a few times that when I'm slowed down, have less going on in my life, am on a news fast, that because there's less information coming in, the emind is less busy. One time, during a month-long break on an island, and me off the internet completely, I noticed after two weeks that my emind didn't really have anything to think about. It was fantastic, me and the nature, such pure joy!

Meditation brings you into conscious living, tunes you into your mind's eye (imind), and I feel that's the important thing.

By contrast, I view mindfulness as the means for concentrating fully on what you are doing, without your emind diverting your focus and distracting you with its thoughts. Try walking, cycling, or driving somewhere without thinking, and observe what happens. That pesky emind will keep on wanting to muscle into your consciousness… and that's okay, the big thing is that you don't have to do what it says, and you can override it any time. But when you're doing something new, learning a new skill, your focus is total and the emind is completely shut out, and this is pure mindfulness, and we enjoy being human!

MY FRIEND, choose to live the **real deal** in life, make your life the real deal, and you shall, and it will be. Imind over emind, conscious living over system conditioned living. Be a confident and grateful dot of existence, and you will thrive. Job done.

18

A DIET FIT FOR THIRD MILLENNIUM CITIZENS

You are what you eat.

Foods and drinks are nutritious, or toxic. Know which is which, take your pick.

Times change, evolution marches on, never stopping for anybody, and we who are alive today are responsible for ushering in the start of a brand new millennium. Various ages and eras have been and gone, and we are exiting the Industrial Age and moving rapidly into the Information Age. We alive today are in transition between Ages, hence our turbulent and uncertain times.

In my view of humanity, we are technologically advanced but psychologically struggling to keep up. In fact, we have not kept up, and something needs to be urgently introduced into our way of life in order to help us catch up. As you know by now, my answer is spiritual revolution for individual citizens. We simply have no choice but to confront the destructive nature that has been programmed into our ego-minds. Running away from it is not an option anymore. This work can only be done by you for you, nobody else can do it for you. This is the urgent message of our times.

I fail to see how we can successfully do this without paying full, immediate and intelligent attention to our diet. Humanity has gone scarily awry when it comes to the growth, production and supply of the very staple of our life, food. Our diet is intimately connected to our emind as well as our body. Our typical 20th century diet is destroying us, it is encouraging our eminds to run amok. We are lost, up shit creek without a paddle!

And it is - we are - destroying Planet Earth with this anti-life diet.

In our understanding of diet here, which we shall explore now, it is more than food. We will include in 'diet' *anything that goes into our body*.

This will include real food from nature, 'foodlike substances' (products from food science, credit to Michael Pollan for this distinction), drinks, herbs, superfoods, air, water, cosmetics, soaps, shampoos, medicines, drugs, anything which goes into our mouth or nose, or onto our skin.

It is vitally necessary we expand our definition in this way to take into account the full picture.

I say humanity urgently needs to address its understanding of its primary relationship with the planet, which gives us our life and sustains it for us. Humanity, through its ignorance and arrogance, does more to harm its own health and that of Mother Earth's than to promote it. It's a colossal nonsense that just has to stop. We are literally on a warpath against ourselves and all life.

Take the SAD for example, the most appropriately-named acronym I've ever come across and I'm an acronym nut. The SAD is *tremendously sad*. It stands for 'standard American diet', but unfortunately, in the name of 'progress', it has increasingly spread all over the world in the last two or three decades. It is the cause of much/most of the illness and disease which is so rampant in many nations these days, and it is behind the dreadful obesity problem which ruins people's health and cuts short their life. It truly is a health destroyer and perhaps its only 'benefit' is that the tongue and emind love such foods.

SAD is fast foods, deep-fried foods, and convenience foods. Look at this list and ask yourself how many of these you eat, and how often: pizzas, burgers, hot dogs, meat, ice-cream, white bread, white sugar, donuts, cakes, pastries, cookies, french fries, chips, crisps, refined oils, junk foods, fast foods, genetically modified foods, processed foods, fizzy drinks?

Toxins and chemicals everywhere, and barely a green thing to be seen.

No whole foods as nature gave us.

All such foods heavily tax the liver, kidneys, heart, arteries, lymphatic system, and your immune system. The whole body. The mind's wellbeing is attacked too, and anybody eating primarily this standard American diet can forget about any spiritual energy. Hundreds of different ailments are treated in hospitals and clinics, and pills (to add further workload to the liver) are the hottest thing in town. Symptoms are treated, but unless we address and remove the causative factor of all these ailments and the internal malfunctioning of the body, then problems will just continue to add up and one day BOOM, it's diabetes, cancer, a stroke, a heart attack, or another nasty. It's truly a modern nightmare for the whole of humanity. And not just for those on such a diet, for we all swim together or sink together, and nobody wants to see friends or loved ones suffering so terribly with their health issues and the horrors of chronic pain.

Just one life we get, no second goes, no dummy runs, no dress rehearsals, no reruns, this is our lot.

These foods are an abomination against the sanctity of the life force beating within each of us. But this is barely scratching the full content of the nightmare…

There is how the food is grown, with systematic spraying of chemicals onto grains, fruits and vegetables. This wanton use of toxic herbicides and pesticides, allied to the mono-cropping practices of 'modern' farming depletes the soil's nutrients, upsets its natural chemistry and biology, and poisons Mother Earth's habitats, waterways and underground reservoirs. Natural ecology and ecological systems are being worn away.

Then there's the 'animals' kept in vast caged houses, aka concentration camps, where they can't move, are fed hormones to make them fatter to produce more meat and profit, and given antibiotics and other medicines because any living being that can't move anywhere is going to be sick all the time. Most meat people eat comes from these imprisoned sick animals.

There are processed and refined foods which are denatured, taking out the nutrients and then having chemicals added synthetically to give taste and increase shelf life. Such toxins are a never-ending burden to one's system if this diet is one's default.

What really got to me, when I was doing all my research, was how even the good foods such as vegetables and fruits are mistreated; as well as being grown with toxic chemicals they are picked too soon, before they are ripe, because they will be transported huge distances. Thus, even most of the nutrients of the good foods are denied us too.

So many books and documentary films have been written and filmed on it all, so we'll stop there. The point is made: modern day eating habits attack the health and wellbeing of humans, and the production and growth of such foods is laying waste to our planet. We can't possibly function anywhere near our potential by eating all these 'foodlike substances'. It's no wonder people put on weight eating such garbage, because the body is desperately craving nutrients and so massive portions go with the territory. If all humans ate natural foods supplied by Mother Earth, rather than these SAD foods, I reckon most hospitals and clinics would go out of business.

From here on in we'll focus on what we should specifically consume, and what to avoid consuming. Then, it's over to the battle between your emind and tongue, and your inner intelligence!

However, I would like to first give you an idea of what my own changes were back in 2008, and what my own diet is these days, and to illustrate to you how it is that I can know what I'm talking about. Then we'll look at what makes for a good diet, and what we can know to be bad one. And then it's over to you to decide how much of the healthy stuff you want and how much of the other addictive but unhealthy stuff you want. Listen to your imind!

I'll just say again though, make it a mission to retrain your tongue, because then eating healthy becomes fun, and once your body is feeling bouncy, energetic, vital, you will have strong defences against any emind muscle memory that seeks to push you back into destructive foods.

So BACK IN 2008, I came out of the Ayurveda Centre that evening, ready and inspired to make changes to my diet and lifestyle, which was the good lady doctor's 'medicine' for me to heal my lower back pains. Within days my body was improving, and I then noticed a greater joy in my mind, and over the coming months due to the nature of my work teaching teachers, I noticed how much more clarity of thinking and brainpower was coming to me as a result. It was abundantly clear from my experience: healthy foods and avoiding toxic ones benefitted both body and mind. It's then that I really started seeing the connections between physical, psychological and spiritual health.

Strangely, she did not put me on a diet according to Ayurveda, rather she gave me lists of foods to take, or avoid, based on one's blood type. Mine is O, and so from memory the main things I had to focus on were no more dairy foods, no pork, and to cut out refined sugars and flours, and of course processed foods. She also gave me another document which listed foods according to their *acid-forming* and *alkaline-forming* properties (see later in the chapter). She told me to try and make sure I ate over half of my foods from the alkaline-forming foods and drinks.

Now, at that time the main losses for my tongue and emind were cheeses, bacon, and sliced ham meats which I loved in those days. I was yet to focus on meats and reducing consumption of them, but having to drop pork was a biggie living in Thailand because, as in most of Asia, pork is the most prevalent meat when eating out, which is a culturally common thing to do. I also had to drop drinking coffee due to me not wanting to drink it without sugar or milk, both of which were out. I found teas instead, and became a professional tea drinker. I love green teas and oolong teas in particular. Cereals were out because the milk and sugar were out. And suddenly most cakes and cookies were out because they're made with white sugar and white flour. And I then began discovering that most breads, even brown breads, had refined sugar in them.

All processed foods were out on account of their 'foodlike' ingredients. I loved crisps/chips in those days with my beers. Now gone.

But in the main I was able to keep much of my usual diet, perhaps because the typical Thai diet includes whole foods and plenty of vegetables, spices, herbs, and of course all the tropical fruits.

I was now focused on buying more fruits, eating lots of vegetables and as time went by my meat consumption went down and down. With no dairy intake, I was barely eating any animal foods at one point. I never did drink fizzy drinks, and had never eaten junk food or gone to fast food outlets, out of protest against the food corporations' destruction of our planet. So, looking back, the key was getting milk, cheese, ice-creams, yoghurt, bacon, ham, pork, white sugar and white flour out of my body.

And it transformed my health.

I went three weeks without any beers, and ever since then I've only got drunk about once a year; my consumption is dramatically reduced. Still haven't kicked it totally, though.

At the same time, because I'm a researcher in my line of work, and because I love reading anyway, I dived right into a concerted and prolonged bout of research. Where I live, we have outstanding second-hand bookshops so I was able to buy lots of books on nutrition, health, various modalities of healthcare, Ayurveda, herbs, superfoods, traditional Chinese medicine,, natural healing methods, and all this kind of thing. I devoured them all, some of them twice. I have a very full bookcase at home. And of course, so much material on websites and on YouTube videos.

I met many like-minded people at workshops, gatherings, and in healthy cafes and restaurants, and learned lots speaking to them and comparing information. I found websites like Happy Cow which lists all vegetarian and vegan establishments in towns across the world, what a brilliant resource! Our town has probably more than almost any other town anywhere else. A new fantastic food world had come to my life. Luckily for me living in Thailand there are such tasty curries and assorted dishes of food which have no meat or dairy in them, and in fact dairy is not really used in Thai food, although as with most countries, the SAD has arrived and taken hold on many citizens.

I kept food and feelings diaries, noting down everything I ate or drank in the day, what time I went to bed, and how I felt each day. I began noticing connections between certain foods and activities which increased or decreased my energy levels, and which influenced my outlook on life, and my ability to sleep soundly. At one point a couple of years into my journey it was clear that I could literally turn my health on or off like a tap based on my own diet and deeds. I clearly saw that more than just a couple of units of alcohol a week, and my body and mind decreased in wellbeing.

Once my body had adjusted to my new diet, detoxing whatever it had to, I noticed eating a cake with lots of sugar in it depleted my spirit and inner essence. I will also say that the longer you go keeping your body clean, the more it notices toxins when exposed to them. As you get time under your belt eating a healthy diet, slowly but surely toxins and other wastes (that your body had stored after years of getting too many for it to process) start moving and releasing themselves from the body. I'm a fan of this slow version of detoxing, where it just happens naturally from eating a healthy diet.

For about six years I just did not stop reading, watching films, talking with others, and learning from other sources, including testing many things out on myself. I went research-mad. I reckoned after six years I had done a good 3000 hours of research based on ten hours a week. But most of the time I was doing much more than that. I had read loads of spiritual books before 2008, and now they barely got a look-in as I focused all my energies on reading books, articles, and websites on food, health and healing. I also tested things out when I had ailments, and availed myself of different kinds of healing, like massage, acupuncture, herbal remedies, cupping. I studied reiki and craniosacral healing, and in general taught myself how to take care of my own health. I learned who was pukka and who was charlatan, and it all went into my mind computer.

I would get ailments still (pretty sure they were from detoxing most of the time, which I suspect takes years), and regress when travelling to England or Australia where I would drop my default diet and enjoy cheeses, eat more meats, fewer veggies and fruits, drink more alcohol, and then by the time I got back to Thailand my body was struggling. But I would get back to my default diet and within a week or two my body was all good again.

I learned to have confidence in my ability to get better without going to a doctor. The trouble was, that modern doctors are trained in treating symptoms, and I was always interested in getting to the root causes so I would know what to change in my life to avoid a repeat. Pills may or may not work today, they certainly don't tell us why we got ill, and they have side effects as per their warning labels. Pills if taken frequently will definitely add to the burden of your liver and other organs too.

Again, a whole book could be written on this, but my main focus here is to give you a boost for wherever you are personally on your dietary, health and healing journey, to offer some good food for thought, and to encourage (inspire?) you to do your own research.

Some really good starting points for doing your own research are: Ayurveda and especially books by Dr David Frawley or Vasant Lad, epigenetics and especially online videos with Dr Bruce Lipton, and traditional Chinese medicine. You will rapidly find yourself branching out from these tremendous starting points.

I would also highly recommend you learn about cancer. My experience tells me that learning about cancer gives us tremendous insights into the whole field of health and disease, a good basic understanding of how the body works, and informs us in how our relationship with the outside world influences everything health-wise. Understand cancer and you pretty much understand how all sickness develops, and therefore how to prevent sickness and how to recover from it.

There are two resources I'd like to offer you to get started. At the outset of my own journey I was recommended to watch Dying to Have Known, made by an Alaskan citizen and film-maker. It's beautifully made, and a really eye-opening film. There is also Ty and Charlene Bollinger's documentary series (three or four of them) called The Truth About Cancer. Each series has about a dozen episodes about an hour long. An absolutely indispensable and all-encompassing resource; you can access hundreds of videos on their website, or buy a complete documentary series.

If you investigate and do research foods and diet (and all spiritual warriors must!), just be warned that conflicting information is everywhere. I would say the best guides to use for choosing your diet are the lists of acid- and alkaline-forming foods, Ayurveda, and common sense. Eat local where you can, avoid corporation foods and drinks, eat minimal or no animal foods, and eat plenty of fruits and vegetables.

So, after 12 years, and as I write, what is my current diet? Well, after about eight years I think, I decided to drink coffee again, and included milk in it, breaking my dairy-free diet, but, I reasoned, three or four coffees a week was not putting much milk into me. I might have bacon and cheese two or three times a year. I was a good boy for all that time only breaking my default diet when on holiday in England or Australia, but I still never had processed foods, pork, coffee, ice-creams or milk until I relaxed things a bit. My key approach was, and still is, to have my default diet and allow in things like sugar just a bit and only infrequently. I felt it good to be flexible if visiting friends or family, or on holidays. I found that the foods I'd taken out of my diet I never pined for. My tongue was retrained very quickly. Feelings of wellness kept it well in check.

In a nutshell (sorry), I eat whole grains, loads of vegetables and fruits, mushrooms, some nuts and seeds, fermented drinks, occasional goats' milk yoghurt, organic eggs from chickens which have a life, butter, raw honey, a little chicken and fish, and very occasionally some beef because I feel instinctively my body wants it from time to time, and only if I know the animals led a free life.

I reckon my diet is about 5% fish and chicken, and just the butter and a bit of milk in my coffee is the only dairy I have. I do sometimes feel torn about eating meat, but ethically speaking it seems to me that whatever we eat - aside from mushrooms, fruits and nuts which are harvested without killing the life form that produces them - means consuming living sentient beings. The planet was made in such a way that all living organisms, to sustain their life, have to eat other life. For me, where humans need to focus is on how they treat their animals while they live. But, also, a spiritual revolution is putting the responsibility for our choices onto the individual citizen, we are trying to get rid of religious or political coercion on how to live our lives.

The foods I eat are easy to digest for my system - fresh foods, local foods, and a minimum of toxic chemicals. It's very easy to do this in Thailand with all its markets everywhere. I'm lucky to have a beautiful wife who cooks such tasty Thai food. I'm not too bad at rustling up my breakfasts, and often go to a veggie place for lunch.

We use sodium bicarbonate to soak produce in for a while before cooking or eating. This definitely removes any surface residue of chemicals. Vinegar is a useful substitute for this work.

My wife uses rice bran oil (high smoke point) for her stir-frying, I use organic cold-pressed coconut oil or ghee when I fry stuff, and we include many spices and herbs from our garden in the cooking. I make simple meals, pasta with lots of veggies and mushrooms, herbs, sometimes with some tuna from a can.

My favourite cooked breakfast which I make is scrambled eggs on toast, shiitake or field mushrooms, asparagus or spinach, and cherry tomatoes, washed down with a pot of finest green or oolong tea. Thailand grows many fine teas and, according to my taste buds, the finest coffees in the world. Another favourite breakfast is fruit with the locally-made granola with nuts and seeds and dried fruits in it. I usually have a mix of about four fruits, add the granola, some cashew nuts, sesame or chia seeds, and some cinnamon. I either have coconut water or rice milk with it. On rare occasions I buy a pot of locally made yoghurt which sends my tongue and mouth into orbit, but it's dairy and my constitution favours minimal dairy. Goats' milk yoghurt is easily digestible.

I drink many herbal teas as well as my greens and oolongs, a coffee every other day, and plenty of water. I can buy green juices locally, and sometimes I make carrot and ginger juice myself.

Oh, I also ensure I don't eat any food for at least three hours before going to bed, then my body can do all its repair work while sleeping instead of still digesting stuff. That's an Ayurveda tip I learned.

I'D NOW LIKE to address superfoods and herbs, which have both heavily featured in my research. I have four fantastic resource books - one is on Ayurvedic Indian herbs, the other on all the traditional Chinese herbs and herb formulas, the other on Thai herbs, and then more of an academic analysis of herbs typically found in US and Britain. I also have an encyclopaedia of herbs and natural healing.

Superfoods to me are those foods which are small in bulk, yet are concentrated in nutrients. They are super for nourishing your body, supporting your wellbeing and preventing ill-health, and they have a great role to play as remedies for various ailments, including colds, sore throats, stomach aches, headaches, constipation, skin issues and so on. Many cutting-edge cancer doctors utilise herbs as central to their protocol of treatment. I know herbs work for health, from my own and my wife's experiences, and those of many people I talk to.

Superfoods are fantastic because they are completely 100% natural foods with no dodgy ingredients, nor are they synthetically produced. Most everybody knows the importance of getting enough vitamins and minerals into their body, and along with essential fatty acids they constitute the vital micro-nutrients we need for our body to function as nature and creation intended. Instead of thinking whether I'm getting enough of the B vitamins, the C, A, D, K vitamins, I simply focus on a wide range of easily available superfoods and herbs, look at their nutrient profile in my books or online, what they're good for, and include them in my daily diet.

My approach is to include a few superfoods in my diet at any one time. I may then stop taking those and take others for a while instead. I like to mix it all up. I did start trying to do it more scientifically at the outset of my journey which proved rather difficult, but in all honesty if we are always taking two or three superfoods we are laughing all the way to the health bank. Some I might only take once or twice a year if they're not common. The key thing for me is to simply always include some of them in my diet. I strongly recommend you do the same.

I only focus on ones I can easily buy for myself, and avoid the mixes which often are sold online at health food stores. Not saying they are no good, but they are usually much more expensive, and there's so many available that we just don't need to spend a lot on superfoods. When it comes to herbs you can find them growing wild, and pick them for free!

I will list only the ones I've taken myself at some time or other, and continue to take at different times. Some you will know, perhaps others you won't. All of them are nutrient powerhouses. You can easily then search them up on the internet, or find a good book or two which gives you the lowdown on their nutrient profile and uses. Some of them you can add to your regular meals, others you may take alone. Choose a few, or lots of them, to add into your diet:

- apple cider vinegar, and ensure it's organic and has the 'mother' in it, Braggs is a long-standing brand
- chia seeds, sesame seeds, flax seeds (be careful about rancidity issues with this one, whereas chia seeds don't have that problem)
- pumpkin and sunflower seeds
- organic cold-pressed coconut oil, sesame oil, cod liver oil and krill oil
- unpasteurised raw honey, manuka honey, bee pollen and royal jelly

- goji berries and all other berries
- amalaki, which is Indian gooseberry
- limes and lemons (and if organic or home-grown use the peel, it's packed with goodies), grapes including the seeds
- dates, raisins, other dried fruits without added sugar
- raw organic cacao powder, maca powder
- wheatgrass or barley grass powder, chlorella, chlorophyll, spirulina powders
- any kind of sprouts, for example mung bean or alfalfa, which you can grow yourself by getting the seeds and a glass jar
- various kinds of seaweeds
- Himalayan pink salt, or that greyish colour sea salt
- ghee (nutritious and great for cooking with), and even grass-fed butter (the benefits or otherwise of butter is a conflicting claim, but I use it and always have done and believe it to be a good source of fat)
- moringa powder or tea, mulberry leaf tea, jiaogulan
- green, oolong, and white teas
- garlic and concentrated allicin from it
- kefir and kombucha drinks (which you can easily make yourself, I've done both in the past, but then got lazy and let it slide)
- all the spices like cinnamon, turmeric, thyme, fennel; make a tea or just add to your cooking
- and so it goes on and on.

This list is certainly not exhaustive, but it gives you a grand start.

All superfoods can be taken to help harmonise our bodily functions, to boost the clarity of mind and brainpower, as well as to treat various ailments, you know, like 'grandmother's home remedies' which modern urban living has to a great extent stamped out. We've successfully used apple cider vinegar for stomachaches, headaches, and once to rapidly fix my wife's food poisoning. I did what my book said, gave her half a teaspoon neat which she could barely swallow so much pain she was in, and then same again 15 minutes later as per my book, and soon after the second teaspoon it was amazing, she was virtually back to normal and nearly all pain gone, didn't even need a third spoonful!

An outstanding resource for such superfoods and other health-boosters and remedies can be found online at Earth Clinic. You get an A-Z of symptoms and remedies, and tens of thousands of anecdotes from the citizens all over the world. Another I like a lot, which is for foods mainly, but has full nutrient profiles for each food, is WH Foods, which stands for the world's healthiest foods. I think it offers 100 such foods and loads of recipes.

Moringa leaves or powder and amalaki powder are two of my favourites which I take more than anything else. Both are packed with vitamin C and a whole host of other vitamins and minerals, all needed by your body for repair work and keeping you healthy. Things like this I simply put one teaspoonful in a cup of hot water and drink it before breakfast. Just keep taking it and let it do its work inside your body.

Let me move onto herbs. Now, really my friend, do learn about herbs and simply include them in your diet, just get them into your life. They are God's medicines growing naturally all over the world, also they are sustainably farmed, and they come in so many various guises. By that I mean some are for treating certain ailments, some for helping certain parts of the body and different bodily processes, others are tonics and can be taken for prevention of ill-health by boosting your immune function and helping your organs to do their work, still others will be good for dispelling gas, relieving constipation, improving digestion and so many other things. Just always remember that everything in your body is all interlinked, so by helping one part or one process it has a knock-on positive effect elsewhere.

I use herbs all the time as preventatives, but also when necessary to treat ailments for our family and for any friends who would like to get advice on them. I have my four books and can look up information about the herbs, their action on the body or mind, and what they treat and how they boost the body. Prevention is cure without the pain!

There are so many for sale, and so many growing everywhere if you know what you are looking for. Two examples for anybody living in Britain, and perhaps in your country if you have a similar climate: milk thistle and stinging nettles. They grow everywhere out in countryside locations. Both of these are very good for the liver, containing good amounts of iron, so particularly good for women every month! Just pick them, take home and soak and wash the dust off them, and then either put fresh in hot water to steep, boil them up to extract even more goodness out of them, or dry them put them in an airtight light-resistant container, and then you have stocks of herbal tea to drink at any time.

Also, if you are picking your own raspberries, get some of the leaves too and make tea out of them, very good news for the body (especially the ladies). Many leaves from common fruit trees are top herbs and easy to make tea out of. Some flowers too.

All herbs have specific functions, and it's just about getting the information and gradually learning things for yourself. One of my mainstays is an Indian tonic herb called ashwaganda, which is similar in its work to ginseng, but far cheaper. I know this herb is a great boost to my energy levels, and will take it every day for two or three months at a time. It's said to work better with men, and a similar one called shatavari is said to be the better choice for women.

When I first began researching everything on nutrition and diet, I found lots of people suggesting we should all eat raw foods because by cooking them we killed all the nutrients through the heat. It made sense, yet humans have cooked their foods for thousands of years, ever since we discovered fire. As usual, I was onto conflicting information. Were we really killing the nutrients through heat?

Then one day I went to our local Chinese herbal dispensary for something or other. The Chinese doctor looks at your tongue, reads your pulse on the wrist, hears about your problem, and then writes out in Chinese about five or more different herbs. These are put together and made into five daily doses. The instructions are to boil one packet in three cups of water for about an hour, and then drink the remaining one cup of herb-infused water. Clearly if the Chinese have been helping people heal from their ailments like this for thousands of years then heating up herbs does not kill the nutrients, so to me that logically means the same goes for our foods. In this way I then trust my own experiences which helps counteract all this conflicting information out there. Ensuring your common sense is active, and not blocked by your emind, is usually a top guide too.

Incidentally, my diet has plenty of cooked foods and quite a lot of raw foods in the form of fruits, nuts, seeds, smoothies, green juices, superfoods and so on, and in my view, you can't go wrong by having a mix. In cold weather, raw foods are less needed, but in the summer more of them can be added to your diet.

Herbs are absolutely amazing, so get yourself a good herb book and learn about them, and incorporate them into your diet. Some that I have used in the past, mostly for general health include burdock, dandelion, ashwaganda, shatavari, pennywort (also called gotu kola; great for the brain and blood circulation), ginkgo biloba, neem, triphala (a three fruit mix from India and also in Thailand, easily available from online stores, great for digestion and relief from constipation), echinacea (in tincture form is great, and take it at first sign of a cold and often this chases the cold away before it can take hold), aloe vera, and many different Thai or Chinese or Indian herbs that I've taken in the past for specific ailments. You can also add all the above spices which technically speaking are from the herb family.

For a few years now I've barely fallen ill with anything, but continue to take superfoods and tonic herbs to help my body take care of itself, and some like pennywort specifically for the brain. I think this is why my general health is good, in part, because they all support my healthy but tasty default diet.

Another thing which is relatively new in my life is using *essential oils*, belonging to the healthcare modality of aromatherapy. I bought a diffuser and a starter kit of twelve different oils. I am now just discovering this new world, and one thing I know already is to ensure one gets good quality oils from a reputable source because there are many synthetic options around. You get what you pay for. I have lemon, frankincense, peppermint (ace to add a drop into my pot of oolong tea), lavender, and some of the company's blends too. They make the air smell so good, and are used for various ailments and to prevent problems too. You can ingest some, topically apply some, and put a drop or two in some water with a candle underneath, thus releasing wonderful aromas into your home. Good for the car, offices, cafes, all buildings.

I THINK I've packed in a load of information in there, so I'd like to summarise the diet bit briefly. If we want to give it a name, how about 'whole foods diet', the 'common sense diet', or '3rd millennium diet'? I like the latter because it emphasises eating for our own health and for helping to heal our planet by not supporting the destructive practices by food corporations.

Eat whole foods and include superfoods and herbs. Minimise animal foods, exclude corporate-made foods and drinks. Eat for health not weight. Your body will find its natural weight in short order.

Avoid all the SAD stuff. Just be shot of it if you can, it's low frequency food. A bit here and there and your body will process it, so if you find you hanker after a hot dog or burger, ice-cream or cake, have it, but more than once a week would not be for me. If you're like me, though, be careful of falling back into old habits. We sometimes go to a quality pizza restaurant and I thoroughly enjoy my dinner, washed down with a bottle of red wine. It's the default diet that is important in my view.

That said, I will never knowingly allow genetically modified food into my body, who knows what it is doing, the corporations got away without fully and properly testing the consequences - research it and find out for yourself. Be aware that so many processed foods include HFCS - high fructose corn syrup - which is made with super cheap genetically modified corn, and must be terrible for one's poor old body. I read once that about 75% of foods sold in American supermarkets have GM ingredients.

Now, it's not just what you eat but *how* you eat that counts. Good advice I've learned and heeded, which I mentioned before: chew your food thoroughly. Enjoy the subtle tastes of whole foods being released in your mouth as you chew well, be kind to your stomach, and get conscious!

I'd like to mention again the acid- and alkaline-forming foods, and how they interact with the body. I'm more than satisfied for myself this is a great guide for what to eat, but again, I have seen some conflicting information; however, over time I've seen for myself that when I have a lot of vegetables and fruits in my diet I thrive, so for me this is a top guide to go by.

You can find lists easily online, but the basic information is that nearly all vegetables and fruits are alkaline-forming, which includes just about all herbs and superfoods, which mostly come from the plant kingdom, while everything else is acid-forming. It's not the make-up of the food that you eat, but rather the nature of the 'ash' after your body has digested it. So, while lemons, limes, pineapple, grapefruit and so on are acidic or sub-acidic fruits, once you digest them, they are alkaline. Meats and dairy as they exist are alkaline in nature, but turn to an acidic ash once digested.

The literature suggests we aim for 60:40 alkaline-forming foods to acid-forming foods, and when we are not well to make it 80:20. You will see from those figures you need lots of fruits and veggies. This is why smoothies, green juices, carrot juice, beetroot juice, and so on are useful, along with superfoods and herbs which all boost your alkaline-forming intake.

When one eats the standard American diet, consuming so many meats, dairy, junk and processed foods, and foods made from refined sugars and flours then this is almost exclusively an acid-forming diet with virtually no nutrients. You are frying and burning yourself up alive. You are methodically and systematically attacking your precious health and life. Sickness is guaranteed, and pills are popped for toffee. Yet, this is the diet for so many people, and is pushed on us all over the world through TV advertising and the corporate juggernaut's reach. I see it as unethical at best, criminal at worst.

Either way, it's for you to know about all these kinds of things, dear reader, and to then make your own informed decisions. Here's the key understanding: when you eat 'too many' acid-forming foods, what happens is that they create a temporary state of acidosis in your body and your blood. The blood cannot move above its neutral pH value, for we would die, and so the body must now take corrective measures to ensure the blood does not go acidic. One of the first places it can turn to is the calcium in your bones, which will neutralise things and avoid a big problem, but in this way, you can see how weaker bones may develop if you have a default diet which is acid-forming. I have also read that acidosis is behind all illnesses and diseases, and I find this compelling.

The books also say we can have acid-forming and alkaline-forming mental input! So a violent movie or horrible boss may elevate your body into a state of acidic stress, while the soothing sounds of a waterfall or birdsong in nature will be a boon to your mental and physical wellbeing.

Last word in the chapter goes to the non-food stuff but which comes into our body mainly through the skin. First is the air you breathe and the sunlight you absorb. Get fresh air as much as you can. Get sunlight for your vitamin D, and because the sun is good for you. Without it we die! If you live in an urban environment get to the parks, wherever trees are, and perhaps put some plants in your home. Get out of the city and into nature whenever you can, and when you do, gulp in that air and really exhale it deeply. Oxygenate your blood.

Second is drinking water. It's been well documented that they add fluoride to municipal tap water, and I accept that this is simply not good for us, and perhaps is a clue behind the increase in Alzheimer's and other brain deterioration in the last few decades. Chlorine is also added. Here in Thailand we get bottled water which is cheap and has been ozonated and subjected to a reverse osmosis process. It takes out all the natural minerals, but also takes out any toxins that got in there. One can easily mineralise it by adding a small amount of sole (pronounced so-lay) which you can make yourself. Get a lump or some crystals of Himalayan salt or sea salt, put it into some clean water in a mason jar overnight, let it dissolve, and then you have natural salt water the same as in your body. Add a teaspoon to a litre of drinking water and there you have natural mineral water! I don't do that, but we get glass bottles delivered which gives us tasty water and avoids plastic. Many friends use filters attached to their taps and water systems.

Now, a real big area of concern you should investigate is the whole array of skin products. This includes your soaps and shampoos, body creams and hair dyes, cosmetics, sun creams, deodorants, anything at all you put on your skin. What goes on it will go through the pores and into your body. Corporate mass-produced skin products are full of toxic chemicals, just check out the list of ingredients. Aluminium-based deodorants block the toxins (which cause the body odour) from coming out, leaving them in your body. When I'm eating a good healthy diet, no excess toxins, so no body odour. See for yourself!

Find alternatives made by ethical companies which are made with natural ingredients, especially soaps and shampoos which we use so often. Some may think this is going over the top, but it's yet one more source of chemicals for your liver and kidneys to process. I've used natural soaps and shampoos for many years. My wife makes liquid soap for washing our dishes and a wonderful shampoo almost entirely made out of kaffir limes from a tree in our garden.

Happy eating, happy living, happy health. Cheers!

19

AYURVEDA: ANCIENT WISDOM FOR MODERN CITIZENS

Timeless wisdoms lead us to timeless truths.

Ayurveda is the art of living, the art of being.

'The person who knows his true self and nature is the greatest person of all.' ~ Dr Sri Brahmananda Swamigal, Ayurveda and Siddha physician

Ayurveda is magic, it's awesome, and it is monumental in its scope and in what it gives to each and every human being who brings it into their lives. I would like to say, without an atom of exaggeration: if our whole world of humans lived by its teachings then humanity would be transformed, almost overnight. We will be aligned with love and nature, not the fear and psychological separation spawned and maintained for centuries by *the system*.

Nothing need be invented, nothing need be written anew, no extra science need be discovered, for with Ayurveda we already have the complete guide to nutrition, lifestyle and healthcare to learn from and implement into our life. Built into it, as with all intelligent and educational human endeavours, is plenty of room for any adjustments we may need to apply, as a consequence of the forces of natural evolution.

The financial, psychological and spiritual resources that we humans collectively waste on sickness and disease are astronomical. Just imagine how, if we banished 90% of this sickness, we could divert those resources instead into promoting, and benefitting from, our innate creativity, productivity and intelligence!

If we all lived an Ayurvedic way of life, the business model and profits of the whole medical system and the corporate cartel who make all the pills would virtually collapse. Our food systems of growth and supply would become local, sustainable and planet-friendly.

We started out on our journey together by recognising that our human family has somehow got itself into a right mess. I trust by now you will agree with me that most of our problems, individually and collectively, are unnecessary. With learning, understanding and application, there is no need to be stressed, struggling and suffering so much of the time.

I would find it hard to disagree with anybody who even suggested that all our conflicts, wars, and brutalities, which humans have committed upon humans for so long now, were in fact caused by the sickness afflicting us in body, mind and spirit.

The collateral damage from our unnatural, unbalanced way of life is staggering. Ignorance is not bliss.

Ayurveda, which in Sanskrit means 'science of life' (veda + ayu), is an astonishing body of knowledge, understandings and ancient wisdoms pertaining to living life in health, happiness and harmony. It is a stunning gift from the people of India from ancient times. I do also believe traditional Chinese medicine to be perhaps of a similar value, yet, for English speakers at least, there is so much more literature and so many more websites informing us about Ayurveda, making its wisdoms widely available in the international language.

Ayurveda is about five or six thousand years old and represents a comprehensive system of wellness and healthcare. Its scope covers three main areas: i) prevention of sickness and disease, ii) early diagnosis and treatment of ailments and diseases, iii) promotion of a lifestyle conducive to harmonious living. Unlike the modern allopathic system which only looks at the body, Ayurveda has a holistic approach, encompassing physical, mental, emotional and spiritual health and wellbeing. It fully recognises the role and influence that our mind has on our overall physical and spiritual health, and that the level of health we experience is always the consequence of our relationship with the external environment.

It simultaneously is able to help us prevent disease, yet treat it when it does occur. It teaches us about the environment we live in, and how to interact with it in a harmonious manner. It does not use medicines that carry side effects or are toxic in any way, and all treatments aim at encouraging the body to heal itself holistically as well as dealing with the specific symptoms. It understands nature, and teaches us to work with it, not against it.

But, dear reader, there is something so very cool about Ayurveda, even after all the benefits I've just outlined: its teachings are available - understandable, doable, achievable - for all citizens, for us laymen and laywomen, not just doctors and health professionals. This means we can learn how to take charge of, and manage, our own health. We can, by a conscious choice, become autonomous and sovereign human beings, no longer dependent on the external authority paradigm. Ayurveda has the power to bust the brutal system. Through applying it we liberate ourselves from the shackles of our schooled ignorance, we become emancipated from that element of our psyche which tells us that external authority always has the answers, not ourselves.

Ayurveda neutralises the anti-life system and veritably chases the pesky operator right out of town. And out of your ego-mind. It empowers you with its time-honoured knowledge and wisdoms, which are more appropriate today than ever before.

I would like to offer you some basic understandings that I have internalised myself from my own study of it. A sort of brief introduction, if you like, which I hope will inspire you to become an Ayurveda advocate! I have several books which I've read and learned from, but which also act as brilliant resources for when I feel my life and health is out of balance. At the end of the chapter I'll recommend a few books and resources that have worked for me.

Just as the natural phenomenon of homeostasis innately works to rebalance an organism which has fallen out of balance, so does Ayurveda. It is a superlative guide for humans to live in a balanced manner, and to help us restore order and health to our body and mind when we fall off our wellness wagon.

THE MAJOR UNDERSTANDING is that there exist, within humans, three major constitution types, or *doshas*, and these in turn are based on the five elements of all life: space, water, air, fire and earth. Our constitution, known as *prakruti*, is determined during our conception, and reflects the relative situation and lifestyle of both parents at that time.

Pitta is the constitution of fire with some water, *kapha* is the constitution of water and earth, while *vata* is of air with some space. Each of us has all three doshas within us, in a unique combination, but usually one predominates, and that is said to be our particular dosha. Whatever your predominant dosha is, means you will have a certain type of body, be prone to a certain kind of mental outlook and capacity for thought, and carry typical emotional traits and characteristics. It will also determine what kind of ailments and illnesses you are likely to get when you fall out of balance.

In our brief guide here we will keep our focus on these three different doshas, but in fact Ayurveda identifies seven different dosha types for all human beings. We can be predominantly one of the three doshas, or we may have roughly equal amounts of two of them and not much of the other, or, not so commonly, one may be a similar amount of all three. Therefore your own dosha could be: pitta, kapha, vata, pitta-kapha, pitta-vata, kapha-vata, or tridoshic pitta-kapha-vata. There are many online resources and websites for you to answer questionnaires to determine what your own constitution or prakruti is.

I have found this is not always easy to know exactly, but it definitely gives us many insights into our own physical, mental and emotional construction! It is an exciting discovery to find out that many of your tendencies towards either negative or positive traits are because of your prakruti, which came about during your conception. We are not bad people! We each have our own unique nature.

This insight is also tremendously helpful to us in our relationships with other people, especially our kids, parents, partner, boyfriend, girlfriend, co-workers, close friends and so on. You will note I'm talking about people we may live with or spend lots of time with. One simple example to illustrate the exciting discoveries to be made… if you are a pitta dosha, then you are prone to impatience, anger, a short temper, and are likely to be on time for meetings; yet if you are married to a kapha, your partner will be prone to laziness, apathy, and envy, and can easily be late for appointments due to their laid-back nature. You might well get into arguments when going out for a meal or to meet others, because you're on time, and your partner is making you fidgety by being too slow or relaxed!

For me the major insight is that by realising I am prone to different things, likes and dislikes than my partner, I can be much more tolerant of her ways, simply because I now realise she was conceived and born that way! We each have our own nature and natural ways of being.

It can be really important to know this kind of thing as a new parent. It's natural for parents to want kids to be like themselves, but if you are a pitta, your partner is a vata, and yet your kid is a kapha, you may be inadvertently trying to bring them up to be somebody against their nature and natural ways. This may cause may tears and misbehaviour at the outset of the little one's life, and may bring them problems in their adulthood. We said at the outset of the book that for us to live in harmony we need our nurture and nature to complement each other, not antagonise. Ayurveda gives us really beneficial insights into building, managing and sustaining healthy relationships with others.

Now, these differences between all of us, depending on the relative and unique combination of the three doshas that we each have within our body and mind, extend to all facets of life. It might explain why in your family somebody likes tomatoes and eggs, yet another member can't stand them. Some may prefer the beach, others the mountains. Some love nature, others prefer the urban streets. You will have different tastes in colours, clothes, possessions, films, music, books, hobbies and so on. Different foods will enhance or antagonise your wellbeing, and the same with weather and climate. Your memory and mind may work differently to others. Different doshas are suited to different kinds of jobs and work, and determine your relationship to things like routine or spontaneity, conservative or rebellious thinking, doing oneself or delegating.

When we consider the relentless march of the corporate mindset of the system, which seeks to impose on us all one voice, one government, one corporation, one media company, one way of life, one ideology, one behaviour, and that it seeks to monopolise and homogenise us all into clones and cut-outs of each other, then we can see, using the teachings and ancient wisdoms of Ayurveda, that we are having our nature and natural impulses completely interfered with, suppressed and antagonised.

What I wanted to do by introducing Ayurveda to you is square the circle, if you like, to end the book by taking us back to the start of it. I said we have been conditioned into ignorance, that our nurture - our upbringing and schooling - in large part antagonises our nature, and that accordingly we don't really know who we are, nor how life works. We have, often, been deeply suppressed from who we are by nature, and out of this suppression comes ignorance, impotence, frustration and illness. We were educated to be compliant, obedient, all the same, robot-like and a shadow of who we can all be. We were all shaped into a one-size-fits-all mould. Emphatically this is not natural!!

Ayurveda is our way out of this unnatural state of affairs. It helps us to decondition and re-educate ourselves, to find out who we naturally are meant to be, and then shows us exactly how to be that person. If we know we are naturally prone to anger, and that if we eat certain foods then this anger is inflamed or pacified, then we can work on our negative traits by avoiding the dietary and lifestyle triggers that lead to them. We become seriously able to really take charge of our health and life, simply by realising who our natural self is.

We learn to eat the foods that support our own constitution, that provide us with physical health, a sound mind and an active soul. We learn what kind of work we are naturally suited to, what our innate skillset is, and how we can best benefit the wider society out there by first living in harmony and good health.

Ayurveda introduces you to you, teaches you about you, and enables you to be this real you. It also clearly teaches us that nothing stays the same, that everything goes round, evolves, grows, decays, regenerates, and dies, and therefore who we are is always open to refinement and our ongoing evolution.

It teaches us what will challenge our health, and what will promote it, and how we can rescue it if we've gone out of tune. We learn how to stop getting in the way of ourselves, and how to enable the harmonious functioning of our body.

With Ayurveda we can become our own lifestyle and health gurus! Read the books and websites, and learn for yourself about the preferred diet, herbs, oils, breathing techniques and exercise types for your own constitution. Learn about treatments for specific ailments, and about Ayurveda's six stages to all diseases. I have read that conventional western healthcare usually only diagnoses and intervenes at the fifth stage, which is when things have started to spread and get serious, and are harder to treat and solve. Ayurveda can diagnose and identify previous stages, and by knowing about them we can spot things early, and treat them much more easily, usually by ourselves. For example, constipation or skin problems are a definite sign that our body is not in harmony, and we are causing stress to it in some way relating to diet, lifestyle, attitude and so on. Being unable to sleep properly is another sign that all is not well. Body odour suggests you are taking in more toxins than your liver and kidneys can process, hence they try to escape the body through the skin. By ignoring our bodily ailments, or taking a pill to 'fix' the pain/problem, we are likely brewing up something bigger in the future.

While it has a complete pharmacology to rival anything else in the human cupboard of treatment modalities, and can treat all manner of health ailments, illnesses, bodily malfunctioning and disease, its true value for me lies in its preventative approach to illness and disease. Thus, when treatment is given it is for both the symptoms and the root causes of the problem, meaning our body can heal itself holistically, and we ourselves can learn what we are doing wrong in our life, or how the external environment impacted on us, and thus take actions to prevent a repeat.

And as we learn more and more, and put into practice what we learn, we are able to more and more successfully avoid getting sick or ill. This is a revelation of the highest order.

When one looks into such things, one will discover that today's cutting edge science in the shape of epigenetics and quantum physics, which have yet to hit mainstream acceptance, bring us a message almost identical to Ayurveda. It would seem all the real truths, understandings, and wisdoms are timeless. But, humanity, driven by greed and fear, seems to forget and unlearn innate wisdoms. Each of us, through our own spiritual revolution, needs to learn about and understand the workings of the environments within and around us, and practise forging an intelligent relationship between the two. Health, harmony and happiness are our reward, and this will automatically confer benefits upon all other life too.

Let's look at some characteristics and aspects of each of the three major doshas. This is to give you a flavour, and to perhaps help you make an initial guess as to which one best fits you. You can then go online and do a test. I'll give you a link to my favourite website at the end of the chapter, but you would do well to take two or three different tests on different sites, or from any book you buy, and in this way get a solid sense for your own dosha. If you were to meet a fully qualified Ayurveda doctor, they could do a pulse diagnosis for you, but until then, the questionnaires will help you.

Perhaps the key understanding from Ayurveda is that like

attracts like, and opposites pacify. This is where the five elements of space, water, air, fire, and earth come in. Also, Ayurveda recognises several pairs of opposites which mark a full spectrum of intermediate stages within, for example, hot and cold, solid and liquid, heavy and light, stable and mobile, dull and sharp and so on. So if you are pitta dosha, which is mainly fire, you will really be struggling if you're standing in the desert drinking a hot Thai soup full of fiery chillies! Use opposites to bring yourself back to balance if you've aggravated your innate state of being.

Okay, let's go…

Fire, the main element of **pitta dosha**, is hot, moves fast, burns things up, and makes solid things into a more liquid state. Some traits and natural ways of a pitta person: has good digestion, finds it hard to put weight on due to excellent digestion and an active disposition, dislikes hot weather, struggles with chillies and spicy foods, hates to miss a meal, is energetic and motivated, is intelligent and ambitious, makes for a good leader, can get impatient and easily angry or inflamed, is often jealous and maybe feels entitled, can be critical and sharp towards others, is kind and loyal, is confident and has no pretence, and is prone to fevers and inflammation within the body. Usually no-nonsense kind of people.

Water, the main element of **kapha dosha**, is heavy and wet, and along with the earth element the attribute of coldness is found. Kapha people are typically heavier and more solid in body structure, likely to have thick and wavy hair, find it easy to put on weight, tend towards laziness, greed and being slow, can be careless, but are thoughtful and caring towards others, are easily apathetic or unmotivated, can produce too much mucous, tend towards colds, are methodical and careful thinkers, are more likely to be balanced, need to eat less and be careful of putting on weight, and are neither argumentative or bossy.

Air, the element of **vata dosha**, blows and is cold, dry and light. Vata people are usually slight in build, tall or short, light in weight, eat irregularly and more often, maybe more angular in face shape, like to keep going with their work but can easily burn themselves out and lose energy, find it hard to maintain attention and focus, have an active mind prone to worry and fear, may feel insecure, are protective and loyal, find plane travel disorienting, can get claustrophobic, like change and new things, need to feel in control but dislike being controlled, tend to being perfectionists, are generous and creative, and they dislike routine, yet it is they who most need it to ground themselves.

These are just some of the physical and mental characteristics typical of each dosha. Remember we all have some of each in us, and many may find they are a bidoshic. I myself am pitta-kapha.

I mentioned above that a great thing about Ayurveda was how it helps us be more understanding in our relationships, and hence we can cultivate more positive energy with people, even when we find differences. We lose that subconscious system-conditioned idea, bubbling away below the radar of our awareness, that there is only one way to live life, only one belief system, and that everybody should do things our way.

So if you're a pitta person married to a kapha person you may often think your partner is lazy, while your partner may find you too active and too impatient. You will get uppity and fidgety if you are hungry, your kapha wife or husband will have no problem if you're out and about and are missing lunch.

If you're a laid-back kapha, who likes to take things easy, then being married to vata will be interesting, because they will be wanting to control you into doing everything now, on time, and in the way they see it should be done. On the other hand, your vata partner will take great care of you and be loyal to you.

If you're both pittas, and the weather is really hot today, and you're caught in a traffic jam, you will compete to see who complains the most! If you're both kaphas, maybe you don't get so much done! Oh, and I think I'm right in saying that vatas have a rather large appetite for sex, so if you're both vatas… wow! On the other hand, vatas are not good at making decisions, in which case just go back to bed!

Bear in mind that the point of life is to be in harmony, and it is when your dosha gets aggravated that you become prone to health issues. When you know your dosha, and your tendencies, you can better take preventative action, and eat the foods right for you so that you maintain balance in your life

If you're a pitta you can easily get hot and irascible, therefore try and choose work and hobbies which cool and slow you down. Avoid traffic jams and be careful of political arguments!

If you're a vata, learn to take rests rather than burning yourself out all the time. And don't take a job which requires you to take responsibility for others, keep away from management unless you have learned how to delegate, because you always want the job doing to your specification, so you'll tend to do everything yourself, and then burn yourself out. Vatas will complain when another person doesn't do the job to their satisfaction, and complaining upsets the harmony of both people.

Kaphas who take an easygoing job may become too slothful and lazy and fall out of balance. They should also partake in more aerobic exercise, and make it a habit in order to make sure they do it. Cultivating habits is really good for kapha, and me being pitta-kapha I know this to be true. On the other hand, vatas who really need the grounding that habits and routines can give them, are the least likely to stick to routines. They also go to bed late when they should do the opposite, and then stress arises. And so it goes on.

We can't finish without a section on diet. Ayurveda recognises six tastes, namely sweet, sour, salty, pungent, bitter and astringent. Each taste, and food, also carries its own energetics, and can be cooling or heating, fast- or slow-digesting. So there is a bit to learn and read about. However, just ensure any book you buy has a list of foods which aggravate or pacify each dosha, and that will be a great starting point for you. In general pitta people should focus on sweet, bitter and astringent foods; kapha people on pungent, bitter and astringent foods; and vatas on sweet, sour and salty foods.

What you will find will call into question all those diet books which recommend this or that diet for people. With barely any exceptions (Dr D'Adamo's blood type diet and Dr Kelley's metabolic typing are the only ones I can think of; both are said to be controversial, although I find them credible myself), all diets offered in books offer the same advice for everybody. But Ayurveda will clearly show this is an error, and you can test things out for yourself. Let's look at two examples to illustrate.

Nuts are said to be healthy foods, and yes, they have high nutrient profiles. But in Ayurveda you will discover that pittas should eat only almonds and coconut, kaphas should keep away from all nuts, while vatas can eat just about all nuts. Now, if you are a kapha and love almonds or cashews, say, then this brings an important point into focus: if you're particularly in robust health, have good peace of mind and feel energetic and joyful, then you're supremely balanced and so eating some of these nuts is unlikely to affect you. Yet, if you are already somewhat stressed, then eating foods like nuts, which naturally aggravate your dosha, should be minimised or avoided.

A popular food with health-oriented people is avocado pears. The food lists will show that pitta and vata people can eat them, but for kaphas it's on the list to avoid! However, it's almost my favourite food (especially a Hass), but I just ensure I don't gorge on them.

The point here is that while all whole foods are healthy foods in and of themselves, they can have different influences on the metabolism and health of different people, depending on their constitution. I mentioned earlier in the *Desserts* section about keeping a 'food and feelings' diary, and perhaps once you discover your dosha, and find the food lists for it, you may decide to start experimenting with your diet to find out how your body and mind respond. By keeping such a diary you can learn what foods and drinks support your health, or aggravate it.

So there you have it, Ayurveda in a nutshell. I think it will be the perfect guide for you to follow up on, having now pretty much finished this book. At first it might seem a bit baffling or overwhelming when you start reading about it, so three tips: i) discover your dosha, ii) focus first on the food lists and character traits, and iii) know that the more effort you put in the easier it all becomes to understand. Some things were confusing and hard for me to understand on first reading, but now I notice no problems when I read things again. Practice is always our friend! I will recommend some outstanding books for you in a mo, and one truly heartwarming documentary film. All are relatively easy to read and understand, and contain a wealth of information for you, and allow you to advance your understandings at your own pace.

My conception of a spiritual revolution, my 3DH5DL framework and formula for life, the cutting edge biology of epigenetics, karma and energy flow, and the ancient wisdom and knowledge of Ayurveda all share the core understanding of life and human life: everything is interconnected and interdependent. When we know deeply that we are connected to the whole grid of life, to the universe, and to each other, and when we learn how to learn so that we can skilfully learn how to achieve health, harmony and happiness, we are set fair for the rest of our life.

The intelligent message must be that we first take care of our health and wellbeing, and then, from this position of strength, we will maximally benefit all other humans and Mother Earth.

Live with HEART my friend, live with honesty, empathy, awareness, responsibility and trust. In so doing, Mother Earth and the God of universal intelligence and cosmic consciousness will protect you. Love will be your currency, not self-doubt. Unconditional ineffable love is our natural way, it was only the system that tried to persuade us otherwise.

You know it makes sense.

* * *

HERE ARE two practical books that I recommend as excellent starting points for you to learn about and enjoy the benefits of Ayurvedic knowledge:

The Book of Ayurveda: A Holistic Approach to Health and Longevity by Judith H. Morrison.

Prakruti: Your Ayurvedic Constitution by Robert E. Svoboda.

Two excellent resource books of mine are:

The Complete Book of Ayurvedic Home Remedies: A Comprehensive Guide to the Ancient Healing of India by Vasant Lad

The Yoga of Herbs: An Ayurvedic Guide to Herbal Medicine by Dr David Frawley and Dr Vasant Lad

Wow, I feel excited simply recommending those four books to you! I've got several books on herbs, but none better than *The Yoga of Herbs*. Both Vasant Lad and David Frawley are huge names in Ayurveda, and each have written loads of books. I have about seven of Dr Frawley's books. I still have a plan one day to study David's online course, but have held off in case I get lots of money and can go to India instead, to study in the temple and holy shrine of Ayurveda!

I'd like to recommend one particular website which to me stands above the others in terms of the comprehensive and easy-to-understand information it offers. The site creator sells herbs and things on her site, but really, just go to the Ayurveda tab and start exploring. They don't ship to Thailand, otherwise I would like to buy from her just by way of saying thank you for such a brilliant free resource. You can also do your dosha test here, and get full diet guides for your constitution.

banyanbotannicals.com

MY LAST RECOMMENDATION is for a film called *Ayurveda: The Art of Being*. It is easily available on Youtube. It's such a beautiful, informative documentary, filmed mostly in India, and gives the viewer so many insights into health and life, and how we can take care of both. Some moments may give your eyes a good cleansing!

Meanwhile, in a final word or two, I'd like to extend an invitation to you, and to ask you for some help…

A CALL TO ACTION

Dear Reader, the end of this book and our culinary adventure is reached! But not, if you so desire it, the journey we've been on together. I would like to extend an invitation for you to continue with our journey, and to enjoy many soul adventures along the way. We need millions of us.

I would therefore like to enlist your help in some matters, should you feel so inclined. Let me explain…

When I set out to write this book, back in 2012, I had one overriding reason almost compelling me to write it, out of which two major objectives emerged.

That reason? Problems.

Everywhere I looked, there they were. The human race was afflicted, especially in the western developed nations. It was by now my view that many of these problems were unnecessary, or at least eminently solvable: people had much less in Thailand, but also fewer problems, less suffering, and more smiles.

I considered that I had answers and solutions. I could help, and wanted to help. I hate seeing pain and suffering in humans and animals alike.

This inner drive and impulse led naturally to the two objectives.

Firstly, I wanted to create a one-stop guide for healthy and happy living *for any citizen at all* who wanted to bring changes into their life, regardless of whether they were just thinking about it for the first time, or were already on their path. I didn't want to preach to the choir, and I didn't want to preclude anybody by using too academic a prose, or boring the pants off them. I wanted my book to be for all humans who wanted a better life, and to help them get what they wanted, to empower themselves.

The second objective was an extension of the first: I wanted to create a book where word of mouth would happily and enthusiastically promote 'a spiritual revolution', and rapidly spread its core message, so urgently necessary in our times: *learn for yourself, liberate yourself, it's up to you; you have to understand life for yourself, you can't depend on gurus or experts.*

I dreamed and envisioned that the concept of 'a spiritual revolution' would become widely known and practised worldwide, and would quickly become synonymous with solutions for individuals, for the whole of humanity, and for Mother Earth. In this way, my thinking went, my book could have maximum positive impact on the world. I want a happy and harmonious humanity, not just you and me!

I decided I would try and write a book that would trigger a spontaneous and organic movement, spreading health and harmony throughout the human world. This movement would have no leaders, no ideology, no headquarters, no pushing or imposing anything onto others, it would simply spring into being, naturally, organically, cumulatively, by the actions of millions of humans conducting their spiritual revolutions. We could all connect with each other using conscious spiritual living as our unifying force.

I didn't want to just sell a book, I wanted to trigger this movement to sweep into the psyche and spirit of humanity. People reading the book would empower themselves and transform their lives, and, with enough numbers doing this, we would definitively heal humanity and the planet.

Little did I know that something else would sweep into the human psyche and spirit before I could finish writing my book, namely the virus of 2020; see how fast a movement can come into being! Well, my good friend, perhaps we've arrived at the very point in time in human history where a spiritual revolution is absolutely and urgently needed.

There is no 'membership' as such, for the movement doesn't exist in any official or physical domain, there are just members united by a desire for a better life for themselves and for the whole world. Each citizen automatically becomes a member by conducting their spiritual revolution, empowering themselves, and turning their life around. No fees to join, just the cost of the book, which is about the price of a yoga lesson!

Okay, that's the background, now the *action*.

And that, fellow spiritual warrior, is where you come in. Assuming I succeeded in my first objective, and that's for you to decide, I would like to invite you to join forces with me and make the second objective become a reality. Also, I have news of a community to which all spiritual revolutionaries and soul adventurers can partake in, and help the movement grow.

This book is just the beginning of my own journey into spreading the practice of conscious living, far and wide, and I'd love you, a fellow spiritual warrior, to stay with me all the way.

Here are some suggestions for you.

i) Help spread the word about the book in your social media channels, recommend it to friends in your community. Tell everybody! Tell them about your experiences of your own spiritual revolution, and what the book has done for you.

ii) Buy a copy of this book for a friend, make it a nice present for them. Maybe give them a beautiful notebook too! If you work as some kind of leader, you could have your organisation purchase several copies for all staff or group members.

iii) It would be tremendous, and a real boon to me, if you could go to the online store where you bought this book, and write me a review and give the book a rating. Reviews are the lifeblood of independent authors, and super-important for helping a book to sell well. I would be delighted for you to leave a *completely honest* review for the book. You can do this at Goodreads too.

iv) My work is only just beginning with this book, and I have plans in the pipeline for a follow-up workbook which will be a practical accompaniment to this book. Also to come will be a series of mini-ebooks for learning about such crucial aspects of human life such as learning, communication, leadership, creating dynamic groups and so on. All such work will belong to 'a spiritual revolution' in that it enhances harmonious living.

Meanwhile I am developing and expanding my wee corner of the cosmic universe on my website through blogging and regular newsletters, and through my Facebook pages. I plan to develop my website into an enterprise for education, entertainment and empowerment. I expect to find time to join the world of podcasting and making videos, both of which may well be up and running by the time you read this.

I have also set up a Facebook group as an HQ for all citizens interested in helping a spiritual revolution movement grow into a powerful and empowering reality. It's a place for you to enjoy the company and camaraderie of fellow citizens who all like exploring and learning about our world and their own inner world. Come by for discussions, insights, ideas and discoveries. It's called 'Pioneers of A Spiritual Revolution', and if you get in quick you can be an *Original Pioneer*, part of my special OPs team!!

In short, I'm putting everything in place to fully promote a spiritual revolution as the solution to our individual and collective ills, and I'd love you to stick with me, be a fellow spiritual warrior and proactive citizen, and help recreate our world into the place of love, peace and harmony we all want it to be. It's up to each of us to overcome division, disconnect and discouragement with compassion, courage and communication.

Multiple thank yous for investing in and reading this book, and I look forward to further soul adventures with you my good friend. May you live in health, harmony and happiness. Namaste and 'Cheers'!

My links and locations where you can find my work:

https://www.aspiritualrevolution.com
https://www.facebook.com/groups/asrpioneers
https://www.facebook.com/asrsouladventurers
I'm also on Facebook as Philip Keay Author
YouTube: A Spiritual Revolution

ACKNOWLEDGMENTS

I would like to offer my eternal gratitude to my parents, Dawn and Bernard, and my sister, Wendy, for enhancing and enriching my life in so many ways. My mum moved onto new pastures in 2001, but always her presence and wisdom are firmly held in my heart and soul. To my brother-in-law Glenn and nephews Oscar and Freddie go heartfelt thanks for being in my life. Same sentiments for Jacque.

I feel much gratitude to all my ex-students who have helped me learn so much on my journey of life. The same goes to all my teaching colleagues I've worked with in Bangkok and Chiang Mai, who became firm friends for life.

I thank every single one of my friends, in various corners of the world, for adding fun and meaning to my life. If I name any of you, others will feel left out. You all know who you are, I love you all! That said, I would like to mention good mate Si Collins and sister Wend who have both given me much help during the publishing process.

Last but not least I thank my lovely beautiful wife Air, my partner in crime since 2005, and our daughter Smile.

ABOUT THE AUTHOR

Philip Keay accidentally emigrated to Thailand in 1991, and has been a transformational teacher of learning, teaching, communication, psychology, leadership, and life skills to students and teachers ever since. He holds a Certificate and Diploma in English Language Teaching from Cambridge University, and a Master of Arts in Applied Linguistics and ELT from King's College, London.

Philip is a soul adventurer, a traveller, a prolific researcher, a writer and photographer. He is a spiritual warrior committed to lifelong learning. Through his teaching and travels he has met, taught, befriended and learned from thousands of people from all corners of the world.

His mission in this life is inspiring people to self-educate and empower themselves to be the best person they can be. He makes this happen in the classroom using his unique brand of task-based, student-centred learning. Now, he brings it to the book world.

Philip lives in northern Thailand with his wife and daughter.

To find more of his work, visit his cosmic corner of the universe at:

www.aspiritualrevolution.com

https://www.facebook.com/groups/asrpioneers

Printed in Great Britain
by Amazon

22393781R00205